A SHAFT
OF SUNLIGHT

Philip Mason

A SHAFT
OF SUNLIGHT

Memories of a Varied Life

ANDRE DEUTSCH

First published 1978 by
André Deutsch Limited
105 Great Russell Street London WC1

Copyright © 1978 by Philip Mason
All rights reserved

Printed in Great Britain by
W & J Mackay Limited, Chatham

British Library Cataloguing in Publication Data

Mason, Philip
  A shaft of sunlight.
  1. Mason, Philip
  I. Title
  325'.341'0954   DS481.M/

ISBN 0-233-96955-1

FOR MARY
to whom it already belongs

For most of us, there is only the unattended
Moment, the moment in and out of time,
The distraction fit, lost in a shaft of sunlight,
The wild thyme unseen, or the winter lightning
Or the waterfall, or music heard so deeply
That it is not heard at all, but you are the music
While the music lasts . . .

T. S. ELIOT, *Four Quartets*: 'The Dry Salvages. V'

CONTENTS

ILLUSTRATIONS

INTRODUCTION

A man who has made great discoveries or taken part in great events may have a positive duty to write some account of his life. That is not the case with me. But I suppose that most writers, as they finish a book, feel that there is still something left to say. And this feeling grows as one gets older. There is so much to explain! So much has had to be left out! There are discoveries made since the last book was finished and there are pictures still vivid in the memory asking to be drawn. They need a thread on which to be strung.

The memories are more insistent if you have lived in a period of rapid change through many kinds of existence that have utterly gone. The moral climate in which my parents lived has disappeared; there are no schools now like those I went to; Oxford is altogether different. The India I knew has vanished; I have not yet seen an account of the British in India that has not left me dissatisfied. What is more, my own life in India fell into several quite distinct sections, as different in flavour as vegetable curry and Lancashire hot-pot. I should like to recall, while I can, something of those lost worlds. What I have to say will not as a rule throw much light on events that figure in the newspaper headlines. To me it is more important to bring to life for a moment some of the people I have known, not necessarily gifted people, nor important in the usual sense of that word, but people I remember, usually with a smile, usually with affection, but each quite different from anyone else. My aim is thus nearer the novelist's than the historian's. In a bookshop, such a book will go under the head of autobiography, but it is not meant to be an autobiography, rather a gallery of portraits and scenes.

It has been hard to choose those scenes. It would have been easy to make each section four times as long but my object has been to record just enough to give the flavour of each stage of experience and to weave the whole into one. I have tried not to clutter the pages with names that are not needed. Some notes are to be found at the end about some of the people mentioned, but there are no numbered references in the text; the reader is advised to glance occasionally at the notes but he will find there are few, either as to people or quotations. The flow of the narrative has been the paramount consideration.

As I thought about this book, it was to have been called *Garlic and Sapphires*, a phrase from Eliot's *Four Quartets* which, whatever Eliot meant by it, to me stood for those momentary interludes that light up the long stretches of monotonous endeavour which come between the beginning of an enterprise and its completion, moments of intense living, full of harsh pungency, and those other moments of sudden realization, moments of vision and understanding, moments out of time. For most of us these come rarely but give meaning to the rest of life. It happened however that, just as I began to write, a period of enforced physical inactivity helped me to dwell longer and more thoughtfully on *Four Quartets*, and what Eliot is saying there about past and present. 'In my beginning is my end,' he writes, reversing the words of Mary Queen of Scots: 'En ma fin est mon commencement,' and again:

> *Time present and time past*
> *Are both perhaps present in time future.*

I found, when I tried to rebuild in memory each of these scenes in turn, that I was living the past a second time, that all my thoughts turned back to one particular phase of my life and that at night in dreams I had conversations with people long since dead. I looked up from the page on which I had been tracing words to find myself miraculously transported into the future. Or was it the present? I found, as I lived again through each of these previous incarnations, that I understood far more clearly and sympathetically than thirty years before why people had behaved as they did. At the end of my book, I came back to those thoughts about time with which I had started and these linked naturally with the last movement of the last of the *Four Quartets*. By now another title seemed more appropriate and the book became *A Shaft of Sunlight*, also a phrase from *Four Quartets*. The reader who knows Eliot will recognize passages in which other thoughts from that series of poems were present as I wrote. But that is not to say that the reader to whom Eliot means nothing need concern himself with anything more than the straightforward pictures of people and events which I present.

P.M.
Hither Daggons, 1977

Part One

IN MY BEGINNING

FOOTFALLS
IN THE MEMORY

1 The Farmer and the Artist

One of my grandfathers voted for Mr Gladstone and one for Mr Disraeli. Two men could hardly have been more different in tastes and interests. George Mason grew first-class malting barley and reared Leicester lambs on the land his father and grandfather had farmed; Mr Disraeli would perhaps hardly have been his own choice as a leader but he was content to follow his landlord the Marquess of Exeter. There were not many books in his house except the big two-volume family Bible, bound in leather, with his children's names written on the fly-leaf. It stands within reach of my arm as I write now. Recreation for him meant a day's hunting if the hounds met near by or an evening walking up partridges in the stubble. He stood for Church and State, the peers and the brewers, a good price for corn and things as they were.

My grandfather Woodruff, on the other hand, was a versatile man of varied intellectual interests. My mother always spoke of him as 'an inventor', a term I found impressive as a small boy and liked to repeat. But inventing things was only one of many occupations. By profession he was an engineer and manager of one of the factories of Cammell Laird, the great Sheffield steel firm. He painted in oils as well as water-colours; he drew in pen-and-ink and experimented with etching; he designed book-plates and illuminated end-papers. He played the violin in an orchestra and hoped that his three children would one day join him to make a string quartet – but alas! only one of the three came up to his standard. He was a Wesleyan Methodist and was admired as a lay preacher; his interest in politics was strong and it was for reasons mainly political that he invested in house property in neighbouring constituencies. In those days, the polls stayed open for a week and at election time he was able to drive over in a pony-trap and vote wherever he had a cottage.

Thus each of my two grandfathers in his different way represented one of the pillars of Victorian greatness. My mother never said that her family was in any way 'better' than my father's. She did not allow herself to think in such terms. She would have considered it disloyal and snobbish and would have reproved me sharply if I had used any expression carrying such an implication. Nonetheless, I had a very definite impression that such was the case. I had far more of my mother's attention than most children of that time. As the wife of a country doctor, she had maids and need not do housework, while she would have repudiated indignantly the aristocratic custom of leaving her children – and especially her eldest – entirely to the care of a nanny. She read aloud to me; she very early taught me to read by what was then an advanced phonetic method; she bought me books. And of course I imbibed from her, and thus from her father, something of his interest in ideas and his belief that education was a key to power, to knowledge, to life.

All his important inventions, my mother explained, had been the property of Cammell Laird; they included spring buffers on railway trucks and engines, from which we should have made millions if he had been able to patent and exploit them himself. The only invention of his that I remember actually seeing was certainly ingenious. It was a flat silver hoop that would hold a folded linen table napkin, but of which one half could be pivoted into the other, making a hook which could be inserted between the lower buttons of the waistcoat; a spring clip, shaped like a shield, would then grip the corner of the napkin and prevent it sliding onto the floor during dinner. It was engraved with ornamental scrolls and was a cherished possession of mine. Another of his creations was a framed drawing called *The Royal Sceptre of England*, a genealogical table starting with William I and ending with Victoria, worked into the shape of a sceptre or cross-shaped truncheon, each sovereign a jewel – the colours a little faded – the lines of descent patiently woven into the minute tracery of the design. The evidence of his industry and his varied gifts was never far away in my childhood.

I had been baptized Philip Mason, with no other name, my mother at that time being impressed by the dignity of simplicity and a dislike of anything pretentious. But since it seemed to me that Woodruff was a prettier, a more unusual, and a more romantic name than plain ordinary Mason – and since I felt that it was from that side of the family alone that I had any hope of proving to be the long-lost heir to a castle and a lake, in the manner of the romances of the period – I decided very early to be Philip Woodruff Mason and was known by that name until I was thirteen and had to produce a birth certificate.

Yet as I have grown older it has been on the background of the farm at Barrowden in Rutland, where Masons had lived so long, that my thoughts have dwelt more and more often. This is partly because I never saw my mother's early home on the outskirts of Sheffield. My grandfather Woodruff had a stroke and retired prematurely from Cammell

Laird, soon after which a financial disaster befell him. My mother, proud though she was of his artistic and intellectual gifts, always said he was no businessman; perhaps he was as loyal, as impulsive and as generous as she was herself. At any rate, he listened to the tale of a cousin who owned a small shipping line which was in that condition so common in business; just one small injection of capital would put everything right. That was the end of my grandfather's savings and he spent the last days of his life in a small house in Finchley, where I was born in 1906. I remember being told of his death early one morning when I went to climb into my mother's bed; in memory it is very close to the death of King Edward VII in 1910 but perhaps it was a year or two later. I made some demonstration of grief; it seemed proper.

'Why are you behaving like that?' said my mother, not at all unkindly but simply seeking the truth with the directness and honesty that some-times made her so disconcerting. 'You didn't really know him.' Then after a pause she went on: 'Perhaps because you are sorry for me.' I accepted with relief this escape from the implication of hypocrisy.

Thus I never saw my mother's old home in what was then wild country on the borders of Yorkshire and Derbyshire. Nor did she speak of it much but everything I did hear was stirring and poetic. She spoke of a favourite horse with a smooth easy action on whose back she would canter for miles along a grass track that followed the line of a high ridge, with wide views over broken wooded country westward towards Kinder Scout and the Peak. She spoke often of the annual holiday of six weeks, when the family took three days to drive over the moors to Robin Hood's Bay, near Whitby on the Yorkshire coast. This little fishing village still tumbles down the cliff from ledge to ledge like a mountain stream, the houses hanging poised as though about to topple into the sea. The cobbled streets, interspersed with steps, are sometimes hardly a yard across. My mother said that in their childhood the Bay folk used among themselves a dialect which no one in England could understand, but that if a Danish fishing boat was blown in, they could make shift to talk to the crew. She told me the legend of St Hilda, the great abbess of Whitby, who had commanded the snakes to be gone from all that wide stretch of moorland that lies inland from Whitby, whereupon they had curled themselves up into hoops and obediently rolled towards the sea and over the cliffs to the beach below. Their heads were knocked off in the fall and they turned to stone and could still be picked up on the beach, being known to the faithless as ammonites. Pools among the rocks on the beach, jelly-fish and anemones, the short steep breakers of the North Sea; the fishing cobles and the smell of fish and seaweed – all the usual ingredients of a northern seaside – all these, though they ran through her

talk of those holidays, were dominated, it seems to me now, by the rolling tangle of moors and becks and gills on which she and her brothers
went for so many expeditions and by the farms where they had tea, feast-
ing with kindly hospitable folk on crumbly turf cakes before the dim
glow of the turf fire.

My grandfather had a cottage at Robin Hood's Bay and there was a
long spell when they went there every year. But at some stage of his life
he became friendly with Professor John Glaister of Glasgow University,
a pioneer in forensic medicine, if not the founder of that field of study.
The Professor one day remarked that of course England could not compare with Scotland for the beauty of its scenery. My grandfather indignantly questioned this opinion and they entered into a kind of pact
to visit each other's countries and compare the splendours they admired.
Mistakenly, it seems to me, my grandfather took the Professor to the
limestone pinnacles of Dovedale in Derbyshire, to Derwentwater and
Grasmere, mountain scenery on a scale much less grand than Scotland,
whereas his only hope of winning any concession from his opponent lay
in showing him something quite different, in which man had played a
greater part – the chalk downs of Dorset, perhaps, or glades of beech in
Wiltshire. But my grandfather was as committed to Wordsworth in
aesthetic taste as to Gladstone in politics and in this my mother followed
him without question. She was always for the hills against the plains and
the tales she told me of Robert the Bruce and William Wallace linked
later with Quentin Durward and Alan Breck to make me cherish a
secret longing to be discovered to be a Scot. I was as pleased about
Bannockburn as about Agincourt.

Against this shadowy hearsay stuff, like a tapestry seen by firelight,
Barrowden was real but prosaic. My Mason grandfather also died when
I was quite small but my grandmother stayed on in the old stone house,
her youngest son managing the farm from the Malting House on the
other side of the lane. She had been Grace Dainty, a name to catch any
man's fancy, and she had a face to match the name, a gentle beautiful old
face when I knew her. We all went to see her three or four times a year
but in the summer I went several times to stay with her alone. The stone
of that part of Rutland is a warm golden brown and I was usually there in
harvest time; there is a literal, visible, colour of gold to all my memories.
There was a stream below the Malting Close where a cousin taught me to
draw the pith from a stick of elder to make a whistle; the sunlight down
there fell through the willows on shallow water running over golden-
brown pebbles. In front of the house was a quadrangle of golden stone;
you came into it from the lane through a gate in a wall of cut stone; on
the right was the high stone wall of the enclosed garden, which was quite

separate from the house. In front was the row of stables and to the left the house itself, with one door to the living part and another to the dairy, where the cream bowls stood on great stone slabs, and to the huge, low-ceilinged kitchen with its floor of stone flags. The roofs of the buildings were also of stone, this of a darker shade, being of a kind that split easily and came from a quarry near by at Colly Weston. Between the house and the stables was the way to the stackyard, the waggon-shed and the barns.

The stackyard was a great playground. By the end of harvest, there would be a city – to a small boy a Manhattan – of towering stacks. They stood on their mushroom-like staddle-stones, safely thatched, for this was before the days of tarpaulin or plastic, waiting for the threshing-machine. Pale bright straw, much paler than the stone, lay everywhere. The hens wandered among the stacks and the barns and we could earn a penny a score for eggs we found. The hay-stacks were at the eastern end of the stackyard. Nowadays it is easy to build a stack of baled hay; it is like a child building with bricks. But in those days the hay was not baled and there was an art in building and thatching a stack which might stand for a full year. When hay was needed, the stack was cut like a cake, with a huge two-handed hay-knife, razor-sharp – an instrument that shared with the chaff-cutter a prohibition so tremendous that we never dared to touch either – and, if a rick of old hay had survived the year through, it might be cut into convenient ledges onto which we could scramble. Our feet would make holes in which rain might collect and if 'the men' caught us they would order us away to a bean-stack where we could do no harm. But we hated bean-straw, which was very hard on bare knees, and had none of the delicious scent of hay. We could do no harm, though, in the waggon-shed, where on Sundays the great curved wooden waggons stood in a row and would serve at will as the *Revenge* or the *Victory* or a long low rakish craft flying the Jolly Roger.

So much has been written in so many books about riding back in the waggons from the harvest fields on top of the piled sheaves of barley that it is hard to be sure what is genuine memory. But I *think* I remember that triumphant return behind the great slow-moving shire horses with their glorious shining quarters of dappled brown and bay and grey. They had names such as Bonny and Snowball, while the cows were always given the names of women or flowers, Molly and Dolly, Daisy and Buttercup. There were not many cows, only some twenty or thirty. Some bullocks were fattened, being brought in during the winter to the stockyard to trample down straw into muck. Barley and sheep were, and still are, the backbone of the farm. The sheep were folded on the stubble after harvest and the hurdles moved on, stage by stage, to cover the whole field. Only the 'golden hoof' of the sheep, it was believed, would produce the best quality of bright malting barley from that light sandy soil. It was a system that needed a good deal of labour, a permanent force of about a dozen men for the five-hundred-acre farm and another dozen of temporary hands for haymaking and harvest. 'But where did they come from?' I asked my father many years later, for it seemed astonishing against that unchanging background that there could be so many temporary hands so conveniently available for less than a quarter of the year. They were Irish, I was told, and went back to Ireland in the autumn.

Permanence seemed the keynote of a life in which the rhythm of the seasons was yearly renewed. But the permanence depended on excellence of quality, maintained by constant effort, the straight lines of good ploughing, generosity with good dung, the skilled construction of well-squared, well-thatched ricks, the unremitting care needed to get good bright barley and to get a good price for it. Only the best barley would make malting barley for the brewers. Prices varied with the quality and also from year to year and market to market. There were some years when the brewers were short and the prices would creep up in January and the man who had kept his barley back till towards the end of the season would score. But this was risky because in March the malting season would come to an end. The price might drop at last and you might even be left with barley unsold. By April you could only sell it as fodder. It was something of a gamble, then, to choose the right moment to sell.

My great-grandfather, Henry Mason, used to brew beer himself on the farm and also to malt barley for his neighbours. He used sometimes to buy barley for his own malting floor when the price was low and sell it to the brewers if it rose; he was in fact, in a small way, a speculator in barley futures. So my father told me, but it was from a cousin of my father's that I heard the story of the lengths to which my great-grandfather Henry would go to get a good price for his barley. I imagine that this took place before the Repeal of the Corn Laws in 1846, when prices must have fluctuated over a wide range.

It was eight miles to Stamford, the natural market for Barrowden. But great-grandfather Henry observed that there were a good many farmers at Stamford with their little bags of samples, while there were very few buyers. It occurred to him that it might be worth going thirty miles in the opposite direction to Leicester, where the balance might be more in his favour. He would go several times in the season, showing his samples, judging the best moment to sell. He would leave home before dawn, have breakfast at an inn in Leicester, see his horse had a good feed, do his business during the morning and ride back in the afternoon. Then one day when the market at Leicester was dull and the buyers cautious, it occurred to him that he might go one stage further. Burton-on-Trent was the place for brewers. He went back to his inn, hired a good stout cob, rode on the thirty miles to Burton and found that he was right; prices *were* better. And so Burton became his market, sixty miles from home. But a neighbour found out what he was doing and decided to follow his example. There were sour looks at first but in the end they decided they would take turns to provide a trap and go together, sharing the price of a hired horse for the second half of the journey from Leicester to Burton.

Then came a year when prices were poor and both of them held on without selling till almost the end of the season. There was only one more chance. It was the neighbour's turn to provide the horse and trap, but when the clock struck five he had not come. He was half an hour late. Great-grandfather Henry realized what he was up to, saddled a horse and set out to make up the lost time. He pushed his horse as fast as he dared, changed horses at Leicester without stopping for breakfast, and when he saw his enemy's head bobbing along over the hedges in front of him, took the next side-road and galloped to get ahead of him. At Burton he would not pause for food until he had taken his samples to the market and made his bargain before his enemy arrived.

That is the story as I heard it. But I knew nothing as a child of this background of self-will and competition, gaining only an impression of permanence, of solidity, of comfort. Would our grandmother provide eight puddings to choose from or would it be only six? (We were allowed to choose two, and two for a second helping.) That was the question we debated when we drove over to see her on a Sunday.

Two pillars of Victorian greatness I have said – the solid background of land and sheep and corn, that seemed as though it would never change, and the new radical questioning spirit of the industrial North – yes, that is what they stood for. But in both traditions it was understood that a man made his own life by his own effort. I was brought up between the two but a child always chooses. I think now of the two traditions as different orders of architecture. When I was a boy, it was the sky-aspiring Gothic that held my fancy; today it is the round arches and ponderous columns of the Romanesque.

2 *Country Doctor*

When my Great-Uncle James retired from medical practice, he lived in a comfortable house in Stamford with a big garden at the back, rising gently to what we called the Roman Wall. I once recounted to my father as much as I could remember of a monologue Uncle James had addressed to me over lunch on the advantage of eating bread with a meal. It had seemed to last a long time.

'Yes,' said my father. 'He has always believed that the best way of fixing what he reads in his memory is to repeat it to someone else at the next meal. I have suffered a good deal from that.'

In fact, my father had suffered a good deal from him in other ways too. Great-Uncle James was older than my grandfather by six years and had left Barrowden at eighteen for the medical school at Glasgow University, where he must have qualified about 1860. He decided to practise in Sheffield, where there were very few doctors for the growing industrial population. After some time he announced that he would 'make a doctor' of my father. Since my father was one of nine children, this was good news and, at the age of about thirteen, my father left Barrowden for Uncle James's house at Sheffield, where he was to be educated by a governess engaged for the purpose. Towards the end of his life, he told me that 'the governess' had made no pretence of teaching him anything. The whole manoeuvre had been simply an excuse for moving her into the house with some semblance of respectability. For two years, my father had no formal education at all. No doubt he learned something from Uncle James's monologues over the dining-table and he had leisure to read. Then Uncle James decided to get married; the 'governess' was sent packing and my father went back to Barrowden.

Nothing was done about his education. No one at Barrowden saw any value in education for its own sake, and country life – closely bound to time by the rhythm of haymaking and harvest, lambing and shearing, the first blackberries and late-keeping apples – is yet, in another sense, timeless. One year missed meant nothing. Uncle James had said he would make him a doctor and that was that. But it was another two years before he suggested that my father should come back to Sheffield and to be in his house, studying to become a doctor and helping in the surgery by making up bottles of medicine. As it was my grandfather who paid the fees for tuition, Uncle James acquired a dispenser and general assistant for the cost of his food. Uncle James usually made a good bargain and this was no exception.

It was Uncle James's intervention that made my father a doctor, but it had interrupted his formal education from about the age of thirteen to seventeen. He found it very difficult to pass the entrance examination for the university and after that the chemistry and physiology were hard going. He had to work long hours to make up for the lost years – and not in the easiest of circumstances. One of Uncle James's less successful bargains was a horse, a fine strong young horse which he thought would do a lot of work. He was right about that but it was one of those indomitably energetic horses which do not understand moderation. It ran away twice with Uncle James and the groom refused to ride it. My father was instructed to keep it exercised. It took him about four hours a day. As Christmas drew near – it would be 1895 or 1896 I suppose – he asked permission to go to Barrowden for Christmas Day. Uncle James agreed, but there were two conditions. He was not to start till he had made up all the medicines prescribed at the surgery on Christmas Eve, and he must take that famous horse. It was nearly nine o'clock before he started and the distance is at least seventy-five miles. He was home in time for breakfast on Christmas Day. It was a fine frosty morning and the hand-bell ringers were lined up in the quadrangle in front of the house. The first carols were ringing out as he arrived.

'You must have been tired,' I said, when he told me this story.

'Not so tired as the horse,' he replied. 'I had to lead him up the hills towards the end. I was in very hard training from riding that horse every day.'

When my father qualified, my grandfather told him that his medical education was his share of the family fortune. He was the fifth of nine children and could expect no more. He took this absolutely literally and never asked for help, even over a loan. In those days, a practice had to be bought, usually for twice the takings of the last year. In order to save some money for the purchase of a practice, my father took a post as surgeon with a line of steamships sailing to the Caribbean and South America. He was already engaged to my mother but they would both have felt it wrong to marry until he had made a start. He saved most of his pay, added to his savings a loan from the bank, and bought a practice on the borders of Cheshire, Lancashire and Derbyshire. It was a mainly working-class practice, worth when he bought it about £200 a year. At first hardly anyone would consult him; they thought he looked too young – and indeed he did always look very young. But one day he was suddenly summoned to the bedside of the most influential old person in the village. She became a firm friend and later told him that that morning she had been on the point of sending for the doctor in the next village, but looking out of the window and seeing him pass she had said: 'Well, that's soomebody's lad!' and decided to give him a trial.

That was a turning-point and after a few more years he was, he felt, in a position to marry and soon after that to move to a practice where there were more possibilities. But in those early days at Broadbottom – it is near Mottram where the artist T. S. Lowry lived – he had made his visits on a bicycle and had lived in a rented cottage, cooking himself porridge for breakfast and porridge for supper. Someone came in and cooked him a midday meal and he was able to save; he was saving to pay off his debt, to buy furniture for his marriage, to help towards that better practice. When he did move, in 1907, a year after I was born, his first practice was worth three times what it had been.

The new practice, five miles from Derby, was centred on what had once been a large country village, now just beginning to turn into a suburb. Already, in 1907, there were residents who went by train to Derby every day, but green fields still came down to the backs of the gardens on either side of the village street. It was a growing place, with a fair cross-section of people from most walks of life in the village itself, and a sprinkling of larger houses and farms in the surrounding country. Altogether, it was a far more ambitious venture than Broadbottom and of course there was now a new and larger debt to the bank.

Few young doctors today would contemplate the kind of life my father lived. It was a firm principle of his that the care of his patients must come first and he must always answer a call for help. The house could never be left empty; there must always be someone to answer the telephone, someone who knew where the doctor was to be found. There were no days off, not even Sundays. Three or four times a year – but this was after the 1914 war when motor-cars were more reliable – arrangements would be made to go to Barrowden, sixty miles away. For that one Sunday, urgent calls would be referred to a friendly neighbour in Belper. Everything possible would be done in advance to clear that day – but there would always be one or two visits to be made on Sunday morning before we could start and we must always be back in good time in case something had cropped up during the day.

The daily routine, six days a week, began with morning surgery and then visits till lunch-time; there would be more visits after a hasty lunch, evening surgery at six, often going on till seven-thirty or eight; after supper there were notes to be written up, and there were often calls in the night. There was no receptionist, no nurse, no secretary; until some time after the First War, there was no dispenser and my father made up the medicines himself. Once a quarter, accounts would be added up and posted to the patients. My father and mother did this secretarial work together, late at night.

There was a great deal of visiting, sometimes to distant farms, and my father was almost always back for lunch later than he had meant to be, sometimes much later. My mother was always disappointed, partly because the food she had arranged had had to be kept hot and would be past its best, partly because he had not been present at the family meal and partly because she did not like him to be overworked and obliged to eat at irregular times. Her nature was so direct and impulsive that she never concealed these feelings and what she said would sound like a reproach. It was not really a reproach; she was committed to him without reservation and shared his belief that his patients must come before his personal convenience. He understood both her concern for his comfort and her dedication to his work. Her words must nonetheless often have been irritating when he came in tired, cold and hungry, but he would gently put them aside. Sometimes he tried to treat them as a joke, saying perhaps: 'I was afraid I should get into hot water.' But that was a mistake. Her disappointment was real, her concern was for him, and she felt it was flippant and even, for the moment, unkind to make light of them. But he was never unkind and that too she understood at a deeper level.

Two sets of motives could hardly be more inseparably welded than they were in my parents' attitude to the practice. Of course there was the plain worldly motive of wanting to get on; there was the debt to be paid off, the children to be educated, provision to be made for old age. In my mother's case there was also a strong desire that her children should achieve the fame and influence which she believed her father had deserved. But they would neither of them have lived so single-minded a life for so long if they had not been convinced that medicine was one of the noblest professions and that every patient bandaged in the surgery, every visit to a bedside, was a good thing done, something to be proud of, so that each day's work brought its own satisfaction.

When my father started medical practice, there was no medical insurance and a doctor charged the fee he thought proper for the patient's position and income. He might charge forty or fifty times as much for half an hour by a bedside in the manor as for the same time spent in a cottage. My father was scrupulous that his working-class patients should be charged fees they could pay and that they should have proper attention. Sometimes he treated them free. Later there began the system of insurance by which 'panel patients' – which in practice meant manual workers paid weekly – were protected against the costs of ill-health, and later still came the National Health Service, which turned almost everyone into 'panel patients', though a few private patients remained. I asked my father how it was possible to be fair to both classes. It was surely wrong to give priority to the rich – but unless they did get priority, what were they paying for? 'National Health patients,' he replied, 'get the attention *I* think they need; private patients get the attention *they* think they need.'

Long after Hitler's war, I once arrived at Derby from London with a heavy suitcase. There seemed to be no one to meet me, so I asked a porter about the next train to Duffield. He looked at my suitcase and exclaimed:

'It's not Dr Mason of Duffield you're visiting? Ah, there's a grand doctor, a real poor man's doctor. We used to live in Duffield and he took as much trouble for us as he could have done for anyone in the world!

What, you may ask, was the background of belief that nurtured this life of happy but unremitting and utterly dedicated endeavour? I can only record an impression. My father in a serious mood once told me that his creed was contained in the one phrase: 'Do as you would be done by.' His was certainly not a philosophical or speculative mind. It was enough to get on with the job to which he had been called; his duty was usually clear enough and he told me on another occasion that he did not think he need bother the Almighty too much about the state of his soul. It was not so important as all that; there were a great many other people who mattered just as much. He went to church when he could, which in the early days was not very often, since there was always some-one who wanted to be visited on Sunday morning. But he did not question the scheme of things; he was on the whole quietly trustful though sometimes a little doubtful about life after death. His compassion for suffering, particularly in children, grew as he grew older – or perhaps it was only that I became more aware of it. In short, I do not think my father's code of behaviour was the product of a personal religious faith; it was rather the outcome in a simple and affectionate nature of a creed hammered out through the centuries which he trustfully accepted and on which he acted.

Much the same might be said of my mother. It might have been expected that she would have been more an asker of questions than my father. Her own father had certainly asked questions and so did her elder brother. My Woodruff grandfather was, as I have said, a Methodist but when he married he came to an unusual agreement with his bride. The boys were to be Methodists, the girls Anglicans. But the home atmosphere of course was the same for both and my mother's approach to religion, as to education, was 'enlightened'. She taught me, for example, that the story of the Creation in Genesis was a myth, not to be taken literally but to be interpreted in the light of modern knowledge. This I am sure she owed to her father. But she was too quick, too practical, to concern herself much with doctrine. For her almost as much as for my father it was conduct that mattered and she took for granted the principles on which she acted, putting all her energy into everything she did.

3 Mrs Binns

The doctor's house stands facing the village street. My brother still lives there. It is a stone house with three sharp high gables and the style of the front is late Stuart, but there is a Georgian addition as well as a Victorian, and a part my father added. I was only a year old when we came to live there, and I remember nothing of Broadbottom. Duffield and Barrowden are the background to my earliest memories. To be brought up in a house three hundred years old that has been altered century by century to fit changing times, to feel that the house goes on though people come and go, must surely have some effect on a growing child, affecting one's attitude to past and present, to human institutions and human endeavour. I made this point many years later, when I was in South Africa and trying to understand the Afrikaaner attempt to construct a quite new society, disentangling and dismissing all the accidents of history. It seemed natural to me, I said to the exponents of apartheid, to add to what you had and go on from there – as the builders had done with the house I had lived in, with the village street, with the church of which the fabric had been begun a thousand years ago by the Normans. They saw the point; that no doubt was the way an English mind would work. But *they* were different; they had carved their farms from the raw *veldt*.

Next door was a house with a Regency front known rather grandly as Duffield House. We understood that this house had once been joined to ours but that they had been separated in Victorian times, when brick additions had been made to both. How different from ours was the house next door! It was altogether more pretentious. You went up steps to a huge front door; the ceilings were much higher, the rooms much larger. The hall, which was very dark, was to a small boy curiously awe-inspiring, resembling one of those chapels in a cathedral where the tattered colours of county regiments hang cased in gauze, dark against the sombre vault-ing of the roof. This was partly because the walls were draped with the cloaks of Maori chiefs, made from the skins of kiwis or cassowaries, skins like those of gigantic hedgehogs, furnished with limp quills, now drab, dark and colourless – surely the gloomiest repositories for dust that ever served as decoration. It was with relief that I used to turn, every Sunday afternoon, from this depressing and rather frightening hall into the drawing-room where Mrs Binns awaited me.

The drawing-room seemed very large and it was a long way to the fireside. There were sofas and chairs covered with shiny white chintz, embellished with a pattern of gigantic pink cabbage roses. The first landmark for a small navigator was the harp, tall, shining, gold and far too august to be twangled. Next, about half way to the fireplace, was one of those triangular seats for three people sitting back to back, called I believe conversation-settees. The fireplace and the looking-glass above it are now inseparably fused in memory with Tenniel's illustration of Alice stepping through the glass into Looking-Glass World; there was a clock in the middle like Alice's and at either end of the chimney-piece a dome of glass. But in Mrs Binns's drawing-room the glass dome covered a Spanish dancer in bright-coloured silk instead of Alice's artificial flowers. On either side of the fireplace were silhouettes of her ancestors.

Mrs Binns was a good deal older than my parents, and her sons, both doctors, lived far away. Soon after we arrived she had suggested that I should come every Sunday afternoon to be read to. I do not remember much of the stories she read – though there seem to have been a good many about American children who unaccountably called a railway station a depot – but I remember fragments of her conversation and her remarkable gift for making me feel that for that afternoon there was no one in the world but the two of us – a rather dumpy little old lady in a silk dress and a little boy. We were engaged in a kind of conspiracy together, with jokes and secrets of our own. She had a small smooth-haired fox-terrier called Spot who was supposed to get very excited if cats were mentioned. So we must never talk of cats; when we looked at Lewis Wain's picture-books, in which – those creatures – are shown in hundreds, doing everything that humans do, we must refer to them as 'giddlies'. Spot never discovered what a giddly was – and the etymology of the word is still a mystery to me.

She was clearly fond of words. 'Never use a short word when a long word will do,' she said to me with her slightly apoplectic chuckle. Among the books she gave me and which I still possess are the *Works* of Charles Stuart Calverley. This was when I was twelve, and too young to enjoy all his verbal felicity and mastery of the anti-climax. But his mimicry of Macaulay appealed to me at once:

> Sikes, housebreaker, of Houndsditch,
>   Habitually swore;
> But so surpassingly profane
>   He never was before,
> As on a night in winter,
>   When – softly as he stole
> In the dim light from stair to stair,
> Noiseless as boys who in her lair
> Seek to surprise a fat old hare –
> He barked his shin-bone, unaware . . .

It was a long time however before I came to appreciate his savage parody of Browning: 'The Cock and the Bull'.

> You see this pebble-stone? It's a thing I bought
> Of a bit of a chit of a boy i' the mid o' the day –
> I like to dock the smaller parts-o'-speech,

As we curtail the already cur-tailed cur
(You catch the paronomasia, play 'po' words?)

A few years later she gave me Brewer's *Dictionary of Phrase and Fable*, the mere sight of which immediately recalls her. It is a book on every page of which some seductive and irrelevant bypath tempts one away from the purpose with which one opened it, and the inconsequent jumble of its contents seems exactly appropriate to my memories of Mrs Binns.

Long before these lasting possessions, she would give me every Christmas a bound volume of *Chums*. This was a magazine for boys, of which the weekly numbers were put together annually to make a fat heavy book in a bright red cover. It could best be read sprawled on the hearth-rug, head supported on elbows. How I despised the *Boy's Own Paper*, full of school stories about winning the house cricket cup! I turned at once to the serials and first to those by S. S. Walkley, who ran a serial every year, alternating between buccaneers, who would tumble into their boats with imprecations fit to poison the moon, and – in the succeeding year – Iroquois and *coureurs-du-bois*, who were incomprehensibly involved in wars in America between the French and the English. I do not think Mrs Binns ever read *Chums* to me herself and it seems to me now remarkable in an old lady to have given a boy something so far removed from her own taste. Only scraps of her varied conversation remain but I remember that she had read Dickens in instalments and how eagerly she had looked forward to the next issue. Mr Dickens, she thought, was the funniest man there had ever been and it had really made her quite ill when the hostler told Mr Pickwick that that horse would not shy, not if it was to meet a vaggin-load of monkeys with their tails burnt off. It did not seem to me very funny. But I must have been impressed – since I remember it so clearly – by something of quite a different order which she told me about Pickwick; the basic idea of the book, she said, was really *Don Quixote* turned inside out, with a fat master and a thin servant instead of a thin master and a fat servant. And of course there is a good deal in this, though Mr Pickwick's innocent benevolence is quite different from Don Quixote's romantic infatuation and Sam is a great deal sharper than Sancho.

Perhaps it was because she talked so much of Pickwick that my memory of my old friend's appearance is influenced by Tony Weller's. You must imagine a large stage-coachman turned into a little old lady but both presented a general effect of shapelessness, of a person muffled up to the chin, with a rubicund complexion. But I do not think small children pay much attention to detail in the appearance of someone they are used to. It is pleasure in the child's company that arouses liking and of this I never had any doubt with Mrs Binns. Her husband was a rather acid little man who had been a mining engineer in New Zealand. He played golf on Sunday afternoons and I doubt whether he would have found much amusement in chuckling over giddlies, but Mrs Binns and I, in the halcyon days before I went away to school, were happy together.

That after all is what matters to a child and I do not think I paid much attention to her views on society, which were those of the Edwardian *Punch*. Servants occasionally figured in her anecdotes but only because their ignorance was funny. There was, for instance, a housemaid who had once said to her that young ladies had nothing to do all day but lie on the sofa and read novels. I did not ask her what she *did* have to do, but I know now, because I heard later how she had replied to my mother's enquiry about music: 'I play seven instruments and all of them perfectly.' She must, I think, have had relations in the Southern States, for she warned me against that wicked and misleading book *Uncle Tom's Cabin*. Slave-owners had been *kind* to their slaves, she told me, and many slaves had fought beside their masters against the upstart dollar-grabbing Northerners. But to me all this was sleet off a duck's back, a proverbial phrase that I heard years later from an Indian prince, which would have pleased Mrs Binns.

Many of my early memories are dated by the coronation of King George V, when I was five. This, I suppose, is the way a pre-literate tribe arranges its chronology, pegging every private event to some natural phenomenon or public day of celebration. No one day could have held all the events that I associate with that occasion. But it must have been on that very morning that I went next door to help Mrs Binns with her preparations for the evening. Every window was to be outlined in little Chinese lanterns, in each of which was a candle; every candle must be lighted in the morning and then blown out, so that it would light again easily in the evening. 'We must black all their little noses,' said Mrs Binns. In the afternoon I was sent to bed, to make up for the sleep I should lose that evening. And there I remember a sensation that recurred. Every toe, every finger, grew to gigantic proportions and tingled faintly and then I too swelled till there was nothing else, no bed, no house, no village, nothing but me. The tide ebbed quickly and there was only a little boy lying in bed and someone – who, I wonder? – was saying: 'What have *I* to do with this round-faced little object? How did *I* get mixed up with this queer little morsel?'

But all that was forgotten in the evening when we drove, in a dog-cart from the *King's Head*, to the top of the Chevin – the 'last hill in the Pennine Range' as my mother used to tell me. It was dark and there was a little green light on the end of the driver's whip which danced here and there like a fire-fly. There was a bonfire, like no bonfire I had ever seen before – a great square tower, hundreds of feet high it seemed, made of old railway sleepers laid crosswise. They must have been soaked in tar or paraffin, for as soon as a light was set to it, the whole structure burst into flame and great spires and ropes of flame roared up to heaven like the tails of ginger tom-cats. And there were rockets, sizzling slowly up into the sky and lazily tumbling in glorious curves into green and silver and crimson globes that burst like bubbles far overhead.

But it cannot really have been on Coronation Day that I was flipped, like a pea from a thumb-nail, from my father's first motor-car, to land by the side of the road at the feet of a shying horse. He had put on the brake very suddenly to avoid the excitable horse and out I went. The car was a De Dion Bouton, one of the earlier models, open of course and with no windscreen to impede my flight; since it was a very tall car in relation to its length, there may have been some play about the upper works. Its number was R2, being the second car to have been registered in the county of Derbyshire. There were two forward gears and no reverse; to turn, it was necessary to find a natural slope leading off the road down which one could run backwards by gravity.

When my father bought that first car, it became necessary to protect against frost a place previously used for keeping a pony-trap. It had been closed by a strong open-work iron gate and all that was necessary was to bolt woodwork on to this gate to close the opening. Bates, the village carpenter, came to inspect it. He measured the gate carefully but said nothing.

'Well,' said my father briskly, 'will you do it?'

'Noa, I wun't,' said Bates.

My father was astonished. 'Why ever not?' he asked.

''Appen thee'll go and soomeone else'll tell me to take it down and a pretty fool I should look,' was his reply.

I have the impression that this was sometimes the reasoning of local craftsmen I had to deal with years later in Dorset, but they would never give so blunt a reply. 'We'll try to look in some time next week,' they would say, with no intention of ever being mixed up in an enterprise they regarded as foolish and unnecessary, but with a carefulness to avoid giving offence which belongs to that part of England south and west of King Alfred's settlement with the Danes. When I went away to school, Bates was instructed to make me a good strong wooden play-box; he made it so large and strong and heavy that I had to endure a good deal of ridicule; it survived at least forty years and was eventually abandoned, not because it was worn out, but because it was too cumbersome for modern railway travel. The village cobbler was a man of similar temperament, who would look gloomily at a pair of shoes brought to him for repair and say he couldn't possibly touch them for six weeks, but in the end he would do them beautifully in half that time.

Duffield was still a village with a corporate life. Sometimes on a Sunday morning there would be a Procession, and that was a great occasion. The church was about a mile from the village, near the bridge across the river Derwent which divided the parish; perhaps the village site too had been there before the Black Death. The Procession would start at the other end of the village and march past our house to the church. There would be the Boy Scouts, with their band, the Church Lads' Brigade, with theirs, the St John Ambulance Brigade – my father as commandant at their head, very smart in a black frogged uniform with a white band round the hat – and I do not remember how many other organizations. The rest of us would follow, on foot. It was proper to walk to church; I remember only two families who went in a carriage and pair.

In a village the size of Duffield, with a sprinkling of retired folk and the beginnings of a suburban middle class, it was necessary, of course, for the doctor to keep up appearances and do some entertaining, which had hardly been necessary at Broadbottom. There were two maids in the house and a woman who came perhaps twice a week to clean the house, an occasional man in the garden and a boy to clean knives and boots and deliver bottles of medicine. There were no vacuum cleaners and all the heating was by coal fires, so that there was a lot of work; grates had to be cleaned and fires laid every morning. My mother had been to a domestic science course and for her there was a right way and a wrong way of doing most things; if there were two ways – as for making raspberry jam – she had long ago decided which was the better and it was incomparably better than anyone else's. As to raspberry jam she was quite right, as about most things; hers really did taste of fresh raspberries. Everything must be home-made; it would have been a disgrace to buy a cake or a pot of jam. It was a waste of money, for one thing, but, quite apart from that, shop cakes and shop jam were not as *good*. They did not taste as good and they were adulterated.

My mother always claimed that her maids stayed with her longer than anyone else's. I think they probably worked harder too; certainly their work was carefully thought out and they were shown exactly how to do it. To be one of our maids was not a post that called for initiative – but it was important to be *responsible*. This word, a favourite with headmistresses, meant reliable or trustworthy – as in the dictionary – but also in my mother's use, exactly obedient, which is not quite according to the dictionary.

Entertainment took several forms. There were days when my mother was 'At Home'; this meant something like twenty ladies dropping in to tea, and they must be entertained with a great variety of delicate little sandwiches and home-made cakes containing confections of raspberries and cream or walnuts and honey; these were days of shared activity, from which everyone – my mother and the maids alike – emerged with a sense of triumph if one of the guests had asked for a recipe. There were also tennis parties, at which no one played tennis very well and a good deal of time was spent looking for lost balls in the shrubbery, and there were dinner parties. None of my father's friends or colleagues had a wife who could organize such a good dinner as my mother – so he told her and so she told me. It meant a sense of tension and excitement throughout the house for at least two days beforehand, mounting steadily till the moment when our parents came to say good-night, my mother radiant in something silvery, filmy and sparkling, my father unfamiliar in a hard shirt-front. It is not surprising that on such nights I would often wake in a state of bewilderment and excitement and patter downstairs to the dining-room.

On one such occasion, a strange thing happened, something for which I could not account at the time. As often before, I was disturbed and frightened, got out of bed and made my way to the drawing-room. But I was quite ready to go back to bed if someone would come and sit by me for a little. And I heard myself say, to my own surprise, that it was my father I wanted, not my mother. It had always been clearly understood by everyone in the house, including myself, that it was my mother to whom I was devoted. How had this strange reversal come about? My mother asked me the direct question. I could only answer that I did not know. But some time later – I cannot say when, but perhaps after many years – the reason became clear to me. My mother would have wanted to know what had frightened me, and of course I should not have been able to say. But my father, I knew instinctively, would say nothing; he would simply sit by the bed and be there, a comforting, reassuring presence.

II

GROWING A SHELL

1 A Hard Decision

At some point before 1914, my parents came to a decision of importance both for them and for me. It was in no way unusual; thousands of English couples made similar resolutions at the same time. But it arose from an institution that to most people not English seems eccentric, if not positively cruel, while to my parents it involved many sacrifices of pleasure and convenience.

The custom of sending away their sons, and later their daughters, had grown steadily among the English from about the time of Waterloo till the end of the era at Sarajevo. 'It is an axiom among the English upper classes,' a Scottish professor remarked drily, 'that the less their children see of their parents the better – and perhaps they are right.' The age at which boys left home crept downwards; the social level to which the custom extended spread wider. New schools such as Marlborough and Cheltenham were founded; old schools, with a reputation that had extended over the neighbouring countryside only, such as Blundell's in the west or Sedbergh in the north, began to draw their pupils from further afield and local boys who came only for the day became fewer and fewer. Preparatory schools, with a few exceptions, came later. In 1834, Tom Brown's private school was a very perfunctory affair; he went to Rugby at eleven and stayed till he was eighteen. But by the time the old Queen died, there was a regular pattern established. The private or prep school took a boy from about eight to thirteen, the public school from thirteen to eighteen. The 'public' schools were so called not merely to confuse Americans; they were trusts, with a board of governors; no one made a profit from them but they were the product of private enterprise and had nothing to do with the state.

It was all very English. G. O. Trevelyan, later to be the biographer of Macaulay, wrote: 'How is it that there are no tradesmen's sons at Eton or Harrow? There is no law, written or unwritten, which excludes them from those schools, and yet the boys take good care that if one comes he shall not stay there very long.' That was in 1864 and by 1900 they were less exclusive. If the father had enough money, if the boy had survived five years at a prep school, if he behaved in the right kind of way, he would be tolerated. And of course there were gradations between schools, as between regiments. Some were socially more esteemed, some were superior academically. Nonetheless, in those Edwardian years, one among the many broad social distinctions dividing the English people, and perhaps one of the most clear-cut, lay between those who had been through a prep school and a public school and those who had not.

There were no rules as to who should go to such schools nor were there any rules as to the benefits they might bring. David Lloyd George became Prime Minister and Wully Robertson a Field-Marshal without such preliminaries. But they were exceptions and in general these pro-longed *rites de passage* were the usual introduction to success in the learned professions as well as in the armed forces, in politics, in banking and large-scale business. My mother, as I have said, thought of education as the key to a richer and fuller life but she was also socially ambitious. It was she, as my father told me much later, who initiated the joint decision to which I have referred. But in a true marriage – a stable marriage regarded by both parties as permanent – it is often a mistake to think of one partner as deciding and the other as following. It is often a truly joint decision, the marriage being like Donne's well-known image of the compasses:

> If they be two, they are two so
> As stiffe twin compasses are two,
> Thy soule the fixt foot, makes no show
> To move, but doth, if the' other doe.
>
> And though it in the center sit,
> Yet when the other far doth rome
> It leanes, and hearkens after it,
> And growes erect, as that comes home.

There appears in such a marriage to be a still point but without the still point there could be no dance.

The decision concerned both my parents deeply and affected their lives for the next twenty-five years. When my father moved to his second practice at Duffield, his income was about seven hundred pounds a year. His aim at the time, he wrote later, was to make it a thousand. To send a boy to a prep school cost something round a hundred and fifty, to a public school rather more, to a university about three hundred. He could hardly do this for one son and not for the other, and I had a sister too.

He was embarking on a course which for about half his working life was likely to commit him to paying out between a third and a half of what he expected to be his income. Such was the force of this strange institution and of my parents' determination to do the best they could for their children.

They went about it with circumspection. Some eight miles distant was Repton, one of those ancient schools which had enlarged its local reputation until it was national. Here my parents knew one of the house-masters and they sought his advice about the prep schools which sent boys to Repton. Which did he think were the best at doing what they were supposed to do – preparing a boy for a public school? He gave them the names of two schools within a radius of fifty miles which he considered outstanding. They visited both and chose Stancliffe Hall, a few miles beyond Matlock, in North Derbyshire, on the edge of the moors.

It was not a school like Summerfields at Oxford with a long-standing reputation for excellence; its quality at that time was entirely the creation of one man who was extraordinarily successful at getting results. He left the school not long after I did and it then changed its character completely. I write only of the time I was there and of that one formidable figure. There was a second headmaster who taught the lowest form geography twice a week, a tall handsome man – complete Dornford Yates – who showed parents round and who, we supposed, supplied most of the capital. But the drive, the management, came from the other partner whom we called HC.

I can still recall in the mind's eye the pictures in the prospectus of boys, relaxed and happy in the soft shady hats they wore in summer, gossiping by the little squares of garden in which they grew mustard and cress and spring onions, at work in the carpenter's shop, or on their rugs under the trees watching a cricket match. But such pictures, true in a sense because those were activities in which we engaged, give no idea of the atmosphere of a place that was intensely, and, as far as the head-master was concerned, unremittingly professional. He impressed my parents; I think it would have been surprising if he had not. They told him quite frankly that my father was still building up a practice and had a mortgage to pay off; it was important that I should win a scholarship. Within a few weeks, he told them with confidence that he would get me a scholarship. But I was idle, he said, and I should need alternate coaxing and driving. I do not recall much coaxing, but perhaps that is an effect of the memory.

On Sundays, we had an extra forty minutes in bed; of course we woke at the same time on Sundays as on weekdays, just as the darkness glimmered into light, and one Sunday morning, early in my first term, we began to whisper. It was strictly forbidden to talk in the dormitory between lights out and the rousing bell but in this, the most junior dormitory in the school, we had a prefect who was new to his job; he was also one of those people who hides indecision behind a pompous manner and never commands respect. His ineffective reprimands encouraged us to talk louder and then one daring malefactor committed the crime of crimes and got out of bed on the wrong side. To each bed was allotted a mat, a basket in which clothes must be neatly folded and stacked, and a jerry. That space, that mat and the territory as far as the next bed was your 'passage'. To go out of your passage was an indictable, almost a capital, offence. This eight-year-old ruffian went so far as to get out of bed into the next boy's passage and shake hands with him. It was done simply to show daring, because it was forbidden. And of course when one had done it, another did. Altogether four of us committed this unspeakable offence.

At this point a master walked along the corridor past the door of the dormitory. There was no riot; there was no pillow-fighting. But there was talking, the feeble protests of the prefect being the loudest. It was enough to be heard through the door; the master looked in and there was a boy out of bed. That Sunday morning we were segregated from the rest of the school; the whole dormitory was 'put into silence', which meant that no one must speak to us nor we to anyone, not even to each other. We must play no games but were sent for silent walks, two by two, in a crocodile, like a girls' school, not actually chained wrist to wrist, but with a strong sensation of being a convict gang. This lasted two days. On Monday night both the headmasters appeared in the dormitory with canes under their arms. They were both very large. They harangued us. Then three of us were told to kneel on their beds in the attitudes of Muslims at prayer. Each received three strokes on the buttocks. They were full strokes delivered with the action of a man driving a golf-ball from the tee. I was spared; I was told I had had a very narrow escape.

Many years later I read a defence of the ancient Indian punishment of blowing to pieces, at the mouth of a cannon, a rebel against his sovereign. It was, argued this writer, painless to the criminal because instantaneous, while the effect on the beholders was deterrent in the extreme. As I read, I recalled this early scene, to which the second part of the argument certainly applied. In fact I do not think that caning was more frequent at Stancliffe than at most other private schools of that period; when it did occur, not many strokes were inflicted and I do not recall them as very painful. But the waiting for execution and the deliberation of the ritual had the effect of concentrating the mind wonderfully.

There was a boy about a year older than myself who for some ancestral reason was going to Rugby. He was an only child and his father was dead; we understood that his father had married in old age and certainly his mother, whom I met only once, seemed much older than anyone else's mother. I associate her with the most delicately cut cucumber sandwiches, with an extreme precision of speech and gentleness of manner, with being, in short, the most old-lady-like of old ladies. Her son was far more like an old lady than a boy. He hated games and the possibility of dirt or physical pain. But he was not unpopular with us; he was a mischievous and witty little being with a quick tongue. On some occasion he had been impertinent in class to one of the mistresses who came to teach us as the war continued. She took him to the headmaster's study to be caned. But at the first stroke he winced and cried out. He was brought into the nearest classroom, which happened to be occupied by class B, the group of seven who were being trained for next year's scholarships. The circumstances were explained to us. Williams must learn to keep still and not cry out and perhaps he would do better if we were there to watch.

He knelt on the floor before us to receive punishment and then suddenly raised his head.

'Sir!' he said in his little old lady's voice: 'I think I might be able to keep still if I knew how many I was to get.'

'Four without flinching or squeaking,' he was told.

But at the first cut he cried: 'Ow!' and put his hand to the place. There would be four more he was told and then:

'Are you going to behave like this next term at Rugby?'

'Oh, sir, I hope not!' he cried in an agony of sincerity.

It was the custom of the day to make jokes about schoolboys being caned. Once when HC was drilling us in Greek irregular verbs an assistant master came to the open window.

'I am going down to the village,' he said. 'Do you want anything?'

'Yes,' said HC jovially, 'I want a cane. A nice swishy one. It's for B, and B likes them swishy.'

We giggled sycophantically.

What cannot be defended even in Edwardian terms was the power entrusted to dormitory prefects, who used to beat us for such offences as not piling our clothes neatly in our baskets or whispering after lights out. These were urchins of twelve or thirteen; the punishment was inflicted when the victim was wearing pyjamas, usually with the heel of a rubber shoe, held by the toe. In memory this was more painful than caning, and ten or eleven with a gym shoe was just as much as I could stand without weeping. One young tyrant decided that it was dull to fit the number of strokes to the crime and he would give two strokes to the first offender, three to the second, whatever the offence, and so to twelve when he would start again. But after eleven, an unnatural virtue set in, so to break the lull he decided to make an arbitrary selection and give someone twelve to bring the figure back to two. Another little monster hit on the ingenious expedient of pricking alternate buttocks with a needle. I have sometimes wondered about his later career.

Perhaps nothing shows more clearly the change in opinion over the last sixty years than the treatment of a boy I shall call Prince. Perhaps he was illegitimate; perhaps it was only that his parents were divorced. But no parents ever came to see him and he had no friends. He was neither stupid nor ugly nor coarse; in fact, he was rather a good-looking little boy. But he stole things. It was not usually difficult to detect the culprit and, since stealing was manifestly different from whispering in the dormitory, caning was not enough and he would be birched. This was rare and we asked him how it was done. He had to remove his lower garments and lie on a cushion so that his bare bottom was slightly raised. He was then beaten with a bundle of birch twigs. By a curious convention it was considered 'swinish' to display the bottom when changing for football but legitimate to 'show your marks' after a beating. Instead of the purple weals left by a cane, to which we were accustomed, the birch left a tangled network of thin red criss-cross lines. Poor little Prince was never so near being a hero as when he 'showed his marks' in the dormitory.

I spoke earlier of unremitting professionalism. This was most clearly manifested in Greek and Latin, for which the two scholarship forms A and B were taken entirely by HC. One evening he announced that tomorrow he would test us on a subject we were supposed to know, the way Latin prepositions combined with the 'principal parts' of Latin irregular verbs. 'Fero, I bear', for instance has highly irregular principal parts; it goes: Fero, ferre, tuli, latum. If combined with 'ad', meaning 'towards', it means 'to fetch' like the French apporter. But the perfect is not ad-tuli but attuli. Child's play, I thought to myself; I have been through all this gibberish before and this part of it is merely a matter of commonsense and euphony. (Oh, yes, I knew that word and more than I now remember about hendiadys, anacoluthon, synecdoche and many other words that Fowler calls technical terms.) It is obviously easier to say attuli than ad-tuli – and no doubt on the same principle it will go allatum instead of adlatum. So I made no special preparations and turned up for this test with no more trepidation than usual. But the combinations are less euphonious than I had supposed and instead of allatum it goes adlatum. There were ten one-word questions. We exchanged papers and marked each other's, handed them back and read out the results. Russell had ten out of ten, Hedley had nine out of ten – Mason was bottom of the class with no more than seven!

'Did you look them up?'

'No, sir.'

'Why not?'

'I thought I knew them, sir.'

I was idle and inaccurate as usual; sentence was immediately pronounced. I was excommunicated, under an interdict; I was 'in silence' and must allow no one to speak to me; I must play no games and hold no book in my hand but Kennedy's Latin Grammar until I could answer correctly twenty consecutive questions on Latin irregular verbs, orally and without hesitation. So for the next four days, Kennedy was my sole companion. Every day I would say: 'Please, sir, I think I know them.'

He would question me. Of course I could easily have recited the principal parts of every verb in the book if given straightforward questions. But it was more often some tortuous conundrum with a trick such as: 'From what two verbs could so-and-so come?' I once got up to seventeen. I never achieved the twenty but after four days I was reprieved – somewhat bemused and probably murmuring Kennedy in my sleep.

We were a small school, of only sixty boys; we got four or five scholarships most years and no one ever failed the Common Entrance Examination to the public schools. Indeed, some boys, those who were far from bright, passed so well that they were put in forms where they stuck for years. HC's word was law. No one ever rebelled. He had power of command. He would have led a Chindit column against the Japanese in Burma and men would have followed him to the death. He told me to write to him twice a term after I left and for years I obeyed. He always answered by return of post, on a single small sheet in a swift illegible handwriting, the kind of letter a boy writes from school: 'We have a useful soccer team and beat Holm Leigh 3–2 and St Anselm's 2–1 . . . I think Waldock minor is safe for his scholarship at Uppingham and Baxter-Brown will get one at Winchester. Some day I shall realize my life's ambition and bring off the top schol. at Eton and Winchester the same year but not this year . . . Glad to hear you have gone up a form . . . Yours ever, HC'. His collection of stamps was immeasurably better than ours and so were his moths and butterflies. He could play six of us simultaneously at chess. He could spot a boy's strong points and exploit them. He knew for instance that while I could be taught to be fourth or fifth in Greek, Latin and Maths, I could usually be relied on to be first in the English essay. To exploit strength is a soldier's art and this he did, but a schoolmaster should also be something of a pastor and reinforce weakness. This he did not do. If he thought a boy lacking in leadership or as an athlete he would write him off and let him see that he was written off. And it might take time to live down that loss of confidence.

Years later someone of my own age said that at school he had come to see that the Old Testament was magnificent literature. 'But I could not see that it had anything to do with *me*!' he went on. I was surprised; the Old Testament I had read at my prep school had seemed to have everything to do with me. There was a jealous and powerful god; if his people did evil in his sight, he would chastise them for forty years. And then, just as unaccountably, they would do good in his sight and would have an easier time for forty years. My life was like that. I would suddenly be told I was working badly and I must 'go on reports'. This meant that after every period I must show the teacher a paper with a square in which he must write: 'Inattentive' or 'Does not try'. This was in itself lowering to any self-esteem one retained and it must be shown to HC at the end of the week – a very anxious moment. I thought I knew just how the Israelites felt about a jealous tribal god.

2 The Worst and the Best

While I was at Stancliffe, men on the Somme and at Paschendaele were walking forward under machine-gun fire against barbed-wire entanglements. Thousands upon thousands were killed in a single day. The names of fathers and brothers who had been killed and of those who were still serving with the forces were read out in chapel every Sunday. Boys leaving public schools at eighteen would be commissioned at once and within six months would be in the trenches. For a subaltern it was long odds that he would never see his twentieth birthday. I do not know what life at a public school was like under these circumstances, but at a prep school death was still remote and seemed to us impossible. We played with French 75-millimetre guns. We had some masters who were past their best; the food was almost always repulsive and we were always a little hungry, but it would be over before it was our turn and then the world would go on as it had before.

Men measure time as though it were a substance like sea-water or treacle or molten copper. But however accurately we measure it, we are not much the wiser as to its nature. It is manifestly not one uniform substance but of a different quality for each of us, at different times for young and for old – for us, learning the principal parts of $\pi\iota\pi\tau\omega$ and the paradigm of $\dot{\epsilon}\beta\eta\nu$ with class B, and for men crouching in the trenches and waiting for zero when, laden with cumbrous gear, they must climb into an open space shredded with flying fragments of steel. It is absurd and irrelevant, you may say, to dwell on these puerile preoccupations when death was so close to so many. But that is to mistake the nature of time, which varies with the circumstances that enfold it. I am trying to remember and describe one pocket of time which I experienced, a pocket of time which had not much more relevance to what was going on in France than the encounter of Atahualpa with Pizarro. And I perceive, as I read again the chapter I have just written, that I have left out both the worst of it and the best.

The worst of it was not sharp discipline and physical punishment. It was lovelessness. I had been under discipline at home. My mother had never heard the word 'confrontation', something which young mothers today are taught to avoid. Indeed, she seemed almost to welcome it; on one occasion, when I wished to take my teddy-bear to some function for which she judged him unsuitable, she had asked whether I loved my teddy-bear better than her. I was far too wise to give the answer which at that moment sprang to mind. No child of the Edwardian age was altogether a stranger to discipline. But it had always been accompanied by love. I had never had any doubt that to my parents I was important. It was indeed at about the time I went to Stancliffe that my mother told me always to put the year as well as the month on my letters since it would be such a help to my biographer. And, since my father was so widely respected, everyone in the village treated me with indulgence.

But as soon as I arrived at Stancliffe everyone regarded me as the meanest and the least of creatures. No one took any interest in me at all, except HC and that was an interest one preferred to escape. The matron was a hard grey-faced woman of whom all my memories are disagreeable. It seemed to me peculiarly chilling that *she* should be unsympathetic. We were supposed to tell her after breakfast if we did not feel well.

'Please, Matron, I think I've got a bit of a sore throat.'

'Did you eat your breakfast?'

'Yes, Matron, I did manage to eat my breakfast.'

'Can't be much of a sore throat then.'

But if later in the day you felt really ill, you would be reprimanded for not having reported the first symptom after breakfast. Once there came an undermatron who was young and pretty and kind. But she did not stay very long.

It was, I suppose, this sense of being unloved and unwanted and even disliked that made me run a temperature and start vomiting the day before my second term began. But that passed. After a year or two, I found two friends who had not much interest in soccer nor cricket nor collecting stamps, still less butterflies with all the revolting paraphernalia of killing bottles, relaxing cabinets and setting trays. (I did begin to collect moths, because it was the proper thing to do. But one night as I lay in bed the killing bottle grew larger and larger, the top unscrewed and out crawled, feathery and fluttery, a gigantic moth, pale and spectral, its eyes glowing ruby-red. I gave up collecting moths.) The three of us read grown-up thrillers and romances – Raffles and Arsène Lupin; E. Phillips Oppenheim and Baroness Orczy; F. Marion Crawford and Stanley J. Weyman. We despised the boy's books on thick paper with large print that the useful left-arm bowlers used to read. As schoolboys, we identified ourselves with *Stalky and Co* in a scornful detachment. That friendship – when one was not 'in silence' – made a constant oasis. And there were other happy memories. Sometimes it was possible to get leave to 'go in the bushes' where among acres of rhododendrons and chestnuts a primitive kind of gang warfare was engrossing, while cricket to me was boring. And sometimes on a fine Sunday in the summer we would go on the moors and construct delectable fortresses among the heather.

Of course I had been spoilt at home and had to be weaned from the infantile illusion that I was the centre of the world. But, you may well ask, why was my mother, who was so deeply loving, not disturbed by the sharpness of the weaning? For that there are several reasons. In the first place I did not tell her a great deal about school. All I wanted in the holidays was to think of something else. It had very soon become evident that she understood very little of what school was like. In an early letter I had mentioned that someone in my form had 'had swish'. She had advised me not to have too much to do with 'boys who get swish as you call it'. This would have condemned me to the membership of a very exclusive club indeed. It was clearly no use asking her advice about school. Life was split into two parts, joyous holidays and stern school. She knew of course that I did not want to go back; indeed, she would have been hurt if I had.

But there is another point which is harder to convey. If some fairy godmother had suddenly offered me the chance of leaving, would I have said yes? To get off the rest of the term, yes, of course, but to leave altogether? 'What might have been is an abstraction' and I do not know what I should have said but I think it quite likely that I should have said no. From both my parents I had drawn a strong feeling that it was proper to finish what you began – and here I was, embarked on a course that seemed inevitable – and after all I had friends and I did not know that any other school would be better. Was not this what life was about? I knew almost by heart the early Kipling stories with their strong sense of commitment to duties usually unpleasant and often dangerous and I had read a great many naval stories by authors such as 'Bartimeus' and 'Taffrail', whose characters were always ending their leave and just going off to the China station. Call it sentimental, call it masochistic, call it what you will, but deep in middle-class Edwardian culture lay this sense of fate, of devotion to a service, of a real life of harsh male endeavour, that was punctuated by a dream life of happiness and affection. The feeling that it was right to march stiff-lipped towards high adventure or a firing-party, a throne or a scaffold, ran through all the books we read, *The Prisoner of Zenda* as well as *The Thirty-Nine Steps*. It was there before the war; during the war it was intensified by everything we read and heard about men going back to the trenches and doing their bit.

Indeed, the unconscious purpose, I believe, of the prep schools and public schools of England was to create just this effect. The child was to be turned into a man – and a man who was prepared to depersonalize himself on demand for war or imperial purposes. Hence Christian names were suppressed, and even twin brothers of eight years old must refer to each other as Smith major and Smith minor. Therefore it was an indelicacy to speak of 'my mother'; if she was referred to at all, it must be in Latin.

It remains surprising that parents not only made such sacrifices to send their children to such places but put up with such autocratic instructions from those they paid. At Stancliffe, for instance, parents were not permitted to take their children to their own houses nor to any but one privileged hotel, 'The Peacock' at Rowsley, an old-fashioned fishing hotel near Haddon Hall. The only alternative was a picnic on the moors. Half-term was for one Saturday and Sunday, during which one might go out for limited periods; if your parents were coming, you asked a friend. A sad abandoned little group stayed behind; one of them was always Prince.

For my parents, the sacrifice was made greater by the war. My father was commissioned in the Royal Army Medical Corps when he was thirty-nine and he was absent for about three years. During that period, he paid a fixed salary to a *locum tenens*, who proved a sad check to a practice that had been growing healthily. My mother explained to me very clearly the effects of war and inflation on professional people like ourselves, who were growing poorer, while our neighbours, who manufactured steel tubes and aeroplane engines, were growing richer. My mother must have needed great courage and resolution to support the doddering *locum* and hold the practice together while at the same time doing various kinds of war work, first as commandant of a convalescent hospital for wounded Belgian soldiers and later as organizer of a scheme for collecting war savings. But she never failed to make our holidays delightful.

For summer holidays we did not usually go far away but to secluded farms in North Derbyshire, and that only for a short stay. One in particular I remember, where I first saw a stoat with a terrified rabbit, a high upland farm near the river Manifold, remote from road or railway, where in memory a golden evening light seems always to be throwing into relief the hummocks in turf kept fine by sheep. There too I watched two horned rams fighting and wondered how each shock could fail to stun them both. But there would be other times when my mother would suddenly decide on an excursion and by ingenious use of the little branch railway line and the main line to Matlock devise new and exciting cross-country walks with picnic lunches. There was a vein of gaiety in her nature that would suddenly break through the vigour and purpose on which I have laid such stress. The air of mountain or moorland would suddenly go to her head and she would want to run down hill or suddenly hold hands and dance like a child. No Greek huntress ever knew a keener thrill of pleasure over a fat buck than she over the first field mushroom. And she had a gift for devising treats, unexpected luxuries which she told us we should enjoy and which we therefore did enjoy. If we had ice cream it was made with real cream and real raspberries, turned by hand in a machine filled with ice from the fishmonger's. Because it did not often happen, it really was a treat. It was a long time before the moment – marking, I suppose, the end of childhood – when it occurred to me to doubt whether I really did like a beverage called raspberry vinegar which she would sometimes make as a treat on a hot summer day.

Bathing, however, was a treat we never questioned. My mother would clasp our hands and fling herself boldly against the short steep waves of the icy North Sea, the rougher the better. When we limped back – sandy and pimply-skinned, our teeth chattering – to the rock where our clothes had been left, we would be enfolded in towels, rubbed dry, stuffed into jerseys and fed on hot milk from a thermos with gingerbread biscuits. Such, we felt obscurely, was life; there would always be enfolding towels and hot milk after cold waves and gritty sand.

Before I come to the new life that began in 1919, there are two unforgettable figures to be sketched. Most prep-school masters in wartime were easy to forget but not these two. One comes straight from fiction. Thirty years later a novel and a film came so close to him that perhaps every school had someone like him. He taught mathematics with the same professionalism as HC taught Latin and Greek; half-holidays were for him days on which he could devote two hours of extra tuition to his most promising pupils. The only peculiarity I remember about his teaching was that in order to turn some mathematical abstraction into concrete terms he used a strange bestiary of his own, of which the most prominent inhabitant was the gephusky, so that instead of a hen and a half laying an egg and a half in a day and a half, it would be a gephusky and a half – but at this point, doubt assails me as to the accuracy of my memory, for I am not sure that gephuskies laid eggs. Though he often made us laugh, no one took liberties with him.

But the remarkable thing about Twitch – so called because his initials were T.W.H. – was his devotion to his profession. He never wanted to escape from us like the others. They had dinner at half past seven; he had supper with us at half past six on a crust and a radish. On Sundays, when we hardly saw the rest, he had breakfast with us, heard each of us repeat the collect for the day, inspected our letters home, making sure that we had covered four pages neatly; marshalled us into chapel, took us for a short walk before lunch and a longer walk after lunch, distributed our weekly ration of sweets, and read to us before supper. The sweets alone were a task at which most men would have rebelled; everyone was expected to bring back something from the holidays but everything went into a common pool and on Sunday – but no other day of the week – each of us was allotted by Twitch exactly the same – two caramel toffees, two peppermint drops and half a bar of chocolate or whatever it might be. That was his Sunday. He never went away in the holidays.

And then the incredible thing happened. For the first time we had mistresses. One of them was an instructress in physical training – trim and slim in a gym tunic. And she married Twitch. It was like the coming of the Arctic summer – thawing ice, green leaf, new life. She died within a year. He told us himself. We were never to mention her name again. The winter came back and once more he was the lonely schoolmaster, the tip of an iceberg, no more.

No one could have been more different than the other figure. One day HC was absent from Stancliffe; he came back as proud as a cat with two tails. He had found an assistant master, shortly to be with us, who was such a paragon as headmasters dare not dream of. He had been a blue at cricket and rugger, he had a VC and a first in Mods; he was connected with half the nobility of Scotland. His name was Egerton-Gordon and he had more initials than anyone except the Prince of Wales. He did not talk like an assistant master at a prep school but like someone who had dropped in from a cricketing weekend at a country house. He had Eton Rambler ties, IZ scarves and Harlequin blazers – all suitably faded. He exuded a faint scent, sharp and agreeable, as though he carried a bottle of smelling-salts in his pocket, and occasionally freshened his brow with eau-de-cologne.

His conversation was entrancing. Once the classroom door was closed, one anecdote would follow another – and always about sides of life quite different from anything we heard from anyone else. There were stories about Oxford, in which undergraduates just back from illicit pleasures in London fled after midnight from proctors' bulldogs; stories of bitter encounters with gangs of poachers – who threw lime in the faces of gamekeepers and the few sporting gentry who had come out for the fun; of old lags – of whom he had once seen a lot when staying on Dartmoor with a friend of his old man's. And there were tales of France, from which he had been invalided after gassing, which were not at all like the stories in *With French at the Front*. 'Imagine a short stretch of the line with a thousand extra men pushed into it, all living on bully-beef, in a blue funk waiting to go over the top and no sanitary arrange-ments – not all violets, I can tell you.' Or the first gas attack, when 'all we knew was that the men must get a wet scarf or a comforter over their mouths and noses and the only way to wet the scarf was to pee on it.' It was much better than talk about stamps and googlies. What was more, Egerton-Gordon appeared to like me. And then, one day, he had gone.

After I left, HC told me how by skilful detective work he had dis-covered that Egerton-Gordon was not the man he had pretended to be and that he had known prison from the inside, for impersonation and false pretences. Rather later I met by chance one of the best of the war-time masters, one saved from the war by extreme short sight. I told him this news and he smiled.

'All the rest of us knew long before the headmaster!' he said.

III

OPENING VISTAS

1 A Team of Eccentrics

After Stancliffe, there followed five years of opening vistas, of growth, of happiness. Part of this was due to the return of my father from the army. He had come back, it seemed, younger, more my own size, more my own age, intensely companionable. 'They are such friends,' my mother used to say, watching us with pleasure and admiration, as we pretended to wrestle or laughed at some absurd joke, but with a touch of envy because she found it as a rule more difficult to cast off 'responsibility', that favourite word of hers. It seems obvious fifty years later that his presence took a strain off her and that I had felt that strain, just as his absence had left me with something missing of which I had not been aware. But outwardly the big change in my life was a new school, which just as much as before was the real business of life, but which now was far less grim.

The freedom and friendliness struck home the first day. New boys came back a day earlier than everyone else. This gave us a moment, a breathing-space, for acclimatization – not so much to the landscape, though the fells, and particularly the hill called Winder, seemed to tower above the little huddle of the tiny market town more strangely close, more intimately, than any hills I had seen before – but to the housemaster, to the matron, to each other and to a world in which you could go for a walk without a watchful master, where you need not change your shoes every time you crossed the sill of the front door.

And the matron! Round and rosy-faced – she was known to us as 'Poms' and looked like an advertisement for cider – she was a daughter of the Dales who had begun her working life as an under-kitchenmaid and now seemed the most grandmotherly, the kindest and the happiest of all old nurses. No one could take liberties with her, but her shining eyes spoke of welcome and friendliness and pure enjoyment of life. After she retired she would give tea parties to new boys in her tiny cottage at the corner of the lane, and the more distinguished an old boy might be the more certain he was to visit Poms – Edith Moorhouse – whenever he came back.

I had started out, in the summer of 1919, entered as a scholarship candidate for Sedbergh, Uppingham and Rugby, and Sedbergh had offered me a much better scholarship than anyone had dared to hope for. In those days, the examination could be taken either at Sedbergh or in Dean's Yard, Westminster. For me the whole affair had been a gorgeous treat. HC had taught me never to look anything up at the last moment and never to give an examination paper a thought once it had been handed in. What was more, he had impressed these ideas on my mother. There was a whole day away from school going to London, and another going back, and there was my mother to meet me, gay and charming and determined to make our little jaunt to Westminster a success, a secret enterprise of our own, meeting me between examinations and giving me delicious lunches. And, fortunately, by a kind of innate irresponsibility – it would be pompous to call it trust in fate – I never felt any apprehension about examinations.

The supreme piece of luck was a question that enabled me to write a whole essay on 'my favourite author'. At that moment, it was Kipling and I had read practically everything he had written. I did not need to nibble my pen and make up my mind; I just wrote as fast as I could. There was, of course, an interview with the headmaster, W. N. Weech, who, on this occasion, was all smiles and twinkles and friendly blue eyes. He was a man who clearly and consciously played a role, putting on for his public appearances a headmaster's mask which he could take off when it suited him. I believe now that his great gift was to recognize enthusiasm. At any rate, he led me on to talk happily about Kipling and he must have judged that, however unfashionable this author might already have become in literary circles, my zestful admiration made up for shortcomings in Greek prose and algebra.

There are minor differences between English public schools, as there were between county regiments. These differences are often picturesque, but I do not mean to dwell on matters which may be relevant to English social history, such as that Sedbergh was founded as a chantry school in 1525 for the soul of Roger Lupton, provost of Eton, or that in the seventeenth century the ushers or junior masters were remunerated by charging a fee called cockpenny on the return of fighting cocks which escaped from the cockpit. Nor shall I dwell on its fierce royalism in the time of the Commonwealth nor its many ups and downs, the most dramatic being between a high point in the early nineteenth century, a very low ebb forty years later, and a revival under Henry Hart, a disciple of Arnold of Rugby. In Hart's time, the school adopted an ideal of simplicity and endurance and took as its motto Homer's description of Odysseus's island kingdom of Ithaca which in Latin becomes *Dura virum nutrix,* a hard nurse of men. It was an ideal appropriate to the Cumbrian hills and in keeping with one aspect of the Arnold tradition. But it is my impression that at this time Weech was trying to steer the school gently away from Sparta and certainly it was the aim of my own housemaster to be Athenian.

It was the freedom that struck me. There were three half-holidays a week and they were free not only from work but quite often from games too. If you found cricket a bore and used a little tact, it was possible in the summer, twice or even three times a week, to go on an expedition in the incomparable country of the Lune and Rawthey valleys or into the tangle of smooth rounded fells that lie north of Sedbergh. One favourite outing was the steady climb, nowhere steep, to the rounded top of the Calf, the knotted heart of that cluster of fells, over two thousand feet above sea level. There you could hear the silence and on a clear day see a glitter of silver threads and sequins that was the sea at Morecambe Bay, thirty miles away to the south-west. From the Calf we would turn east and make our way through broken peaty ground to the head of Cautley Spout, where the little Cautley Beck fell in three long wavering falls almost a thousand feet to the plain below and then went linking and looping to join the Rawthey near the Crosskeys. It was a sharp scramble down the Spout and then a moorland trudge to the Crosskeys. This was a roadside farm that years ago had been an inn but now provided wonderful teas with eggs and scones and rich plum cake with a slice of almond paste through the middle. From there it was four miles and a quarter – heel and toe, brisk as you could – by a winding lane, to and fro, back and forth over the Rawthey, to be back at the house in time for a second tea. Or there was tiled and cobbled Dent six miles away towards Whernside, or to the west the deep clear green pools of the Lune.

It was not so easy to make use of an ordinary half-holiday in winter because Rugby football was taken much more seriously than cricket but it did happen now and then, while in each term, winter and summer alike, there were three or four 'extra halves' when there were no games and everyone was expected to go on some expedition, one that would reach a point at least three miles from the school. And sometimes in the winter there would be a morning-half, starting at eleven o'clock, and off we would go with thick sandwiches in our pockets and the day before us. But to preserve the almost sacred tradition of seeing the countryside on foot, motor-cars were forbidden, even with one's parents.

The admiration for the headmaster which I have come to feel increasingly as I look back rests largely on his encouragement of the eccentric and inspiring men who were his colleagues. He played in public a role that was sometimes dampening, sometimes provocative, almost always steadying – but his staff was unconventional in the extreme. One of these, certainly eccentric but not exactly inspiring, was A. J. Fowler, brother of the famous H. J. Fowler, of the *Oxford Dictionary* and *Modern English Usage*. To me he is the essence of that strand of Victorian England expressed in Lewis Carroll, Edward Lear and C. S. Calverley, the don who loved puns and nonsense. It was he who first lent me Trollope and I think of him as essentially a character from Trollope, though not very like any particular character unless perhaps there is a touch of the Warden. He had never shaved in his life and wore a trimly clipped full set of beard, moustache and whiskers, like King George V. He said: 'ain't it, old man', and "otel'; he was full of riddles, puns and catches, sometimes in Latin or Greek or a mixture of both with English. Sometimes everyone except one recent arrival knew the answer to one of his macaronic riddles and we would sit round like hunting dogs with our tongues lolling out till the victim was entrapped and the incident closed with the bearded aside: 'Haven't caught anyone with that for years.' It was he who taught me that a situation or an object cannot be more unique or less unique; it is either unique or it is not. You must never say 'plausible' without realizing that it is derogatory to the hearer, because it suggests that only the speaker can see through the smooth fellow to whom it is applied. And I still wince at mention of a third alternative.

He was sometimes hazily unaware of his immediate surroundings. Once, when everyone else was joyously embarking on an extra half, he put on his cap and gown and walked as usual dreamily up the hill from his house to find the school buildings deserted. 'I felt like the Queen of Sheba,' he said when he told the story. 'The half was not told to me.' He was born, characteristically, on 29 February and on his thirteenth birthday his form gave him a football, which we judged appropriate. I have a feeling that no one who had not met him could truly understand Victorian England.

After Fowler, for four full years I was in the hands of enthusiasts. In my second year I came into the form of S. C. Sharland. He had been a Blundell's scholar at Balliol in Jowett's day. Perhaps some of his enthusiasms were a little too short-lived, his convictions a little too facile. But that did not reduce his value for us. We were with him for only a year, and he bubbled, he indubitably bubbled, with more than anyone could tire of in a year.

It was the Lower VI Classical and we were still doing Latin and Greek. But Sharland was not a polished classical scholar. It was the freshness of his interests and his excitement about them that made him a good teacher. His abiding joy was in the beauty of language, in particular Keats, Matthew Arnold and Dante Gabriel Rossetti. He could 'do' a Shakespeare

play for an examination without poisoning it. He contrasted Shake-
peare's Richard II with what was known of the historical Richard, and
then we were invited to consider whether he was a first study, a sketch,
for Hamlet. He found us historical novels to illustrate any period of
history that he taught. But as a teacher I chiefly remember him sitting on
his desk with his hands beneath him, shifting his weight from one to the
other in his eagerness to convey to us the full meaning of a stanza of
Keats, to bring out the harmonies, to give the verse its full ring, the full
range of sonorous, sensuous many-coloured sound. He made us all
learn poetry and persuaded many of us to write poetry, to read poetry,
to hear poetry in our heads.

What was also exciting was that he taught us to work on our own.
Everyone in the form had a 'stunt', usually I think two 'stunts' a term.
The stunt might be on almost any subject; I did a long one on the
organization and field system of a mediaeval village and a short one on a
book of poems by J. C. Squire. Whatever it was, you had to get it up on
your own and read a paper on it to the class; there were about eighteen in
the class. We were never under the shadow of examinations; of course
we took the School Certificate and the Higher Certificate but entirely in
our stride.

Sharland also made us look at pictures and gave gramophone recitals,
with a gramophone of high quality for its day, running by clockwork
which was wound by hand, with a huge red horn, like that in the famous
old advertisement for His Master's Voice. Sometimes on an extra half
he would invite two of us to tea, usually at the tiny village of Howgill –
where he had a favourite cottage for teas – a village reached over the fells,
through heather and over sheep-bitten turf, skirting the western slopes
of Winder, and crossing I forget how many valleys carved by the becks
running down from Winder and the Calf. There would be eggs for tea
and apple pasty and talk, schoolmaster's talk no doubt, but enjoyable
because of its zest. And then we would go back along Howgill Lane,
just wide enough for three, going down to cross a beck by a fern-sprinkled
stone bridge, and up between high hedges where in June the dark
northern dog-rose was brilliant. It was not only because of the tea that
we enjoyed such outings.

But my deepest and most permanent debt to Sharland is a mental
image. I have written of this before but the justification for saying some
things again is simply that all your life they colour what you think and
much that you do. It is a metaphor, a way of looking at life, a vision to
which often experience can be related.

Picture a globe, sometimes quite small, sometimes immense. It is
opaque, or mainly opaque and partly translucent, thinly swathed in

swirling mist. It is not the terrestrial globe but an entire universe of space and time and spirit. Within it is a light, a glory, too bright for human eyes to stand, but the whole globe is pricked and starred and studded with tiny points of light of different colours and intensities where the radiance from within comes through. It is all one radiance. You are seeing these points of light when you listen to a Brandenburg Concerto or a Beethoven symphony; if you read with care the *Bhagavad Gita* or Dante or the poems of Kabir or Tagore.

No doubt the picture has changed in my mind and I have added new bits and forgotten others, but I should now include among these points of light, these pinpricks in the formless fog of the opacity, the life of some quite simple person, a woman perhaps who had scrubbed floors all her days for other people in order to supplement her husband's earnings, who had brought up her children decently and seen them through their troubles. And I should include a field well ploughed, a hedge well cut and laid, a well-grown rose-bush and a cutter close-hauled slicing into a Force 6 south-wester in the Solent. I would go on almost indefinitely and include James Thurber and Beachcomber as well as Eliot and Gerard Manley Hopkins – but the colours are as varied as the colours of the rainbow, and some are far more intense than others, shining through the swirling fog like the beam of a lighthouse, while others are so faint you cannot be sure from one minute to the next that they are there at all.

In Sharland's picture there was one clear point where the light from within the globe shone through quite clearly, and it was white – and white is simply the presence of all the colours at once. I am not sure that I can now regard that as an adequate image of the Incarnation – but then no image is ever adequate and this is not a theological treatise. But the enduring habit of thought that image gave me helped me to see why Hindu pilgrims went to bathe wherever two streams joined near the sources of the Ganges. And again I have seldom been more aware of that lighthouse beam than in Akbar's great lonely mosque at Fatehpur Sikri.

We were with Sharland for a year, and that left three years of preparation for a university. I ventured to ask if I might read English Literature at Oxford. Weech, now at his most headmasterly and Johnsonian, opened his eyes – no longer twinkling – to their widest and informed me that English literature was a subject women read. Only a second-rate college would permit it in a man. I must try for a scholarship in history and even that must be stiffened by at least some knowledge of Spanish or German.

So for the next three years it was history for about two-thirds of my time under the most inspiring man I have ever had the good fortune to meet.

2 *A Most Inspiring Man*

Until I came to know him I had thought of Neville Gorton as something of a joke. His clothes were always incredibly old and incongruous – bright blue, thick woollen stockings, shapeless breeches, a ragged cardigan, a fragment of clerical waistcoat that was always escaping and having to be pushed back by an eagerly gesticulating hand, a mere wisp of a tattered gown slung round the neck like a scarf. I had seen him at school concerts; he had a fine tenor voice and would attempt ambitious songs that moved him but he would suddenly break down and exclaim: 'Dash it, I've forgotten the words!' When his turn came to preach in chapel, he was quite likely to throw away his script as he entered the pulpit; there was something wrong with it, it was not what he wanted to say, he must start all over again with a new intensity. A phrase from one of his sermons comes back: 'What the Lord said was: "Peter, you are a *brick*!"'

Years later, when he was Bishop of Coventry the Archbishop of the day said that he was a man through whom the Holy Spirit blew in great gusts – and that was exactly right. Of the dozens of stories told of him when he was Bishop of Coventry, my favourite – and it is true – is of the procession which was moving through the streets to a church where a new vicar was to be inducted. They formed up and moved off in all their robes, the Bishop in the rear with mitre, cope and crozier. But at the church door he was not to be found – he had seen an old lady leaning over her gate to watch the procession, stopped to chat with her and become so interested that he went into the house with her and there they found him – mitre and all – sitting on a corner of her kitchen table deep in conversation.

It was not surprising then that to boys of fourteen who did not know him, Neville* seemed at first a comic figure. But it was altogether different when I came under his guidance. There were only six or seven of us who meant to try for history scholarships; officially we were part of the Upper Sixth Classical. They, poor dears, sat doing so many lines a day of Aeschylus or Thucydides, while we sat at the back doing our own thing. Of the two-thirds of our time spent on what was loosely called history, only about a third was actually in class with Neville. The rest of the time was given to what Sharland had called 'stunts' and the object was not to make us pass an examination but to educate us.

---

* Neville Gorton was known at this time to masters and boys alike as Gorty. But after I left he always signed his letters to me Neville and I called him by that name, so it seems sensible to keep to that. The same consideration makes me speak of Gerald Meister throughout this chapter by his Christian name, though at school we referred to him by a nickname for which I never heard a convincing explanation.

Neville's method was to give you a book, discuss it with you a little, and then tell you to get on with it. After a little there would be more discussion. 'What do you like in it? What interests you? What would you like to write an essay on?' And after a bit you would do your essay and there would be another discussion. 'Good phrase that. Is that your own?' But much more often: 'Weak phrase that. Can't you see how much stronger it would be if you put it the other way round?' He taught us to use metaphor, to break up our sentences, to search for epigram, to despise flabby writing. We had to be terse, Tacitean, sharp. Every sentence must *mean* something. And the whole must hang together and the argument flow. He gave us dangerous models, Chesterton, Guedalla, Belloc. But above all he kept us interested. I read Grant Robertson's book on Bismarck and wrote an essay on the unification of Germany. Can it really have been planned step by step with such exact foresight as I then supposed? But Neville spent his criticism on the shape, the clarity with which events were presented, the vigour of the phraseology. Then he remarked that that had been a good solid bit of history and I probably needed a change, so he gave me a lovely great illustrated book on Italian Renaissance painters. I read *The Brothers Karamazov* and *Crime and Punishment* and von Hügel on *The Mystical Element in Religion* and de Tocqueville's *Ancien Régime* and Maine's *Ancient Law* and Tawney's *Acquisitive Society* – a mixed bag indeed, but running through it always the basic idea of keeping us on our toes, of alternating tough going with something more congenial, always with the knowledge that we should have to comment and to justify what we said.

As well as finding time for guiding us in all these different ploys, he would talk to us a great deal, quite unpredictably, sometimes for several days together on some many-volumed account of the French Revolution that he was deep in himself and then quite suddenly he would switch to some philosophical or theological problem that he was wrestling with or something to do with painting. He never talked down to us; he never potted anything for us to learn. He was always trying to work something out for himself and give us a share in it; we must keep up as best we could and let it flow over us and then try to reconstruct on our own lines. Emotionally he was deeply Catholic; socially he was radical and a socialist of the school of R. H. Tawney; at the same time he was a humanist and passionately moved by beauty.

It sounds very haphazard and in detail it was. Perhaps if you had only a year with him it would not have worked. Undoubtedly I was idle at first. But before long, every one of us came to recognize a new sort of discipline; we were aware of a fierceness in him, an intolerance of the second-best – not of the intellectual second-best, of dullness, of mere failure to comprehend, but of lack of sympathy, of lack of consideration for others, of the closed, callous, indifferent mind. One Sunday evening a colleague preached a sermon in chapel to the effect that there always had been war and that to prepare for war was the best way to get peace; indeed, it might be justifiable to get your blow in first. The delivery was dull, the style prosaic, the matter conventional and insensitive. 'How did you like the sermon, sir?' one of us asked next morning with more than a touch of slyness. Neville sprang to his feet and paced fiercely to and fro. At last he burst out: 'Mr . . . ought to be burnt! No, I mean it. I really mean it. He is the sort of person who justifies everything done by the Inquisition.' But, if that man had been in trouble, he would have given him his last penny. I do in fact remember two friends of his who fell into what might be called disgrace and lonely poverty, to whom he gave a home in their last days. But the fierceness was always there. I can see him in the sharp shapes and colours of El Greco, driving the money-changers from the temple with knotted cords.

I still bear from those cords one deep scar which I deserved. Unemployment was not yet as bad as it became in the Thirties but it was bad. One day Neville told us all to leave whatever we were doing and write a leading article on unemployment, taking as our model any newspaper we liked. I suppose I was sulky at being taken off whatever I was working on; I know I didn't want to do it. Instead of taking it seriously I scribbled off at top speed something meant to be funny in what I imagined was the style of left-wing demagogy at its worst. Next day, Neville talked about unemployment and what it meant to men and what could be done about it. Then he commented on what the others had done, picturing themselves on the staff of *The Times* or the *Guardian*. Mine he threw back, saying in biting tones: 'As for this, I can only call it an appalling example of moral obliquity in the face of a serious problem.' I felt my face slowly turn a dark red. He was right and I knew it. It happened in the first few months of my time with him. It would not have crossed my mind a year later. Even today I can think of no sharper test to apply to any moral dilemma than to consider what his reaction would be.

I am making him sound solemn but peals of happy laughter, often at himself, would break into any conversation with him and I have never known anyone who was less a respecter of persons. His affection included the latest joined and most ignorant urchin at the bottom of the school and the boy who spent all his time watching ravens and catching moles as well as his most promising pupil. It included a shepherd he had met on the fells; Harvey Askew, the shoemaker behind his counter in the town – interrupting his trade to demonstrate a nice point in the tying of a fly for the Rawthey – whoever, in short, he was talking to, unless he showed himself callous or cruel or brutal. He never looked like a clergyman nor talked like a clergyman but in a mysterious way he was always a priest. He never preached a finished sermon nor wrote a finished piece of prose, because he was always wrestling with principalities and powers and could never be sure he had got them down. But when he turned to the people and said: 'Therefore with angels and archangels and with all the company of heaven we laud and magnify thy glorious Name . . .' you knew that they were there. You could hear the beat of mighty pinions beneath the vaulted roof, crowding for a timeless moment out of time-lessness into time.

He was quite sure about the intersection of timelessness with time. Just before I left, I remember saying to him one day as we walked down from school – in exactly the mood which I can see now he had tried to induce in me – that there were so many marvellous things in the world to see and rejoice in and try to do that one life was far too short. 'All the more reason,' he replied with his happy smile, 'for hurrying on to the next life where you'll be able to do them all superlatively.'

While I knew him he became a housemaster and he married, events that might have been expected to exercise a stabilizing influence and so I suppose to a minimal extent they did. He became a trifle less noticeably a stranger upon earth. He became a trifle more likely to answer a letter – though just as illegibly – a trifle more likely to keep an appointment – though still at breakneck speed in an ancient car of once high quality – but essentially he was the same. Other men have dwindled as I have grown older but not Neville Gorton. I never met him without feeling braced, invigorated, refreshed, aware that for a moment I had seen a tongue of flame.

Three years of such a man, from fifteen to eighteen, mark you for life. You may disregard or forget, perhaps for years, but you are bound to come back. It is as though you had been brought up by Jesuits. My house-master, Gerald Meister, was almost as different from Neville Gorton as were my two grandfathers from each other. His trim spare figure was always neatly dressed, usually in a well-cut but old and well-worn suit of grey flannel. How do such men avoid the solecism of ever wearing a new suit and yet never show a frayed cuff or elbow? He was precise in speech and thought, exact in punctuality; his writing was legible, he was con-ventional though abstemious in his way of life. He was a mathematician. Yet he and Neville were close friends. They were both affectionate; they both enjoyed games without any stupid idolatry; they both liked to talk ideas, they liked *fresh* ideas. But there was something deeper than that. Both, I think, were what soldiers call a good officer. Each put the care of the men under his command before his own convenience.

Over Gerald's desk hung a reproduction of Ghirlandaio's well-known picture of the man with a carbuncular nose looking with affection at his grandson. He often spoke of this picture; he loved the beauty of the man's expression in spite of his deformity. It was perhaps the key to his nature, his concern for people. He had become a housemaster when young and kept his house for about twenty-one years; he had to give it up some time before retiring age, but he could not bear the thought of staying on at Sedbergh without his beloved house.

There was a standard of esteem in our house which had very little to do with games or success of any kind. We had a brilliant athlete among us who won his colours for cricket in his first year and for rugger in his second. He became a rugger international later and he could play any game brilliantly. 'Up at school' he was a hero but in the house, though there was nothing against him and no one disliked him, there was a slight but quite perceptible feeling that he should be kept in his place; all this athletic success was creditable but it should not promote him in either the official or the unofficial hierarchy. On the other hand, we had a boy in pebble glasses who could not see a cricket ball till it almost touched his bat, who could not see even a high-kicked rugger ball till it began to drop towards him, and who yet by the gallantry of his tackling made himself a creditable full back; he was of no more than average competence in any other field, but he was one of the most respected boys in the house. He never showed off and he had guts; he was modest, straightforward, kind and funny, in a simple absurd unhurtful way of his own. Everyone liked him and paid attention to what he said. I am sure that in part this standard of values was due to our housemaster.

In my last year, I used to stay behind after house prayers for ten minutes in the interval before the beginning of late prep. It was a moment to which I looked forward. I could not talk to Gerald about mathematics but he could talk to me about anything with which I was bubbling at the moment; in particular he loved to talk about the Renaissance in Italy. He spoke once of the widow of a former headmaster who was a friend of his. 'If it weren't for her,' he said once, 'I think I should say that no one could be truly civilized – whatever that may mean – without at least a grounding in Latin and Greek. But then she studies Dante, and that of course is a life's work in itself.' I could talk to him on almost any subject in carpet slippers without that sense that one might at any moment see a kingfisher catch fire that was always there with Neville.

There was also the senior science master, universally known as Bobby, with whom I never had any contact. He was grimily negligent, like a caricature of a science master, and was reputed to speak through clenched teeth, as a skull might speak. He was a mountaineer and took boys on

Lakeland climbs. On one occasion he lost his foothold on an exposed and precipitous face. When at last the incident came to an end without disaster, he was heard, by those near enough, to say in his usual close-bitten tones: 'Lucky I've got strong fingernails.' He spent some twenty-five years in trying to perfect a seven-day clock which for every form in the school would announce by bells the beginning and end of every period, with the addition of an admonitory cough five minutes before the end. It was easy enough, apparently, to adapt it for a week with three whole schooldays and three half-holidays and with shorter periods in the Lower school than in the Upper, but he could never quite make it record the fact that on some days the break was five minutes longer than on others.

I do not pretend fully to understand Weech. I have said that as head-master he put on a mask. It was ponderous, Johnsonian, apparently pompous. As a teacher he made a point of being extremely exacting but unaccountable. He challenged, he provoked, he allowed himself to be led into digressions. These were interesting, varied and often funny – but it was unwise to laugh. The Scythians were reported to drink blood, mare's milk and water. 'They seem to have kept a very unhealthy cellar' was his comment, accompanied by a challenging stare that quelled even a nervous giggle. On one occasion he was holding forth on tyranny and the assassination of Julius Caesar: 'Brutus,' he announced in his most ponderous Johnsonian manner, 'was a Whig and a prig.' I treasured this, and a fortnight later – the subject now being The Hero in Antiquity – my chance came. 'And who, Mason, would be *your* hero in antiquity?' 'Brutus, sir,' I piped, innocent as a lamb – and believed he had fallen into my trap.

But I fell unhesitatingly into his traps. His main purpose, I think now, was to make us defend the radicalism we imbibed from Neville. He referred one day to the unemployed as men who refuse to work – and gazed round with a challenging blue stare. I jumped into the pit at once. 'But where are they to get work, sir?' 'In Australia,' he replied and made me try – splutteringly – to explain why the whole of the Rhondda valley could not be sentenced to transportation for life without having even poached a hare.

Of course he was being deliberately provocative. The man he pretended to be would never have allowed Brendan Bracken, the day before the beginning of term, to turn up newly landed from Australia, without appointment or previous arrangement, sign a cheque for his first term's fees and come in to School House as a new boy of at least sixteen. To me it now seems that there was magnanimity in holding together so eccentric and heterogeneous a team and allowing himself so often to appear in a role sometimes ogreish, frequently pompous and repressive. But why it should have been necessary to disguise himself so heavily I have never understood. There must somewhere I suppose have been some deep diffidence – but we never saw a sign of it.

'In my end is my beginning' and to have lived five years in so beautiful a place can never be forgotten. When I was a boy it was the fells that stirred me. You could see them from near Danny Bridge on the road to Wensleydale, like a cluster of great golden elephants – round domestic Indian elephants of course, not the gaunt black African variety with their vast ears and inadequate hindquarters. And when I had reached the top of Calf and heard the curlew and the blackcock, there would come over me sometimes that gaiety that invaded my mother in the mountains, or sometimes instead a longing to be alone, to be quiet, to soak in the solitude. But when I came back forty years later, though the fells, even after the Himalayas, were no less impressive, there was a new pull at the heart, something I had taken for granted before, something that would take me unawares, almost like the clutch of a baby's hand on your finger. It would be a corner where a lane turned to the round arch of a little stone bridge beneath a rowan, or it would be the entrance to a farm with its roughly cut stones of slate-blue and brownish-grey and its stand of six or seven ash trees. Such a picture might confront the eyes whenever the winding dipping lane below the fells crossed a beck.

There was one moment of a special, an unexpected consciousness. The light was fading in a clear sky. It was my last summer at Sedbergh and everyone else was in bed; I suppose it was in May. I stood at a window at the top of the house with my elbows on the sill and looked across the tiled roofs and narrow back streets of the stony little town. Winder, the nearest, the steepest, the most intimate, of all the hills, hung strangely close, sombre already and almost menacing. There was a tree in blossom, perhaps a very late apple in someone's back garden. I felt I could not bear to leave so much beauty. In a sense I never have.

It was a moment in and out of time. But it is only in time that you recall it.

IV

BLISS WAS IT...

1 Finding Friends

'Tea is served, gentlemen.'

We were scribbling away, several hundred of us, about the Industrial Revolution or the liberation of Italy and a dozen other subjects, on a December afternoon – one of those cheerless afternoons to which Oxford contributes a chill damp mugginess all its own – when the doors of the vast Victorian Gothic hall opened and closed behind a butler, in a morning coat and a black bow tie.

We left the enclosure of the common land or the rise of the Jacobins in the French revolution and went to get a cup of tea, a thin sandwich and a pink sugary cake, which we took to our places and went on scribbling. It seemed a very civilized way of conducting an examination. We were suddenly being treated as grown-ups. Collectively, we were addressed as 'gentlemen', instead of 'boys'; formally I was Mr Mason. I was invited to dine at High Table in Balliol; after dinner, back in the Senior Common Room, Kenneth Bell, who was my host, said; 'I've been reading your stuff. Like it. Like your style. Very few adjectives.' To be told, at seventeen, that one *had* a style! Neither he nor I realized that it was really Neville Gorton's style.

I was never Kenneth Bell's pupil and I am told he was not a successful tutor in the sense of getting good results in examinations. But Anthony Powell writes of him as an educating influence and he was certainly excellent at making a scholarship candidate feel at home. In any case, after four years of Balliol indoctrination, I felt I almost belonged to the place already; it had hardly crossed my mind as a serious proposition that I might have to go somewhere else. I must have chattered away, quite at ease. Kenneth Bell later made a remark that I treasure. 'There are two schools,' he said, 'which send up young men who talk freely about their ideas. One is Eton, where they have been taught to talk; the other is Sedbergh, where they have never been taught not to.'

This readiness to talk was something of an obstacle in finding a place among those of my own age. There was a note of guarded smoothness

which sometimes met any step towards friendliness, the note which
Americans so often resent in the English. At Sedbergh, I had hardly
encountered this polite, defensive, glacial veneer. Something of the
heather and the curlew still hung about me. I was certainly rural and
possibly rustic.

Balliol was a strange society, varied, tolerant and exciting, and there
is still something mysterious to me about the opening moves – like the
first notes of drowsy birds waking in spring, like an orchestra tuning up,
perhaps like the first stirring of a tune in a composer's mind – that
helped us to get a 'fit', to find the particular place that we did, and to
determine which of the many influences that surrounded us should claim
our affections and lead to life-long friendships. How did we sort ourselves
out and work ourselves into the network of overlapping groups that
began to coalesce and separate themselves and form themselves again?

There were about two hundred undergraduates, which for an Oxford
college was large, and there was very little conventional division into
'years'. Of course a fresher was a little uncertain in his first term, but
after that there was hardly any feeling that to be 'senior' meant anything
at all. On the other hand, there was a wide social range. Crown Prince
Olaf of Norway – now the King – came up in my year; he was in himself
a friendly, rather middle-class, figure, much more approachable than
some of the English, for whom that guarded smoothness was never
relaxed. But in his case most of us felt a certain reluctance to seek a
closer acquaintance which might earn the reproach of tuft-hunting. We
had a marquis who would later be a duke, an Arab royalty, a Polish prince,
an Irish peer or two, more than our share of Rhodes scholars, particularly
American, two or three Indians, not a single African, more Scots than
most colleges, more than a handful of Etonians, a sample or two from
most public schools and a sprinkling from 'grammar schools' which were
still day schools and therefore still local – but not, in those far-off days,
one member of the college who could be thought of as 'working class'.

But of course interests, temperaments and social background formed
us into groups, most of which overlapped. There were a few at one end
of the scale who could be clearly labelled 'hearties', a few at the other
who were just as clearly 'aesthetes'. Some of the latter in fact labelled
themselves by a uniform which I still think was picturesque. It was the
day of 'Oxford bags'; all trousers bought in Oxford were a little wider
than they would have been in London, but the aesthetes wore trousers
extravagantly wide, sometimes as much as twenty-four inches at the
ankle, really twin skirts, and of delicate pastel shades, mauve or lilac
or strawberry-and-cream, worn usually with a dark, close-fitting, rather
formal jacket and a flowing tie, also in a pastel shade. Peter Quennell,

being tall, looked splendid in such clothes; Cyril Connolly was less impressive. The literary figure who was later to be the most famous, Graham Greene, appeared aloof from the committed aesthetes, already distinguished by an expression of sad awareness. Anthony Powell was already playing to perfection the part for which he casts the narrator in his novels, the almost invisible man, the universal unobtrusive confidant and observer. The central group of committed aesthetes to my nostril distilled a distinctly feline effluence, not quite what one might expect from a couched Brazilian jaguar, not so rank nor so feral, but distinctly catty.

In the middle ground between these extremes lay most of the college. It was in the first few weeks that the process of trying each other out was most tentative. My first close contact was with Dingle Foot, then an ardent Liberal, later Solicitor-General in a Labour administration. But he was a committed politician and it soon became clear to me that I was not; we drifted apart. We were all feeling our way; we would ask each other to tea, ordering hot anchovy toast to be sent up to our rooms from the Junior Common Room in a covered dish to go in front of the fire, perhaps with thin little sandwiches of foie gras, adding perhaps a walnut cake from Fuller's in the Cornmarket.

In those far-off days the dons felt a concern for their pupils in every aspect of their lives. There were distinct attempts to help us to mix. One of these was 'Freshers' Essays'. The newcomers were divided into batches of four, who had embarked on different subjects and otherwise might not have been thrown together. Each batch was allotted for half a term to a tutor to whom they would not normally show work. The first don to whom my batch went was Cyril Bailey, famous for his lectures on Lucretius. Most of the dons we met in this way asked us to a meal; Cyril made me almost part of his household at 'The King's Mound', as he did to many others. But most of them were pupils of his own, reading the classics. For me his kindness was a special gift; the people he helped me to meet were the main influence of my time at Balliol. In my first Easter Vacation, he invited me to a reading party at a farm house, at Little Stretton near the Long Mynd.

The party consisted of Cyril and his wife Gemma and six undergraduates, three in their third year, three in their first. The older three included Henry Brooke, one day to be Home Secretary, and Walter Oakeshott, later Headmaster of Winchester; among the three freshers Morris Whitehouse and I had already begun to be friends. The life we led would seem to the modern undergraduate as remote as though we had been on the moon. It was a big comfortable farmhouse, with a dining-room that had once been a kitchen, where hams hung to be smoked. After breakfast we settled down to our books, all eight of us, and read till lunch. After lunch, we might split into parties but as a rule did something together, walking on the Long Mynd – where I felt almost as though I were back on the fells at Sedbergh – or using bicycles for a longer excursion to Stokesay Castle or some such place. Back to tea at the farm, two hours reading before dinner, another hour after dinner, and then – would you believe it? – Gemma read to us before we went to bed, from a long nineteenth-century Scandinavian novel, called *Gösta Berling*, in which neither plot nor character seemed to matter but every chapter had a stirring incident.

Gemma was deaf and that was why she read to us; she found it hard to take a full part in the conversation. She was a daughter of Bishop Creighton, who had been Bishop of London. She read with dramatic force and we enjoyed this evening session, after which we went to bed. How docile and submissive it must sound to a later generation! But we were linked not only by the fact that we did all want to get some work done but by our affection for Cyril and Gemma.

Not that Gemma was exactly a *comfortable* person to be with. Of Cyril, the reverse was true. Although he was in his fifties, we talked to him on most subjects as though he were our own age. Indeed, in my case there were reticences with even the closest of my own age on subjects I might have discussed with Cyril and of course the reverse was true too. He had a power of evoking friendship and confidence without imposing himself. But I do not intend to try to describe Cyril Bailey; he was a well-known figure in Oxford and not – as Sligger was – controversial.

The quality in Gemma which made it difficult to relax in her presence was partly due to her deafness but only partly. She would sometimes appear remote, utterly closed to her surroundings. She had a face with fine bone that would please a sculptor; in wind and sunshine her fair skin tanned quickly; her beauty was Norse rather than English. But that look of remoteness, which the deaf sometimes share with the blind, would disappear in a sudden flash of happiness or kindness or sometimes of impatience or irritation.

There was a tenseness about her. She was fifteen or twenty years younger than Cyril and a much fiercer, more decisive character. The difference between them – that of temperament as much as of age – sometimes stoked her inner fire, as did her evangelical upbringing and above all her deafness. She was both a scholar and a musician and she was continually aware of being kept out of things by her disability. She chafed inwardly but somehow she was able by continual effort to overcome it in part and the Bach Choir was one of the joys of her life. Joy often broke through the remoteness, the austerity and the repressed fire that this effort entailed. Once, on one of those expeditions with bicycles, we reached the top of a long hill up which we had pushed our machines. Before us lay a wide stretch of the lovely border country from Shropshire into Wales. We were breathless from the long ascent; her face broke into a smile of joy, of pure happiness. 'I suppose some people, when they talk of the pleasures of the body, mean nothing but eating and drinking – not this!' she said. Years later, when Cyril had retired and they lived at East Hannay, I arrived at the house unexpectedly on a Saturday afternoon and found her playing the piano. I said I was glad she found some time for recreation. 'Recreation!' she said indignantly, repudiating the very thought. 'The organist is away and I have to deputize for him tomorrow. So I was practising the hymn tunes.' 'Get out of my kitchen!' she would say fiercely if a guest, in those days of retirement, tried to help with the washing up.

That is partly a digression from my main theme, but not entirely, because it is strange that Cyril and Gemma should have been the link which drew together, over several undergraduate generations, the group of young men who constituted a continuing tradition, of which Walter Oakeshott represented the second generation and Morris Whitehouse and myself the third.

Morris and I came to the college in 1924. The men who had been through the war and survived it had begun to come up in 1919; by now they had all gone down and so had the generation who had been suddenly reprieved on 11 November 1918. But they must have dominated those five years. It is not surprising then to find among them a strain of gaiety, of quite unconditional joy in just being alive, of joy in all the possibilities and absurdities of life, together with another strain, beneath the surface, much less apparent, a feeling that if only people would be reasonable, nothing so dreadful as *that* need ever happen again. It couldn't happen again – could it? – but there was nonetheless a disturbed consciousness that there was a great deal of injustice to be put right – but that could wait until one was out of the charmed circle of Oxford in the great world. And so, for the moment . . .!

That, at least, is how I imagine they felt, the young men, most of them pupils of Cyril's, who began the tradition into the tail end of which I stumbled. They did absurd things, ambitious things, exciting things, picturesque things. There was certainly a touch of arrogance about some of it; the rest of Oxford was hardly needed – it was a mere background to their absorbing activities. There were gifted and amusing people enough in the college, all anyone could need. It was, for the moment, like the court of some small Italian dukedom in the Renaissance.

No doubt it was arrogant of Anthony Asquith to decide that he could get along without the Oxford University Dramatic Society and to take a party of his friends, whom he called the Balliol Players, into the border country of Shropshire, Hereford and Wales to surprise, enlighten and entertain the rustics with Aeschylus and *The Merry Wives of Windsor*. Arrogant or no, it was much more fun than the administrative tedium and semi-political bickering that always seemed to go with any production of the OUDS. And it was done with grace and charm and spontaneity. Again, it was not exactly modest, in the middle of the General Strike of 1926, when people talked of civil war, to start a national newspaper in the cause of peace. But it was youth at its most joyous and most exciting.

The comparison with a Renaissance court occurred to me only recently, as I read in Castiglione's *Book of the Courtier* of the group of friends who used to meet after supper in the palace at Urbino in the presence of the Duchess and play 'games'. Most of their games were discussions of imaginary situations to which everyone present was expected to make a witty and agreeable contribution. Not only did we play games of that kind, but the intention in ordinary conversation was similar; it was to please, to amuse, to decorate.

The most absurd activity of this group was called, after one of those technical terms (to use Fowler's expression again) which I had learnt at my prep school, the Hysteron Proteron Society, the Back-to-Front Club. They set aside one day to living backwards, getting dressed in the early morning in a white tie and tails and eating a rather grand dinner backwards, beginning with cigars, coffee and liqueurs, working back through the savoury to the soup, and ending late at night, grumpily, with marmalade, eggs and bacon, porridge and a cold bath. Opinion differed as to whether the opening cigar or the closing cold bath was the more unpleasant. It raised a number of interesting points; it is obvious that one can reverse the order in which events succeed each other, but the actual event cannot be reversed; you cannot start smoking the stub of a cigar and watch it grow longer; you cannot start with an empty glass and see it gradually fill.

That society was not long-lived; it went on to a competition as to who could boil an egg in the most surprising circumstances, such as a tube train in London or a lecture on Logic, and after one or two more irrelevancies it died a natural death just before I came up. The Heptarchy on the other hand lived much longer. It supposed a Britain divided into seven kingdoms, in a mythical period based loosely on Geoffrey of Monmouth's account of Britain. But you were permitted, in this game, to draw on any source you liked; the Heptarch of Wessex and Lyonesse used for his public documents a stately prose from the early seventeenth century; James Fergusson of Valentia – that is, Lowland Scotland, the Roman province – expressed himself in a lawyer's Lallans, full of 'quhilks' and 'quherefores'.

The game had three main departments – war, diplomacy and ceremony. If one of the Heptarchs felt it was time, he might summon a meeting and state a grievance against a brother Heptarch. The matter might be settled amicably by bargaining but it might lead to war, sometimes after two or three evenings of diplomacy. War again might take several evenings; it was played on a huge map of England and Scotland with flags on pins.

When I succeeded Robert Birley as Heptarch of Northumbria, my kingdom was in rather a poor position; I suspect that he had only given half his attention to the last war. Wales held Cheshire and Lancashire, while a previous King of Valentia had encroached so far down the Cumbrian coast that I had no outlet to the western sea. I felt I owed it to my people to restore the ancient glory and freedom of Northumbria so I made secret treaties with the wild Highlanders of Caledonia and I think with Mercia and Kent and assumed the title of Prince of Strathclyde, which I knew James Fergusson of Valentia would regard as a *casus belli*. It was a very glorious war and I took *two* outlets to the sea, leaving a Valentian enclave south of Carlisle ripe for later acquisition.

There were many other 'games', in this Renaissance sense, of which perhaps the nearest to those played at the courts of Urbino was one I associate chiefly with Robert Birley. It was named after a quite undistinguished seventeenth-century bishop whose portrait hung in the hall. It would discuss some broad subject such as the drama but everyone who took part represented a historical figure and was supposed to speak in character. There were many other societies; some met after dinner to engage in some activity that was stimulating, entertaining or absurd, and incidentally to drink mulled claret. One read plays, usually Elizabethan or Restoration. There was one to which I read a paper on decorative heraldry and the language of heraldry while Morris Whitehouse read one on alchemy and the philosopher's stone. There were others with no damned merit about them, groups which met merely to dine and to drink too much, to which you were elected if the others found you acceptable.

I even became a member of a cricket club, which played the only kind of cricket I have ever enjoyed, against neighbouring villages on Saturday afternoons. We were called the Balliol Erratics and were more pleased if we lost than if we won. It was unnecessary, for membership, ever to have played cricket before and we included one or two Americans who had not. The order of batting was decided by drawing from a hat. On one famous occasion, we put the village in to bat and had them all out for 51. We had that day two good players but they drew the last two places. When the first of these two went in to bat, the score on our side was 2 runs for 8 wickets. The heroic two made it up to 49 before one of them was run out – so the village had just won in a perfect finish. There would be elms round the village green and very often rabbit-scrapes on the pitch.

2 *Arrogant Absurdities*

Of all our activities the two most exciting were the Balliol Players and the *British Independent*. But before I come to them, I want to emphasize the variety of flavour in these different groups. Their membership overlapped but it did not coincide. There was nonetheless a similarity and a continuity in the tradition.

One element in the continuity was 58 Holywell, a house on the Balliol side of New College, kept as 'digs' by one Walter Dore, who had once been Cyril Bailey's scout. The house would hold six, and there were usually three in their third year and three in their fourth. The inhabitants invited their successors. They were most desirable digs; Mrs Dore was a reasonable cook and instantly became motherly if anyone was indisposed; there was a bell and, if you rang, it would be answered; the Dores kept a maid. Dore could usually find a drink and, with warning, the pair could lay on a lunch party. 'What would you say to a little dressed crab, sir?' was always Dore's opening gambit. Such occasions were rare, but tea, with cakes and hot buttered toast for any number, could always be produced without hesitation and friends would drop in on us for tea without notice – something few Oxford landladies would tolerate. We had a great chest there containing the robes of the Heptarchy and the costumes of all the Balliol Player productions.

Of the ramifications of interest and affection that I have left out, the principal centres on Sligger, Francis Fortescue Urquhart, who except for a year in Paris had been at Balliol since 1890. He figures in many memoirs and has been thought to provide one element at least in many characters in novels – and he is a controversial figure, standing for much that a later generation was to dislike. He came of an old Highland family; he belonged to a generation who did not consider it of supreme importance to publish academic work; he did not enjoy writing nor seek fame. Nor did he consider himself a trainer for the final examinations and to a pupil who had in fact got his First, he once wrote: 'What do these things matter! You are, I am sure, quite indifferent to your little First by now.'

He conceived it the duty of a don to be a companion and a friend to as many as he could of the young men. But he knew he could not be a friend to everyone; he knew his limitations and was indeed one of the most modest of men. He could not *force* his affections and knew that it was by affectionate friendship that he could be of most help to the young. He was accused of favouritism and of preferring young men from Eton and Winchester; he was aware of this and deliberately tried to widen his circle – but not beyond the limits of those he liked and who liked him. It was in fact a very wide circle of close friends and to them he brought an understanding of Europe, particularly of mediaeval Europe and of Catholic Latin Europe. He had a 'mission civilisatrice', as the French used to claim of their colonial empire. But he would not have said that himself; he would have thought it pompous. Nonetheless, you could not be with him long without feeling more civilized, in the sense of perceiving something more of the beauty of the European heritage at its best.

He had thought as a young man of joining the Society of Jesus but once he had decided that that was not his vocation, he put it firmly behind him and had no afterthoughts. Nor did he have doubts about the essential tenets of Christianity. It was the centre of his life, but he never pushed it on other people and in my experience was rather reluctant to speak of it. He wrote once in a letter to an Anglican friend: 'Surely it is natural (that) those who believe in the Divinity of Our Lord and in the mysteries of His life and passion and His love for us must have much, most in common. The division comes when it is a question of what He intended His Church to be.'

Personally I felt drawn to him from my first meeting and to me he was always kindness itself. He was not inspiring or exciting, as Neville Gorton was, but to know him was to be gently, imperceptibly *widened* in one's interests and affections. My first summer vacation I was invited to the Châlet des Mélèzes, his summer home in the Alps above St Gervais-les-Bains. You were expected to walk up the last three thousand feet; a mule brought the suitcase. I am always slightly intoxicated by mountain air and this was my first encounter with the Alps – but I shall have enough to say of mountains later and I shall not now dwell on that first climb, on the scent of pine trees and fresh clean wood, on the torrent of lupins which had seeded themselves from the garden that Sligger's father had planted and which poured down along the course of the stream, nor on the first walk up to the col from which the whole Mont Blanc range dawned on one. Much better, Sligger always maintained, not to have the snows before one's eyes all the time but to have to take that short walk and to see them fresh in their splendour when you reached the top. The daily routine at the châlet was very like it had been at the farm near the Long Mynd except that instead of Gemma reading to us in the evening we played round games such as: 'I packed my Saratoga trunk...' or did Nebs, a variant of charades, named I believe after a distinguished performance by Raymond Asquith as Nebuchadnezzar eating grass.

Morris Whitehouse and I often visited Sligger at night in college; he kept open house to his friends from ten-thirty till midnight; up till ten-thirty we were all supposed to be working. He would turn from his books and join you, if you were the first to arrive, or there might be half a dozen there already. It was always a refreshing experience and we met people from other colleges whom we should not otherwise have known. His rooms were full of portraits of his friends, '*les beaux jeunes hommes de M. Urquhart*', as they were called by the villagers from near the Châlet. Rupert Brooke hung just to the right of the window. I have argued elsewhere – and do not propose to repeat the argument – that much of Victorian greatness was due to celibate schoolmasters, dons and officers who dedicated themselves to young men, and it is of the aftermath of the Victorian age that I am writing. The grosser implications of some attacks on Sligger are unthinkable to anyone who knew him. Indeed, most attacks on him have proceeded from envy. He chose his friends and sometimes those left out resented exclusion. He was good – and goodness attracts malice.

I have spoken of the Balliol Players. The first tour in the Welsh Marches was altogether too romantic; the intention was simply that the party should go, with bicycles and sleeping bags, to this lovely stretch of country and act in the kind of setting where *Comus* was first performed. The strolling, or rather pedalling, players would announce their arrival by trumpet and town crier and give their performance the same day. It was absurdly ambitious to take two plays on a fortnight's tour, and, whatever may have been the experience of strolling players in Elizabethan times, in the twentieth century people will not drop all they are doing and run to see a play at a moment's notice. That first tour was financially a failure, though it provided some useful lessons about what not to do, and those who took part remembered many moments with pleasure.

The second tour was produced by Anthony Asquith and the business side was organized by Walter Oakeshott, who took enormous trouble to find local agents who would look after the advertising and seating and the issue of tickets. This tour went to the Hardy country and included, as a tribute, a performance in the garden at Max Gate. The play was a contracted form of three plays by Aeschylus – *The Curse of the House of Atreus* – and the doom-laden atmosphere represented just that element in Greek tragedy that had appealed to Hardy. There was also a performance at Corfe Castle, arranged simply on account of the magnificence of the setting; it was not thought likely that there would be much of an audience. In fact, Corfe Castle proved to be the success of the tour. People came from far and near. In the third, fourth and fifth tours, we always had seven or eight hundred people at Corfe Castle.

Why did we do it? Why did we put in the effort and enthusiasm involved? The answer in a word is youth but of course everyone who took
part would give different reasons as well. For myself, I enjoyed acting;
like the founders, I felt that it was good to pass on something of the
intellectual excitement which we were experiencing in Oxford; and to
go with friends to beautiful places in England in late June is in itself an
attraction that needs no explanation. On the third tour, Morris produced
the play; it was the *Hippolytus* of Euripides and Walter Oakeshott played
Hippolytus. We liked none of the existing translations, so Kenneth
translated it for us into a verse nearer the original than Gilbert Murray's,
perhaps harsher but often achieving a moving simplicity. That year
Jack Westrup wrote music meant for unaccompanied male voices in the
open air; Morris wrote the music for the fourth and fifth tours.

So there we were, with our own translation, our own music, our own
production. Since I was the business manager for the third tour, it is the
effort involved in that side of it that sticks in my memory and I am impressed today by the financial audacity of the whole affair. We had no
ongoing funds and did everything on credit. We published Kenneth's
translation, Blackwell's printing and binding it for us, and sold copies
at the performances. We printed programmes, handbills, posters and
distributed them to local agents – usually a bookshop or a stationer. They
hired chairs for us and put them on the site; they did the local advertising. We engaged, where possible, a hall where we could go if it rained;
we also insured against rain. We designed and had built, by a carpenter
near Folly Bridge, the façade of a Greek palace which could be bolted
together on the site, and also a chariot; we hired a Foden steam traction
engine to carry the palace and the sleeping bags of the cyclists. Morris
and I went some months beforehand to every site where we would act
and I saw all the agents. It was then that we paid the first of many visits
to Max Gate. The cost of the production – scenery, payments to agents,
hire of lorry, costumes, printing, properties – came to between £500 and
£600 and we covered it, with a few pounds over.

When at last the day came and we were off, I felt like a child on his
birthday. The memory of that whole fortnight and of those that came
later is one of lyrical delight – but very hard work. We had to get the
palace off the Foden and bolt it together on the site. We must make sure
at each site that everyone understood where he should go on or come off
– and we liked distant entries, particularly for the chariot, which used to
come on with a lusty chorus from some distant glade or the buttress of
some ruined castle. The production had to be redesigned in minor ways at
each new site. We had to make sure that shields and swords and helmets
were in the right place and that programme sellers knew what they had

to do and had sufficient copies of the translation ready for sale. Then we would act the play, have a splendid supper of bacon and eggs and beer at the pub and make for some romantic and inaccessible place where we meant to sleep. We slept on the top of Glastonbury Tor; on a bastion of the Bishop's Palace at Wells, where we woke up among birds because trees from beyond the moat reached almost to the outer walls of the Palace; in Maiden Castle and in Corfe Castle. When I told Thomas Hardy of this, he shuddered: 'I wouldn't sleep in Corfe Castle for anything,' he said. 'Think of those thirteen knights King John starved to death in the dungeons! Think of the traitor Lady Bankes hanged from the battlements in the Civil War! And the poor boy stabbed as he took the stirrup-cup. The place must be full of ghosts.' But usually Mrs Hardy would say, 'Mr Hardy thinks . . .' or 'Mr Hardy means . . .' He was very gentle and much concerned for our welfare. Once we went to see him when it had been raining and he was afraid our trousers were wet; it didn't matter *below* the knee, but it was serious if you went about in trousers wet *above* the knee, he explained, feeling my trousers to make sure.

Dorchester was the hardest day of all. We acted at Max Gate in the afternoon and then there was afternoon tea in the garden with straw-berries and cream and then – as soon as politeness would permit – we had to tear the palace down, get it on to the Foden and put it up again in Dorchester for the public performance in the evening.

There were moments of beauty, of visual beauty as the dying Hippo-lytus was carried away by torch-bearers in the fading light; of shields and helmets crossing the rampart at Old Sarum against the setting sun; of a sentinel crying his warning from a pinnacle at Corfe. There was sometimes another kind of beauty too; Theseus' lament for Phaedra; Hippolytus and his huntsmen making their vows to Artemis; Agamem-non in agony because the oracle declared the army could not sail for Troy unless he sacrificed his daughter. That was on the fourth tour; I had to learn my part rather quickly that year because I had just done my final examinations but for me it was the most interesting play to act in. I was Clytaemnestra and I had to fight for the life of Iphigeneia, my daughter, the destined victim. I knew, and of course the audience knew too, that when the army came back Clytaemnestra would kill Agamemnon and start a blood feud within the family; it would become the duty of her own children to kill her. Trying to act the part, one felt how modern Euripides was in his understanding of character; Clytaemnestra fought for her child and brushed aside nonsense about oracles and honour and the need to humiliate Troy. That was men's talk – but here was a loved daughter. But Agamemnon of course had to think about his job; he was leader of a band of kings and nobles bent on war. 'I *must* do this!' he cried. Clytaemnestra is usually portrayed as merely a fiend, but in this play Euripides sees her as a woman of strong affections whose husband had killed her child and betrayed her – and she would have ten years to brood on that while the army was at Troy.

To act a play is to understand it as you never can by reading it or watching it. We came to think of the figures of Greek mythology as people. The whole experience, with all its blunders and absurdities, and perhaps just because of the outlay of nervous energy that went into it, still has for me the colours of the rainbow. Someone produced a book with accounts of the first few tours. I quoted, for the piece I wrote, a verse of Housman's which still seems to me to express the feeling of those days:

> Once in the wind of morning
> I ranged the thymy wold;
> The world-wide air was azure
> And all the brooks ran gold.

Much of the picture I have tried to draw, not of the whole of Oxford but of my Oxford, will seem insufferable to a later generation. I have said that beneath the gaiety and irrelevance of our behaviour there was a consciousness of the injustice in the world outside. For most of us the main response to that was the recognition that because we were privileged we must make the most of our time at Oxford and go away with the equipment for a career, as leaders of a kind in some field. And we did in fact work hard in the vacations, if more intermittently in term. Most of the people I have mentioned did get first-class honours. But we did accept the need for leadership; we would exercise it ourselves one day and meanwhile – and that is where our successors seem different – we thought our elders had something to teach us; we were certainly not in a rage with them.

One tribute that we paid uneasily to the injustice of the world was the Boys' Club, for 'those less fortunate than ourselves'. Sedbergh had one in Bradford; Balliol had one in Oxford, in a poor district on the outskirts. On arrival one was asked to go down one night a week and mingle with the boys. They had a football team and a cricket team and in the evening came to the club premises to play table tennis or billiards or snooker, or use the gym. Of course it was good that there should be such a place and yet – and yet – I was always a little unhappy. A placebo to the conscience – a mild anaesthetic for a symptom – and I didn't feel I was getting anywhere. They called us 'the toffs'; I remember one of my contemporaries lighting a Turkish cigarette: 'Cor,' they cried, 'bang goes 'alf-a-crown.'

Morris and I decided that instead of going down once a week we would go every night for a month before Christmas and produce a one-act play for them to do at their Christmas concert. The play must be funny and simple and be written with the Oxford dialect in mind. And, since we had the best dressing-up box in Oxford, they must involve fancy dress. We wrote a short play based on the scene in *The Merry Wives* when Falstaff is carried out in the washing-basket and tipped into the Thames; it went quite well and we wrote another based on an episode from *Don Quixote*; the third we gave a Greek setting, because we had plenty of Greek clothes, but the story came from *The Laird of Cockpen* in the Scottish Students' song book. He married a wife, his braw house to keep, but the poor lass was dumb, so he called in a doctor to cut her clacking-strings and she began immediately to scold – and it was beyond the doctor's art to tie them up again – one of the world's simple basic jokes. That was great fun because the doctor was a magician and was attended by a variety of familiars – which gave everyone a chance to dress up. There was a splendid operation – in which the wife blew out one of those whistles which unroll into a long pink paper sausage with a feather on the end. Afterwards Mrs Dore provided a stupendous high tea at 58 Holywell and they sang songs. We overheard one of them say to another: 'That was a rare bit of fun; hope I'll be in the play next year.'

For audacity, of course, the *British Independent* easily took the prize. In the general strike of 1926, there were tanks rumbling through the streets of London. It really did seem that there was danger of something very like civil war. The Government seemed determined to crush the Trade Unions, the Unions to overthrow the Government. Both parties tried to make things seem worse than they were – the Government to justify the use of force, the Trade Unions to show that they could paralyse the country. Walter Oakeshott conceived the quite simple idea that we should start a newspaper that would tell the truth and express the views of anyone who was on the side of peace – Labour, Liberal or Conservative. He borrowed a working capital of £500, an office just off the Strand and a number of Gestetner machines and typewriters; he obtained a grudging concession from the TUC that they would not interfere if it was not *printed*, a promise of news from some agency temporarily out of business, and some facilities from the *Spectator*. And he summoned twenty or thirty of his friends.

As with the Balliol Players, everyone had to do something of everything. I had borrowed my tutor's car and once the enterprise got off the ground my day settled into a demanding routine. I slept in the Oakeshott family's kitchen, got up at four-thirty and made myself a cup of tea and then went off with loads of the *British Independent*, doing a round of the bookstalls at tube stations, working gradually in towards the City, where there were not only bookstalls but men anxious to sell anything in the streets. By about nine I had got rid of my cargo, had some breakfast in the Strand and reported at the office. For the rest of the day, it was my task to interview people with well-known names and get something we could publish. By evening, having flown in with what honey I could gather throughout the day, I came back to the office and turned the handles of the duplicating machines or stapled sheets together or made up parcels of the finished paper or made posters saying BUY THE B.I. We usually finished about midnight and got three hours' sleep.

Neither the police nor the TUC were quite sure that they approved of peace and sometimes we were being watched by both. I was sent to see Lord Grey of Falloden, Ramsay Macdonald, the Bishop of London (he was Winnington-Ingram), Wedgwood Benn (the father of the present Cabinet Minister), Lord Parmoor and St Loe Strachey, the editor of the *Spectator*, who was very much on our side.

We produced five numbers, and the sales grew; the last day we did twenty thousand copies. How much longer we could have stood the strain I do not know but after the fifth number, and the tenth day of the crisis, the strike collapsed. For us, disappointment mingled with our relief, and exhaustion with both. That it should end just when we had got the organization going and sales going up every day! But of course it was to end the crisis that we had worked. I do not suppose we affected the course of events one way or the other.

For Walter, who had been the mainspring of the whole enterprise, there was a good deal of tidying up to do before he could hurry back to Oxford in time for his final examinations in Greats. He got his First. I returned his car to Charles Morris, my tutor, not in the best of shape. I had bumped a taxi, not very hard, at Hyde Park Corner. Also the car had disappeared for about twenty-four hours. It had not been there one morning when I went out in the small hours with my load of papers; of course I reported it to the police but it was embarrassing that I could not remember the registration number. That night, at about two in the morning, I was roused from the drugged sleep of utter exhaustion to find the Oakeshotts' kitchen full of gigantic policemen, all laughing at me. I have never understood how they got in. They made me come to the station to identify the car, which they had found the other side of the block. They thought it had been there all the time but it was full of orange peel and chocolate wrappings and seemed to me to have been lived in. When the strike was over and we were on the way back to Oxford, I was surprised, at the top of a steep hill, to be passed by one of the back wheels, which went bounding away past the car down the hill. Charles was extremely forbearing about it all; he felt, I think, that it was part of his contribution to the Great Strike.

Most of our contemporaries came back to Oxford with money in their pockets because they had gone to drive trains or be special constables – whereas we were not sure for some time that we should not have to stump up towards the deficit. I had no regrets about that but was conscious of a barrier between myself and some of the special constables, who were disappointed that they had not had a bash at the strikers, or who rejoiced that they had.

Some of us stayed on at Oxford and became dons. For most of us the time came to go, and we knew that we must go, just as we now know that we must die. This was a kind of death; it meant saying good-bye to so much. Since I was going to the other side of the world, the wrench was sharper for me than for most. But there was the excitement of starting a new life which I had chosen myself. More than one of us yielded to persuasion and became an accountant or a manufacturer or a diplomat instead of following the calling that most appealed to him – the stage for one, archaeology for another, music perhaps for a third. They became reconciled no doubt, but, however pointless it may seem, there is a sadness in recalling:

> ... the passage which we did not take
> Towards the door we never opened
> Into the rose-garden ...

Part Two

FIELDS
AND PEASANTS

V

LONELINESS

1 Wolves and Locusts

The journey from Bombay to Saharanpur, in the north-western corner of the United Provinces, took some fifteen or sixteen hours. For most of the way I had the great bare compartment to myself; I lolled on the bunk and watched the brown dusty land slide past. But for the first stage I had a companion; he was the Indian editor of a Bombay newspaper. We began to talk and I explained that I was in the Indian Civil Service and on my way to my first posting as Assistant Magistrate. He said something that, in various forms and in various countries, I was to hear for the next forty years or so. As an Indian, he wanted his country to stand on its own feet, to be a nation in its own right among the nations of the world. But there was no ill feeling; India had learnt much from England, he had been brought up in the English tradition and he did not want all the English to go – but they should stay as friends, as helpers, as advisers, not as masters.

Of course this agreed with the general lines on which I had been brought up at Oxford. When I was asked, at the interview which was part of the ICS examination, why I wanted to go to India, I replied that I thought India was going to be a most exciting place politically. 'Here we are,' I said, with enthusiasm, 'having successfully devolved power to Canada, Australia, New Zealand' – and in my ignorance I fear I added South Africa – 'and it has worked. We are still part of one organism. Now we have embarked on the enormous experiment of trying to do the same thing with a people who differ from us in language, culture and religion. Will this work too?' I believed every word I said – and fortunately it was just the right thing to say to that board of interviewers at that moment. So my conversation with the editor ran smoothly and we parted with mutual good wishes. But when he went, his hair left on the window-pane where he had leaned a thick smear of some greasy substance, at which I looked with distaste, reflecting how often it is little things that keep people apart.

As we went north and the light began to fade, it became colder – it was mid-December – and I became aware of a sensation almost of coming home. This was because, in the days when I had adored Kipling, I had read so much about Northern India that even now, when I was estranged from him, the scents of dust and spices were familiar and many of the sights. In Delhi, the train stood a long time and I looked out at the platform, covered with sleeping figures, wrapped from head to foot like corpses in their rough white cotton cloths or their coloured quilts. I saw what I had expected; I had known it would be like that.

It was midnight when we reached Saharanpur, where I was met by a large young man whose name was George Fisher. He and his young bride were staying the night with Grant, the District Magistrate, so there was no room in the house for me. For the moment, I was to sleep in a tent. How sharp the night air of December seems in Northern India! It is actually not much above freezing but the contrast with the bright dry heat of midday makes it seem colder and gives it a rasp and a tingle that are invigorating if you have a thick warm coat – but stupefying for a villager on a poor diet who has not. There will be more later about George Fisher; that night we did not talk much. He showed me the tent – almost a marquee, twenty-four-foot square, with a bathroom behind and an office room in front. By December the ground is baked dry; covered with three inches of straw, on which is laid a coarse cotton carpet, it makes a splendid floor for a tent. It was my first Indian tent and I can still savour that faint dusty smell of dry straw and canvas that was always to be the herald of delight when the time of winter camping began. The bed was the usual Indian pattern – a wooden frame criss-crossed with stiff tight webbing. By its side was a small table with the traditional symbol of Indian hospitality – a miniature cut-glass decanter of whisky.

Next morning I was astonished and delighted by the crispness and freshness of the air, by dew on the grass and by the sight of trees that looked like elms. I went into the house for breakfast and began to apologize to Mrs Grant for the inconvenience of arriving when the house was full. At that moment Grant himself came in from his morning ride. He was a tall lightly built man in his late forties, fair, with that leathery sun-dried look that fair men sometimes get if they are much out of doors in hot climates. His manner was brisk and businesslike, his speech rather clipped.

'Hello, Mason,' he said, 'I've got a pony outside which might suit you. Native dealer over from Meerut. Have a look at her when you've had breakfast.'

Within an hour, I was the owner of Tessa, half-thoroughbred, half-trained for polo, the most lively and responsive horse I was ever to own. She was small and light for cavalry polo, but we learnt to play together and took part in many small tournaments. At getting quickly off the mark and spinning round she was hard to beat; a touch was enough and she would be round; she was a darling and I loved her dearly. I never had any other pony about whom I felt like that.

My next step on that first day was to go to Grant in his study.

'What am I to do about work, sir?' I asked.

'Don't call me sir. Within our service, keep it for those two steps above you – the Commissioner or the Chief Secretary. Don't bother about work yet. What you have to do is to get the feel of the country. Here's a book about polo. I'll examine you on it this evening. Ah!'

At that moment, the mosquito-proof spring door opened to admit a slightly built Indian with a face heavily marked by smallpox, dressed as we were, in a tweed coat and grey flannel trousers. He had disregarded the row of visitors in Indian clothes who had come 'to pay their respects'.

'Ah, Mirza,' Grant continued, 'Just the man. Here's young Mason, just arrived from England. Take him out and show him the Exhibition. Bring him back for lunch. You'll stay for lunch, won't you?'

So off we went, Mirza and I, to look at the Exhibition. It was full of steel ploughs and prize bulls and pumps for tube-wells. Mirza had been to Cambridge and eaten his dinners at Gray's Inn to become a barrister. But he did not practise law nor, so far as I know, had he tried to enter Government service and this made him unusual for a man with such qualifications. He had some land near Roorkee, at the other end of the district, but he was mainly a businessman, experimenting in the manufacture of a variety of things, including a rather coarse white pottery covered with gilt or silver which he sold to Indian landowners who wished to entertain English officials. George Fisher, who was posted at Roorkee, told me later that he had come to know Mirza well and he had heard from him strange confidences about the perils and vices in London that in those days beset an Indian student with a moderate income. But that morning he and I merely made conversation.

Grant had great confidence in Mirza and had made him a Special Magistrate, which meant that he sat alone and for such offences as burglary could sentence to two years imprisonment. Grant and Fisher both treated him as a social equal, which would hardly have been possible with any other Indian in Saharanpur at that time. The gentlemen in Indian clothes with titles such as Khan Bahadur and Rai Bahadur who did not speak English would be given a chair and treated with great courtesy when they came to call but would have been much embarrassed to be asked to lunch. Alas, Grant and Fisher, with whom Mirza had been so happy, were succeeded by officers more suspicious or less gullible – I do not know the rights of it. A scandal arose – perhaps it was brought to light or even manufactured by an enemy. It appeared to be proved – and everything fell about Mirza's ears. His credit collapsed, he went bankrupt and ceased to be a Special Magistrate. But that was later.

Of course I was lonely at Saharanpur. On my twenty-third birthday I was in bed recovering from concussion. I had gone out as usual with Tessa in the early morning and we had spent a few minutes in the riding school, cantering, pulling up and reining back, then swinging round on the hocks – for a polo pony must not be allowed to get into bad habits and turn on its forehand – and then we had gone to a beginner's circuit of low jumps and ditches in the Remount Depot. We did one round and started on a second – and then I woke up with a bad headache, no horse and no idea where I was. But by my birthday I was well enough to read my letters. My mother wrote: 'You gave us great happiness twenty-three years ago' and suddenly I felt just as I had done when I first went to my prep school and dared not open a letter from home if there was anyone looking.

It was remarkable that she had not stood in my way about going to India. By nature my mother was possessive, and everything of hers had special virtues – recipes, china, furniture and most of all her children. Once on a family holiday, we made the acquaintance of an exceptionally agreeable man who must have listened courteously to much of her conversation. 'Your mother does have the most *wonderful* children,' he said to me when we were alone, releasing a good deal of pent-up mirth. She had always been happy for me to ask a school friend to stay with us but she had never liked me to go away in the holidays on a return visit and I had had the greatest difficulty in persuading her to let me go to an OTC camp which bit a week out of the summer holidays – not that I wanted to go, but it was the decent thing to do. Nor did she hesitate for a moment to express her criticism if any of her children showed the least sign of friendship with anyone of the opposite sex. She could never believe that anyone could be good enough for *her* children. Yet she raised no objection to India. Perhaps this was because she already saw me as a Governor and did not perceive, as I did, that there would not be time for that; perhaps it was my father who for once took the initiative with her and persuaded her that it would be unwise to intervene.

He, I think, had made up his mind, perhaps without putting it into words, that he would let me go my own way, though there could never be any doubt of his unfailing interest and affection. In the years after the war, he continued to look after his patients with the same steady devoted attention; he made up the ground he had lost by his absence with the army and the practice grew, until he took a partner in the mid Thirties when he was nearing sixty. He was the still centre, observing with understanding and interest, if sometimes an affectionate amusement, my mother's energetic devotion to fund-raising for the Village Hall, to the Women's Institute and to the Rural Community Council. She became a County Organizer and went all over Derbyshire; she organized the County Exhibition of Women's Institute handicrafts – and year after year her own Institute won the County Banner. Nor did she merely organize; she won prizes herself for glove-making and basket-work.

I recall only one occasion when my father tried to deflect me from any course of importance that he thought I might pursue. He feared I might go over to the Church of Rome. His arguments against it were not doctrinal; he felt it was too monolithic and too political and he was distrustful of an over-anxious and self-centred religiosity. I am doubtful whether the discussion had much effect on me at the time; it did help me later to understand my father's position. The grounds for his disturbance were genuine enough. I had gone up to Oxford with a strong feeling that the Protestant forms of Christianity had often been harsh and unforgiving, that the identification of Sunday with the Sabbath was Pharisaical and un-Christian and that what I knew of Calvinism was altogether repellent. At Duffield, where the evangelical tradition was strong, the form of worship seemed to me dreary beyond belief. The accent, if there was one, was on duty – and on a rather negative concept of duty. On the other hand, St Mary Magdalene stood for forgiveness, Our Lady for suffering and renunciation, St Francis and his canticle of the Sun for joy and praise and adoration.

I found my way therefore down the Cowley Road to the Society of St John the Evangelist. The lovely plainsong of their celebration sent my spirit soaring. I made my first confession, the sweat pouring down my back. The father to whom I went was a famous interpreter of the spiritual exercises of St Ignatius Loyola. Perhaps he thought he would make a monk of me; certainly he tried me too hard and I fell away – not because of intellectual doubt but because of sheer inability to maintain such high standards. I was still on the same side but I was deep in the cares and pleasures of the world.

If, on that twenty-third birthday in 1929, I remembered my parents with a sense of guilt, it was only the generalized guilt that I suppose most sons sometimes feel, because they cannot repay all the love they have received. My father was a still centre for me, as he was for my mother. I was altogether part of the family, and I was sad only because I was ill and alone in a strange land. But I was not sad the whole time; the first morning's walk with Mirza had been followed by a rather exciting succession of bewilderments. Someone called on me:

'Sir, I am the Nāzir,' he said. 'Are there any orders for me, sir?'

But I did not know what the Nāzir did and I had to question him to find out. He was the Quartermaster, more or less, of the District Magistrate's office and he had already supplied me with a messenger and a clerk and a rack of official stationery – but to whom should I write?

My clerk, by Grant's arrangement, spoke no English. He brought me records in Urdu of old cases already settled and filed and we went through them together. Urdu is a composite language with fragments of Persian and Arabic embedded in Hindi. Once we came on the Persian phrase: Huzūr Shāhānshāh-i-Mu'allā. Its literal meaning is The Presence, The King of Kings, The Exalted, but I did not understand. 'What does it mean?' I asked him in Urdu. 'It means –' he paused and thought and two English words emerged '– it means Queen Victoria!' So strong had been the hold of that august lady.

A day came when Grant suddenly told me I should 'try a case'. I was a magistrate with third-class powers, which meant I could send someone to prison for three months or fine someone fifty rupees (then £4 or $16). Someone's buffalo had strayed into someone else's sugar-cane and in the ensuing quarrel blows had been exchanged. Since the villagers of Northern India often carry a six-foot quarter-staff with brass at either end, such quarrels can be fatal; this however was trivial. It was only 'Simple Hurt'; no bones had been broken, which would have made it 'Grievous Hurt' and beyond my powers. Slowly, slowly, almost word by word I puzzled out the stories of each party. There were in fact two cases, since each party brought charges against the other. No one spoke English; the pleaders on either side had the minimum qualifications and the Urdu I had learned at Oxford was like schoolboy French. In the end I fined one party ten rupees each and acquitted the other, but it took a long time.

Odd jobs were felt to be the right thing for me. There was a reward of five rupees for a dead wolf. A party of a very low caste, nomadic gipsy folk called Kanjars (pronounced as in conjuror) came in with thirteen dead wolves, which they had collected in the course of a trip into the jungles of the Siwālik foothills, away to the north. There was a strong stink, and so of course it was I who was sent to certify that they were genuine wolves, not jackals. They were covered with dried mud and blood and not very easy to see but they seemed far too big for jackals so I certified that they were wolves and ordered the Nāzir to pay the rewards. The Kanjars were told to cut off their ears and tails and burn them; I waited till I had seen these grisly relics thrown on the fire. It was a strange task for a student of philosophy.

The Kanjars were back again next month with more wolves. It was on their third visit that I discovered that they had kept the sun-dried carcasses of the original wolves, inserted a freshly killed jackal inside the rib-cage – as the chef of a Victorian duke would stuff a quail inside an ortolan – and sewn on new ears and tails manufactured from hessian and smeared with fresh blood. My formal education being over, my true education had begun.

A swarm of flying locusts had passed over a corner of the district some time before. Now it appeared that they had laid eggs which had hatched out. The Entomologist to Government sent us instructions. The real remedy, he said, was to observe where the flying locusts settled and dig up their eggs – but it was too late for that. When they hatched, locusts, he said, went through various stages of growth, in the earliest of which they could not fly but could only hop; it was in these stages that they would strip every vestige of green from a crop. So long as they were pink, they could not fly; when they could fly they turned olive green. Hoppers could be destroyed by digging a V-shaped trench. The outer side of the trench could be made impassable to hoppers by nailing to it a strip of American cloth dipped in paraffin. The hoppers should be driven into the V by a line of men beating tin cans or brass gongs; at the sharp point of the V would be a deep pit in which they would collect, and where they could be trampled to death.

With these instructions I set out for the north-western corner of the district on the banks of the Jumna, where the hoppers had emerged. There they were, twice the size of grasshoppers, munching and crunching at crops already ruined, the bare stalks stirring and rustling beneath the weight of their attack. They were undoubtedly pink, a darkish shrimp colour. So I planned an enormous V with a pit at the point. The villagers were very unwilling to co-operate. In the first place, it was wrong to kill locusts – it was a Hindu village; a man across the river in the Punjab had killed locusts and all his cattle had died and two of his sons. In the second place, it would not work. But I had with me a vigorous junior official and we bullied them into it, grumbling and unwilling. The earthworks completed, we attempted to nail American cloth – it would now be plastic – to the far side of the trench. I suppose this might be possible in heavy English clay – where locusts are rare; it was obviously impossible in the light sandy soil by the river – which is the kind of place where locusts lay eggs. I wondered whether the Entomologist had ever left his office. However, we propped up the strip with splinters of bamboo. Then we started our beat. The pink hoppers immediately took off and flew away in a dark cloud – as the villagers had said they would, as the Entomologist had said they could not.

The Grants took me into camp with them. Mrs Grant was gentle and kind; she went home every summer to be with the children and in the winter made her husband comfortable. She liked to sit on the verandah

and watch her cow milked, making sure that everything was clean and
that the milk was not diluted. She saw that drinking water from the well
was boiled and filtered every day. She enjoyed life in camp, which could
be made very comfortable if the moves were kept short, but she would
have preferred a larger place than Saharanpur, a place where she could
have turned over the pages of the *Tatler* in the company of other ladies.
She was the daughter of an officer in the Indian Army and I do not think
her outlook on India was very different from that of her parents.

Grant resembled a number of ICS officers of his generation in his
scepticism about schemes for improving life in the villages. The Indian
peasant had ways of doing things which had evolved over thousands of
years; it was no use trying to persuade him to plough cow-dung into his
field instead of burning it unless you could provide him with an alternative form of fuel. Grant would have expected my adventures with the
wolves and the locusts to end as they did. Experts in Lucknow seldom
understood the facts of life. But he differed from most of the service, even
of his own generation, in tending to support the landowner against the
cultivator. He was never a man to put his ideas in abstract form, but I
suspect that an unformulated theory about the evolution of human society
lay behind his attitude to the lower strata in the villages; they had got
used to living as they did – but a go-ahead landowner could be helped
by a tube-well or a better breed of bull.

To landowners, Grant was always polite and he took trouble to see
they should have access to him. He was the only man I have ever known
who thought it proper to snub his personal servant in front of visitors
so that they should not bribe him to influence his decisions. I have the
impression that his head messenger received a more liberal harvest in
consequence. Grant was also, I believe, the last man in India to sit on
the bed while his bearer rolled his socks on to his feet and tied his
shoelaces. He told me to do the same and I did as I was told until I
found that the practice had begun to go out long before the Great
Queen died.

Once when we were in camp we rode over to visit a large landowner
who was also an Honorary Magistrate. He held the title of Khan Bahadur,
by which he was addressed. His full style was Khan Bahadur Maqsud Ali
Khan Sahib. He was a tall portly man of dignified appearance, light of
complexion and probably of Afghan ancestry. We entered the enclosure
to his house through a decorative arch of banana fronds, topped with an
inscription in gilt and tinsel lettering on a scarlet ground. 'Well Come!'
it said. Inside, there were garlands and table and chairs and oranges.
Grant instantly noticed that since his last visit the floor of the enclosure,
formerly of dried mud, had been paved with the substance called *kankar*

As a family, we seem to have had little desire to preserve a record of our lives. This photograph, taken after my christening, is all we have of my mother in her youth.

I can just remember this sailor suit, which I wore at family weddings and children's parties and which made me feel very grown-up.

My father was about eighty-eight when this was taken and was still driving himself, spending every morning on visiting his old patients and taking an occasional surgery.

George Fisher addressing villagers on the subject of sanitation.

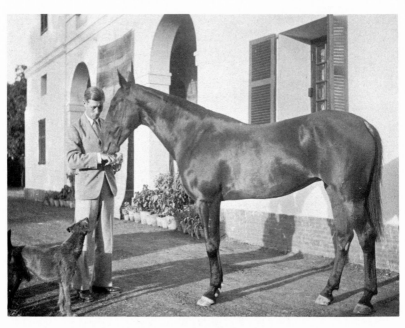

P.M. with Tessa.

P.M. at work in camp.

An elephant pulling a bus out of a river-bed. It was not done
for a young ICS officer to have a car but we would
occasionally hire a bus, which often broke down. But
someone could usually be found to help.

Crushing sugar-cane near Bareilly. From January to February, they cut sugar-cane in the villages near Bareilly; buffaloes or bullocks would walk in a circle crushing the cane in a machine like an old-fashioned coffee-grinder, and the pulp was burnt under pans in which the juice thickened into brown toffee-like molasses.

left A Rajput villager near Bareilly.

The basic means of transport: a bullock-cart near Bareilly with a full load.

(to rhyme with bunker) which was then generally used in the United Provinces to make roads. It is a volcanic material which is used because there is no stone, and it is found only in certain deposits. Grant complimented the Khan Bahadur on this improvement. 'But where did you get the *kankar*?' he asked. The Khan Bahadur became less dignified and giggled sheepishly, but at last confessed that the railway authorities had deposited some piles of the stuff preparatory to refreshing the ballast on the main line near by and he had sent over a few carts to collect some. It was not really stealing – that was clearly his view – to take from the railway, particularly for a Magistrate who was paid nothing for his work.

Grant merely laughed. Some officers would have been outraged – but then such officers would not have been told the story. He was good-humoured, if cynical about what one should expect from the natives – a term which he continued to use long after anyone else. He did not enjoy the society at the Saharanpur Club but considered it a duty to go there at regular intervals when not in camp. There he liked to drink a quarter-peg – that is, half a small whisky – and usually no more than one of those. Usually there was work to be done before dinner, after which he would read the paper and go to bed early so as to be out in good time with his ponies. He had four or five ponies and came perilously near breaking the ancient rule of our service by making a business of them. He would buy ponies almost raw from Dhalip Chand, who had sold me Tessa, teach them to rein back, to change feet at the canter, to passage sideways and turn, get them used to a polo stick and play them in slow polo, at the canter. When they were almost ready to play at the gallop he would sell them, and make enough on the deal to pay for his hobby. He got through his work quickly and if he made no innovations he kept his district in good order and knew a good deal about the crops, keeping about two acres under cultivation himself to provide fodder for his horses. He had obtained a Second in Greats at Oxford but showed no sign of it; it had just been work that he had got through. As a newcomer to India, I was an object of dry but kindly humour. The first night I spent in the Siwalik jungle, some kind of wild jungle cat came into my tent. Not being used to wild animals in my bedroom, I mentioned it next morning. 'Better sit up for it over a saucer of milk,' he said. I cannot recall conversation with him on any subject more serious than the training of ponies.

2 *Illusion and Embarrassment*

All but the most far-sighted of Grant's generation had lived in the illusion of permanence. There had seemed little reason before 1914 to suppose that the India they knew would change for a century at least. They were aware of course that there were constitutional reforms, with which Viceroys and Governors concerned themselves; but these had little impact in an old-fashioned district. The Indian gentlemen who came to 'pay their respects' expressed the most conservative sentiments; peasants, if questioned, would prudently – and with some historical truth – indicate that British rule was preferable to anything their ancestors had experienced and that it was better than the rule of a Maharaja or a Nawab. It was easy in such a place to make light of the opinions of – famous phrase! – a handful of agitators.

In contrast, the young Englishman who came to the Indian Civil Service in the Twenties could hardly fail to understand that an experiment had begun which was designed to make great changes. It was the intention that half the service should be Indian, and in the years from 1920 to 1925 nearly all the new entry had been Indian. In the United Provinces, there was an elected Assembly and the Governor's Council included two Ministers with a responsibility to the Assembly as well as two Members responsible to the Governor – and one of these was an Indian. These four headed all the departments of the provincial Government and only one, the Finance Member, was British.

Yet so strong was the illusion of permanence that it was easy to forget all this. The awareness of change had still hardly soaked through to Saharanpur. Such a man as Grant of course knew what was happening but he thought of his duty as he had always done; he was responsible for keeping Hindus and Muslims from killing each other, for ensuring that people could go peacefully about their affairs without being robbed, for the regular collection of the land revenue, for keeping bribery and oppression within bounds. Beyond that, if he could help to improve the breed of cattle or the output of the soil, he would; he would have made an admirable estate agent to an English duke. But he did not think much about preparing Indians for self-government.

George Fisher, on the other hand, was in spirit a missionary. Saharanpur was unusual among UP districts in having an 'independent' subdivision at Roorkee, fifty miles away to the south, and here he reigned, in semi-independent state, under Grant's general supervision. He was vigorous in the inspection of village committees. There were some which were supposed to enforce simple regulations for cleanliness and others to settle minor disputes. He was full of schemes for improvement. There was something which in 1928 was called Village Uplift, later renamed Rural Development. Its beginnings must always be associated with F. L. Brayne in the Punjab, who preached a doctrine of better agriculture and cleaner villages with the fervour of the prophet of a new religion. Grant regarded this new faith with sceptical amusement, but others of his generation were slightly outraged, as a canon of Barchester might be by the onset of Methodism.

George, however, believed that rural development was an essential part of the new approach without which constitutional reforms would be meaningless. He felt about it passionately and he was impatient with the conservatism of some of his elders. He was equally impatient with something of far less importance, India's deep-rooted official respect for seniority. 'A senior man' was a phrase he always greeted with ribald mirth. In this, of course, India was a sharp change from Oxford, where undergraduates had addressed dons by their Christian names and had been encouraged to express their views freely; to be young in Oxford was nothing to be ashamed of. But India was an official hierarchy in which age was important. To me, it seemed wise to recognize that we were back in the Victorian age and that it cost little to preface one's opinions with a deferential tribute to the value of experience. But George was so set on the importance of what he wanted to say that he would not pause to consider how it might strike someone else, and there were some of his seniors who deplored, as opinionated and dogmatic, proposals which they might have taken up as their own had they been presented with tact.

One of his passions was for structural development at Hardwar, a holy place where the Ganges comes out of the hills. Every twelfth year there is a tremendous pilgrimage to Hardwar, when Hindus come from all over India in hundreds of thousands. Such crowds are hard to control and access to the most sacred part of the Ganges was by a narrow funnel, between buildings, where people had often been crushed to death. There had been deaths on the last such occasion. Another would soon arise, and George felt responsible for what might happen. The way to the holy pool – the Har-ki-pairi – could, and should, be opened up. To alter anything at Hardwar involved getting the consent of the Hindu religious authorities – all the property belonged to temples – and in this George was successful. When I knew him it was with the official hierarchy that he was struggling, and this demanded diplomacy of the highest order.

At some stage of my year at Saharanpur, some change in plan, or perhaps a sudden illness, summoned Grant to Meerut to act as Commissioner and gave George Fisher the opportunity to act for two months as District Magistrate. In this he was fortunate, for it was only his third year. For me of course it was welcome too, because, kind though the Grants had been, we had few ideas in common, while George Fisher, a parson's son who had been at Repton and Christchurch, belonged to my own generation and had had a similar upbringing. He was a friend. He was a big man, generous, determined, courageous. I admired his enthusiasm even though I sometimes wished that his immediate object did not have so complete a monopoly of his attention. He was so single-minded that I have seen him walk out of his tent, deep in discussion about a drainage scheme, and bump unseeing straight into his own wife, who was standing waiting for him.

They had been married for only a few months and were deeply happy. She was a sensitive, intelligent girl, brown of hair and eyes, slim, graceful, like a deer in the movements of head and neck. It was a marriage of opposites; she was acutely aware of many things at the same time. 'Oh, I'm not *educated*,' she would say, with a peculiar mocking intonation aimed at him or at me for some Oxford pedantry and mocking herself and formal education at the same time. She laughed a great deal in those days, at herself and us and at the absurdities of Indian life. And George too could laugh. One of the plagues of the municipal board at Hardwar was the presence of innumerable monkeys, which, being holy, could not be killed. Many were sent to Hardwar as a holy place by other municipal boards far away, who thus at the same time rid themselves of a pest and performed an act pleasing to Hindu piety. In Hardwar, where the street lamps were still lighted by kerosene oil, the monkeys learnt that they could pull out the wicks and drink the oil, from which they obtained a gratifying exhilaration. 'There's a problem,' said George, 'that the London County Council doesn't have to face.'

So we laughed together, but her laughter and her happiness ended suddenly. George was killed at polo a few months later; in his utter absorption, he crossed the line of the ball, breaking the most fundamental rule of the game – as essential for safety as obeying the rule of the road in a car. When I saw her after that, I wondered how she could ever take up the pieces of her life again. But she did; she went back to England and became a medical student, married again, was happy again and then – but she was one of those people whom life tries by a succession of sorrows. I shall not follow her out of the field that the lens of my camera covers.

There was one other sadness in that first year. On the voyage out by P & O, I had two companions, both from King's College, Cambridge, and we had become friends. One of them was soaked in *A Passage to India* and had made up his mind that he would not get on with his compatriots. He did not expect to be happy. He was as much of a missionary as George Fisher, but far less robust, both in temperament and physique. As we looked over the side at the shimmer and glare of Bombay harbour, I was conscious of slight nausea and headache; dark glasses were hardly known. 'Sad that we shall never feel really well again,' he said. And in his own case he was right; he was dead before the year ended. He was sent into camp on famine duty in May, when it is very hot; he had an attack of appendicitis and by the time he had been jolted thirty miles in a bullock-cart to a hospital, his appendix had burst. Useless no doubt to ponder on what might have been; useless to think of the steps we did not take towards the door we never opened – still more useless in the case of someone else. Nonetheless, I have often wondered what might have been the fate, if they had lived, of those two idealists, both too brave and too devoted to conceal their criticism of what they disliked.

In Grant and Fisher I met in dramatic contrast two aspects of the British approach to India. But there was a side of life in India which I saw in Saharanpur and was never to see again – the hot weather in a small station. Saharanpur was far indeed from being what was known as a penal station; it had a longer cold weather than places further east, less extreme hot weather than places more central. There were many places that were 'smaller', in that there were fewer Europeans. But for my part I feel less lonely when surrounded by people who make no social demands, peasants and servants, who are content to be different, than when bound to associate with uncongenial companions.

At Saharanpur, there were three officers at the Remount Depot, which received horses for the Indian cavalry and gave them an elementary training. The Commandant, a Major, had been an international athlete but had run to fat; he was reputed to weigh 20 stone – 280 pounds – and had become too heavy to ride, though he was said to be still a wonderful judge of a horse. He drank a bottle of whisky a day, but it did not seem to make much difference to him. He was a Canadian and told us that when he went on leave he had encountered a law permitting only two bottles a month, and that only on medical certificate. So he had to go through the telephone directory and find fifteen doctors he knew. But he was a pleasanter companion than his two colleagues. There was an Irish vet and the second-in-command, a little man who looked like a jockey; he had had a wartime commission and had somehow kept it. They were both hard drinkers, too, men with whom I felt no sympathy. But in the Remount Depot they played just the right kind of polo for me, at the canter, with ponies that were all learning the game. They both drank whisky between the chukkers, a thing I have never seen done anywhere else. Indian orderlies would make up the numbers to eight and there was one Risaldar, an Indian officer who would join us afterwards for a glass of lemonade. A Risaldar was a cavalry officer who had risen from the ranks and held a commission from the Viceroy, not from the King; he was a subordinate officer but was given a chair and addressed with the polite honorific forms of speech, like the Spanish *Usted*. But all ranks of Indian cavalry came of good stock, holding land and paying for their own horses when they joined the regiment. They were of warrior castes with a high concept of personal honour. This Risaldar was a tall Punjabi Muslim, very handsome and scrupulously neat in his breeches and boots; how dignified he seemed, sipping his lemonade, how much more of a gentleman – there is no other word – than those two brutalized representatives of Western culture!

There was also the Club and from time to time it was a duty to go there – but to me it was always a duty, indeed something of an ordeal. I did not care for bridge or billiards; if there was conversation, it was always reminiscence about old so-and-so, whom I did not know. It was hard to find any common ground. When the hot weather began, there were two middle-aged women usually to be found at the Club; both came from the community of mixed descent which had once been called Eurasian and at the time I am speaking of was officially known as Anglo-Indian. They had been brought up in India and their menfolk had belonged to subordinate departments; one had been in the Indian Medical Department, which consisted of doctors qualified by a short period of study not internationally recognized. In a country desperately in need of both doctors and money, it was not a bad arrangement – but in the lives of individuals it might be cruel. They might rise to the rank of Captain or even Major, but British India was as much infected by caste as Indian India and they were never socially or professionally the equals of the Indian Medical Service, who had qualifications recognized in Britain. There was something pathetic in their talk of a 'home' they had never seen, in their obstinate – and perhaps partly assumed – ignorance of the India that lay all round them. Poor ladies! The powder lay in violet drifts in the shadows below their eyes; their skin turned grey instead of olive as they grew older; pretence seemed to dominate their lives. But each of these two had one love; each had an Alsatian dog, bred by the Irish vet in the Remount Depot, pedigree dogs of great beauty. Each was sure that hers was incomparably the better and each confidently entered her favourite for a show in the hill station of Mussoorie not far away. One took the first prize, the other was defeated. Perhaps the winner triumphed too openly and the loser said something unforgivable in reply; at any rate from that moment neither would meet the other. Before going to the Club, each would send a servant to enquire whether the other was there, and if so sit gloomily at home.

It was embarrassment at the danger of being thought stand-offish and superior that made it an ordeal to go to the Club at Saharanpur. I could not enter into conversation which concerned experiences quite foreign to mine, nor could those I found there have entered into talk about recent life at Oxford. The one thing that concerned us all was the future of India, and on this we were bound to disagree. It was easy for me to picture leaving India and finding some different way of life in England – not so for them. There might be six or seven denizens of the Club on a hot weather evening, half of them born in India with no knowledge of any other world, and to talk to them as I had talked to the Board which interviewed me in London, or to the editor in the train, would have meant shocked incomprehension – not to say anger that anyone so young and inexperienced should have views on what affected them so deeply. And to talk about politics to the polo players from the Remount Depot would have met with uncomprehending contempt.

How agonizing to the young is embarrassment! I have one memory of embarrassment which is out of place here in time – but time is a way of perceiving human experience and in terms of the emotional response it belongs here. In Heidelberg, three years earlier, I had lived with a German family who provided a midday and an evening meal for half-a-dozen young unmarried people. It was not with them that my difficulty arose but with an older man, a Prussian from the eastern marches near the Baltic. He was not a *junker* but of the professional middle classes; he had a degree and before 1914 had been the headmaster and proprietor of a private school in Heidelberg, run on what he believed were the lines of an English public school. Let us call him Herr Pfeiffer. I went to him three times a week for German conversation and paid him two marks an hour, the mark being then about ten to the pound. He was at this time desperately poor; all his capital had been swallowed up in the inflation and he had not been able to find regular employment. I was supposed to pay him at the end of each week, but about midweek, with acute embarrassment, he would always ask for an advance. His wife felt there must be flowers on the table where we worked, but they were obviously flowers that someone else had thrown away.

He had been an officer in the regular reserve and had joined his regiment at the outbreak of war in 1914 and before the end of the year had been wounded in the hip by a fragment of shell. He was bitter about British propaganda, which had been so much better than German. There was a story about a German soldier who went peacefully into a ✓ butcher's shop in Brussels and asked for a piece of sausage. He held out his hand for the change and the butcher whipped out a cleaver from below the counter and chopped off his right hand. His comrades took that butcher, drove one of his own meathooks into his back and left him hanging. Of course the British press splashed that – but said nothing about what the butcher had done with the cleaver – and they said nothing of how Belgian nuns had crept out of their convent at night and hacked off the sexual organs of wounded German soldiers.

German war guilt was a myth; war had been inevitable; it was part of the dialectic of history, as between Rome and Carthage. The British had won by the power of the Royal Navy and the blockade, by the cunning of their propaganda; it was hard for a German to forget the turnip year, when German children had died of bowel complaints because they had had to eat raw turnips. Still, he was prepared to look on the war in a sporting spirit as far as the British were concerned. The Germans had lost – but were prepared to forget and forgive. But the French – and here his face would grow dark with passion – the French and their vindictive occupation of the Rhineland with Senegalese troops! To see a German *mädchen* sitting on the knee of a black soldier! *'Der Englander,'* he broke out *'ist ein* gentleman *aber der Französe ist ein – ein maudit bête!'* – the last French phrase being used because he did not think I would understand any German expression strong enough for his feelings. I tried to keep off the subject of the French in the Rhineland; it seemed likely to bring on a stroke.

I cannot say that I exactly liked Herr Pfeiffer but I did feel sad about his personal and national misfortunes; he felt so deeply the humiliation of poverty and defeat. I listened with fascination to some of his stories. He had at some stage been sent with two German NCOs to stiffen an Austrian regiment of Czechs – or perhaps some other kind of *untermensch* – and had put his revolver to the head of the colonel and forbidden him to retreat.

In the operations against the Bolsheviks (after the armistice with the West) he had put on the uniform and taken the papers of a Red Russian colonel who had been captured and had spent six weeks in Moscow, never knowing when he might meet someone who knew the man he was impersonating. And though his political ideas were very different from mine, I could see why he felt as he did. He was altogether Cromwellian; *'sein mehr als schein'* – 'Be more than you seem' – was a favourite saying, and he was all for cold baths, short hair, hard exercise and rigorous discipline. He hated the black, red and yellow flag of the Weimar Republic; it stood for priests, socialists and Jews. All the seeds of Nazism were there in him; Germans must obey one leader, it is in their blood, he would say.

In all this, I was not exactly embarrassed. I was there to learn German but also something about Germany and it would clearly be hopeless to argue with a man of his age about views so strongly held. So I listened and encouraged him to tell me more. One of his angers was against Americans because they were *nouveaux riches* who did not know how to behave. He had once been with an American who had offered him a meal or a bottle of wine with some phrase such as: 'It's all right, I'll pay.' He had found it deeply insulting that he, an officer of the Kaiser, who had fought duels as a student, should be treated like that. I only partly understood the affront, but dared not ask for elucidation.

Some days later he offered to show me the Schloss, the residence of the Elector Palatine. Afterwards, I thoughtlessly suggested that we should have a cup of coffee and a cake. He was reluctant but I pressed him and we sat down. I had meant to pay – but suddenly I remembered that mannerless American. My German was still clumsy; how could I avoid committing the same offence? But I also remembered those midweek advances of half-a-dozen marks. Frozen with embarrassment, I sat tongue-tied; I watched his reluctant fingers find a thin little purse and slowly, slowly, draw out a few coins desperately needed at home. If only I had thought beforehand and prepared a little speech: 'May I ask you to do me the honour to allow me . . .!' It was a failure in forethought and in powers of expression. Sympathy and understanding came too late.

It was not quite like that at the Saharanpur Club – but there was a resemblance. I did not actually offend against the code of those grey-faced ladies, but I was always afraid of upsetting them by condescension. I was ashamed of my own good fortune and they seemed to me pathetic and slightly ridiculous. And so – there was nothing to say. The days grew hotter, till to draw a breath through the nose out of doors in the daytime was to scorch the inner membranes of the nostrils. It was a sensation I was to recall thirty years later in Saskatchewan, in midwinter, with the temperature many degrees below zero, when I ran from the aeroplane through the frozen snow to the warmth of the reception hall – with its peanut machines and magazine stalls – and discovered my nostrils to be scorched with cold and blocked with ice.

That was simply an inconvenient sensation that did not last long – but I was conscious of a lassitude and exhaustion that continued all morning. I consulted the IMD doctor – the IMS man had gone on leave. He told me to eat two boiled eggs before my morning ride and two more when I came back; a pint of salty water would have been better advice, but it was a long time before I learnt that.

Heat and lassitude combined with uncongenial company are perhaps some excuse for the childishness of fantasy – and it was certainly childish to picture to myself, as I rode in through the gates of the burnt dusty compound that lay round the District Magistrate's house, the miraculous arrival – through what chain of impossible circumstance I could not guess – of some Oxford friend who would be waiting for me on the verandah.

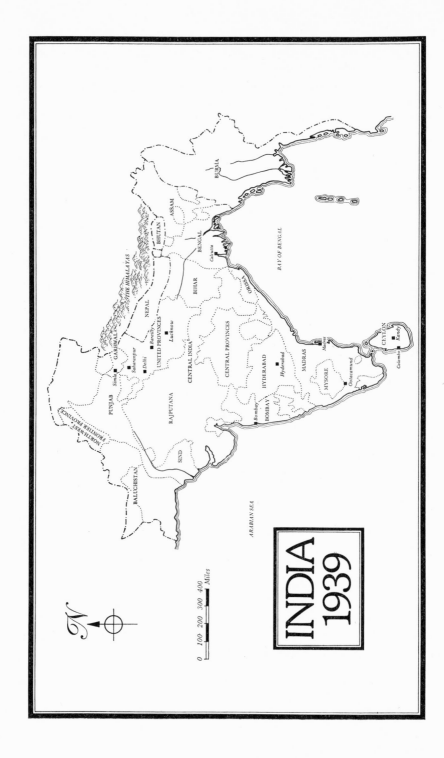

INDIA
1939

VI

THE FIRST JOB

1 Almost a Great Man

It was easy to forget that we were in India to help Indians to govern themselves. This was partly because they showed few signs of wanting to be helped – the passive majority, like most of the world, being on the whole more interested in the next meal, the active minority unconvinced that they needed any instruction. But our forgetfulness was also due to the interest of the work that confronted us. Every day seemed to be full. That at least was the case with me when the first eighteen months were over and I had a real job – in charge of a sub-division.

I knew, as my mother did not, that I should never be a Governor, not only because I did not think British rule would last long enough but because I had already decided to retire from India at an age when I could still do something else – at about the age, to make a presumptuous comparison, when Conrad ceased to follow the sea. Nonetheless, I did occasionally consider what reforms a Governor might have made in the training of young officers. It was probably right to spend the first six months with a good district officer, learning the feel of the country, acquiring some immunity to the intestinal disturbances which result from breathing India's richly organic dust, disposing of a few simple criminal cases ending in fines of ten rupees, and doing a few odd jobs such as my wolves and locusts. But six months was enough for that and it would surely have been better to make the first hot weather more of a mental and less of a physical ordeal. I would, I decided, have let my young man have a sniff at the hot weather but about the middle of May I would have taken him away to the cool of the hills and made arrangements so that for three months at least he spoke and read nothing but Urdu and had to pass a really difficult examination. As it was, being a bad linguist, and idle, I picked up rustic phrases from villagers in court and did no work to perfect my Urdu. Years after independence, in Pakistan, I apologized for my Urdu, which I had learnt, I said, in the fields and villages of Rohilkand. 'We can hear that,' said my host. A few of my service took the trouble to speak with propriety a language that is both subtle and literary; most of us were content to be fluent but with an atrocious accent and no mastery of shades of meaning.

After that intensive course in spoken and written Urdu, the young man in my ideal system would have had a month's leave and then started his second winter in a tent near a village where he would have laboriously and painstakingly prepared the record of crops and ownership of fields for that one village. This was the document which in a thousand other villages would be the basis of much of his later work. He would have worked under the guidance of a man who had been doing this kind of thing for twenty years – a man who would never do anything else and was far below him in the official hierarchy – but he would have learnt the backbone of his profession.

What in fact did happen next is a matter on which I do not mean to dwell. Each of us spent a year as odd-job man in various districts and then we were brought together for a training course where we had lectures – formal lectures, monotonously read. I have never liked lectures and felt I was being treated as a schoolboy – and a schoolboy of about fifteen at that. The man in charge of the whole training camp was a scholar of some repute in Eastern Hindi. He had published collections of folklore in that dialect and translated them. He was a gentle, kindly man and one cannot avoid describing him as well-meaning. Unfortunately, he was indecisive and at the same time given to making petty rules which invited defiance. These he would see defied and remain silent. He made a rule that lights in tents must be out by some very early hour; we took not the faintest notice. He forbade us to heat our tents by anything but one special kind of stove; we told him of another kind of stove that was cheaper, safer and warmer but he forbade us to use it. We installed it and asked him to dinner and he warmed his hands at it with docility. He met me out riding at the very beginning of the camp and said he wanted me to be in charge of polo. When should we play?

'Mondays, Wednesdays and Fridays,' I replied. It was the usual arrangement and was best both for ponies and young players.

'Oh,' he said doubtfully, 'I had thought we should play only twice a week.'

'Of course,' I replied, 'if that is the time-table you have decided, we must fit into it. But since you ask my advice, three days would be better.'

'Very well,' he replied, 'I want you to be in charge. We will do as you say.' And he rode away, magnanimously though rather sadly, but soon turned and came back with an objection.

I repeated my suggestion and once again he gave in and rode away, only to come back with another difficulty. I continued to give the same advice and in the end we did as I wanted. He brought out the worst in me – and not only in me. Years later, after independence, three of us tried to make amends by asking him to lunch in London. We knew we had behaved badly – but he had asked for it. It is hard to understand how he ever managed a district; perhaps he was always given a particularly good policeman. I learnt hardly anything in those four months.

By March of 1930, aged twenty-four, I was posted to my first real job. I was Subdivisional Officer – commonly called SDO – at Bareilly. For most of the time I was there, the District Magistrate was Michael Nethersole, a remarkable man, very nearly a great man, one who a century and a half earlier might have carved out a kingdom for himself, one whom it is easy to see as a dictator in Paraguay or Guatemala, a Conradian figure of destiny. He was the background to my time in Bareilly and lessons I learnt from him were of great help to me later.

Nethersole had been at Oxford at the outbreak of war but had immediately enlisted and served in France as a despatch rider. As though riding a motor-bicycle through shell-fire were not dangerous enough, he had volunteered for the Royal Flying Corps, which eventually combined with its naval opposite number to become the Royal Air Force. He had risen to the rank of Major or Squadron-Leader and had led a squadron of the primitive aircraft of World War I in what was technically an innovation – the first low-level attack by aircraft on German troops. By this feat he won the Distinguished Service Order.

This was the military background of Micky Nethersole, whose character was almost diametrically opposed to that of my well-meaning but indecisive superior at the training camp. The only thing they had in common was a respect for the language of the country. Micky spoke Urdu not only with fluency but with great clarity and precision; it was like listening to a public speech by an educated Frenchman, with none of that slurring of consonants and prolongation of vowels that is so common in the English. He had been born in India, his father – who was of Kentish stock – holding high office as an engineer; it was his mother, however, who was remembered. She was Irish and a character, and it must have been from her that he inherited his swiftness of decision, his passionate and sometimes moody temperament.

He had taken trouble not only to learn Urdu well, but also to understand the ways of the people. He enjoyed Indian food and accepted Indian hospitality with pleasure, not, as some of us undoubtedly did, as a rather disagreeable duty. Because of his understanding of Indian ways, he was able to follow his temperamental inclination and rule his district by Indian methods – despotic methods, fully understood by Indians but by no means always in accord with British law. He never defied the law but frequently disregarded it, operating usually by hints in the right quarter to trusted henchmen. But he was scrupulous in two respects. There must be no personal advantage to himself of a pecuniary kind, and nothing must be put in writing that would bring a blush to the cheek of a High Court Judge.

Judicious favouritism was one of the keys, he maintained, to efficient rule. Pick a good man and do all you can for him; trust him; expect a great deal from him but don't keep asking him questions. Tell him what to do and see that he does it but leave him to do it in his own way. He will be your man and he will die for you. This applied not only to subordinate officials but to friendly landowners all over the district. And he certainly won this kind of devotion from those he picked; something very deep in Indian character and culture responded to such treatment with complete emotional fidelity. I recall an intelligent and hard-working young Muslim, an executive officer who ought to have been promoted; with a little more luck in his examinations he might have started in the Indian Civil Service, but he had started two grades below that level and in the ordinary way it would take him thirty years to catch up. Micky did everything in his power to accelerate his advance and the young man spoke to me of these efforts with tears in his eyes. He really would have died for Micky. Claude Auchinleck, the Field-Marshal, had the same power of winning Indian devotion. On the other hand, Micky could be ruthless towards an official whom he believed to be corrupt.

When I knew him, he was perhaps a little less of the Mughal than he had once been. But he told me of an incident in his first spell in charge of a district which shows to what lengths he would go. He regarded this district as his personal property. It was a district near Bareilly, almost entirely rural and with no other European inhabitant – but about a million Indians. Nethersole arrived one morning at a stretch of shallow water near his camp which he expected to find covered with wild duck – but there were none. Two young British gunner officers from Bareilly, sixty miles away, had arrived the night before in time for the evening flight and had shot some duck; they had slept in the open on the edge of the water and before it was light had waded out to islands where they could hide and could shoot a few more – and within half an hour of sunrise the water was deserted; the duck had moved on to some neighbouring marsh. There were no laws in India preserving shooting for the owner of the land; anyone who had a gun could shoot in the proper season. But the neighbouring landowners would of course prefer the duck on their water to be shot by the District Officer rather than by some unknown soldiers. What was more, they had invited him. Micky was furious; he regarded it as poaching. He calculated that those two officers would keep the knowledge of this place to themselves and come again in about a fortnight, when the duck might be expected to be back. They did; they had their evening shoot; as before, they slept in the open by the water's edge. But this time they woke to find they had no guns.

They went to the nearest police station and reported the crime. The police wrote down all they said with meticulous care but the sub-inspector shook his head; he would do all he could of course but the whole affair was inexplicable – far too ambitious a crime for any of his local bad men. The two young officers waited a week, but heard nothing; they went again to see the sub-inspector but he had no clues. At last, after another week, they went to see the District Magistrate, who listened to what they told him and then, with apparent irrelevance, gave them a lecture on the difference between life in a place like Budaon, where there was no recreation but shooting, and life in Bareilly, where there was the Club, regimental messes, the polo ground and a wide variety of company. He then offered to strike a bargain with them. They would undertake not to shoot in his district without letting him know. For his part, he would provide them with hospitality when they came, but he would join them. They agreed to this bargain, and nothing was said about guns. Micky then promised to see if he could help the police with their enquiries and the guns were found within a week. They had been well looked after.

This incident illustrates an unusual attitude to the law but also a remarkable degree of confidence between the district officer and quite a number of other people. I imagine, though he never told me the details, that in that particular affair the sub-inspector of police and probably some gipsy-like folk, such as the Kanjars of my wolf story, or the Nats or some other nomad tribe, knew what had happened. A despot must trust his instruments and they him – and when Nethersole applied these despotic methods on a larger scale to the government of his district he had to have the absolute confidence of those he used.

I was in Bareilly for three years, 1930, 1931 and 1932. During that time a reader of the world press would have supposed the whole of India to be seething with unrest. My sister, who came to visit me, went to a hairdresser in Marseille, who cried in horror: '*Vous allez aux Indes! On vous coupera la gorge!*' but in fact she was allowed to go wherever she liked; she would go off and explore the city while I was at work; we would be greeted in any village we entered with embarrassing hospitality. Of course most of the lawyers and schoolmasters in the city – like my editor in the train – wanted India to be independent, and probably many of the shopkeepers too. But the middle classes in India were a small part of the population, and the number of active politicians was very small indeed. Many of the landowners were suspicious of the Socialist tendencies of the Congress and many of the Muslims – who were in a majority in the city – regarded the Congress as dangerously Hindu.

But we *were* of course living through a revolution – a long-drawn-out revolution which lasted thirty years – and there were some political activists. As in all revolutions, some of these were idealists and some were men who had failed to find regular employment and had drifted into politics as a road to power and wealth. Some were men who would have been professional criminals if they had not been able to find a political cover for their activities. Any active politician, however much an idealist, presented a District Magistrate with a problem; their aims were directly opposed. The politician wanted to stir people up; the District Magistrate wanted to calm people down. He knew that political meetings and demonstrations would lead to broken heads and looted shops.

Edwin Montagu, the reforming Secretary of State for India of 1919, had said that the Indian peasant must be roused from his 'pathetic contentment'. But had he considered, I wonder, what tasks this would impose on the District Magistrate, whose job it was to keep the peace? Was it not inevitable, in the light of hindsight, that the result should have been an 'undeclared, intermittent and surreptitious civil war'?

Some twenty-five miles north of Bareilly lay the country town of Shahi, the marketing centre for the villages ten miles around in each direction. It was run by an efficient municipal board presided over by one Khan Bahadur Mohammad Reza Khan Sahib. He saw to it that the streets were clean and that the customs of the neighbourhood were observed. He was not a large landowner but he was a magistrate as well as chairman of the board and he had a wide network of influence. He was a Rohilla Pathan; his ancestors had come from Afghanistan and possessed themselves of the land by force. Courage was the virtue he admired and he spoke with contempt of his neighbours as 'natives'. He did not speak English and disapproved of education, which made people cowardly. He had openly and irretrievably committed himself to the cause of British rule. So far had we come from the concept of 'helping Indians to learn to govern themselves' that the nationalists, who were supporters of the Congress, had come to be looked on as enemies by most Government servants, still more emphatically by such a man as the Khan Bahadur. His ideas of rule were simple; a good ruler was one who saw that his orders were obeyed and the idea of paying a leader of the Opposition to criticize the Government was something quite unintelligible to him. It was a crime; it was treason. The area round Shahi was peaceful and he meant to keep it so.

The Khan Bahadur and Nethersole felt an immediate affinity for each other and when he learnt that the activists of Bareilly planned a political demonstration in Shahi, the Khan Bahadur paid a visit to the District Magistrate and sought his advice. He did not want a political disturbance in his town; the Congress marchers would be Hindus and inevitably the Muslims of Shahi would attack them; there would not only be rioting between the two communities but gangsters and criminals from miles around would use the political disturbance as cover and there would be knives used in dark alleys, lonely people robbed, the shutters of shops broken. He thought it would be better if the police kept out of this – there was a sub-inspector with a head constable and eight constables at Shahi. He could muster a force of henchmen – I use a deliberately vague expression – and they would be quite sufficient to stop the march before it reached the town. All he wanted was a nod – the flutter of an eyelid.

He got rather more. There must be no fire-arms or knives, he was told; no one must be killed – but if the local tenantry turned out with their bamboo poles to keep undesirable elements out of their town – why, that was something no one could have foreseen and they could not be blamed. The District Magistrate would have known nothing about it beforehand. The Khan Bahadur told me the story when it was all over. He had collected a considerable body of men, over a thousand he said, and had divided them into two divisions, Hindus and Muslims. The Muslims he held in reserve; he wanted if possible to avoid all communal feeling. He met the marchers two or three miles short of the town and confronted them with superior force; he told them that he would not permit a large and apparently organized body to enter a peaceful town with the clear intention of causing a disturbance. He had carefully obtained the signatures of all the property owners of Shahi to a statement indicating their fears of a disturbance. The marchers sat down, intending, he judged, to wait until dark and slip past his guards. He urged them to disperse peacefully, but they continued to sit. An hour before sunset he gave them a final warning; since they did not respond, he ordered his men to charge and disperse them. A six-foot bamboo pole is a formidable weapon and can be lethal, but though there were bruises and perhaps some broken bones, no one was killed.

That is how the Khan Bahadur told me the story and I tell it again now, partly as an example of Nethersole's methods but also to show how very different things were – at least in this corner of India – from either the constitutional theory or the picture in the world's press. Nethersole had the Khan Bahadur's confidence, without which this could not have happened; the operation – to give it a grandiose name – was completely successful, not only in keeping Shahi quiet for the moment but in keeping the whole district quiet for the next three years. There had been no official action; Nethersole would if necessary have maintained that it was a spontaneous ebullition of popular feeling but would have stood by the Khan Bahadur through thick and thin. How different from my simple-minded picture of the peaceful devolution of power, with Nationalist India walking hand-in-hand with Official India and gratefully picking up tips on how to run an empire! And how far removed, at the same time, from the picture of a nation seething with nationalist fervour!

I cannot remember that I ever discussed India's future with Micky. We talked a great deal about running a district, about Indian customs, about Hindu and Muslim beliefs. 'Ladies sometimes ask me if I like Indians,' he said, 'and I say that it entirely depends on the person. Some Indians I like very much indeed – and some Englishmen too. Some Indians I absolutely detest – and some Englishmen too.' And no one could really understand the word detest unless he had heard it pronounced by Nethersole. He was almost pathological in his irritation with the Government he served. Pedantry, insistence on precedent, official parsimony, were red rags to him. On one occasion he recommended spending money on repairing the jail, but he was told that 'owing to financial stringency' he could not have it. 'I shall write them,' he announced, 'a really intemperate letter. I shall say that I do not make such recommendations lightly and I cannot accept responsibility for the lives of the prisoners confined in this jail unless the matter is attended to at once. I see no other course but to release the prisoners from the most dangerous parts.' He got the prison repaired.

With all his intense hostility to the Secretariat in Lucknow, this illogical man combined a certain envy. 'Of course I should like to be in the Secretariat,' I once heard him say. 'Extra pay and a hot weather in the hills with one's wife – who would say no to that? But they say I have no secretariat experience. How can you get experience if they never let you have it?' But really of course he would have hated it.

When his wife Hermione came out in the beginning of the cold weather, I took to her at once. She looked very young and strangely demure to be the wife of a man so violent, so headstrong and so positive in his convictions. I call her to mind most easily in a dress that was I think then old-fashioned, of black velvet or perhaps a very dark brown, slightly lustrous, with a white collar, looking not unlike the well-known self-portrait by Madame Vigée le Brun. She did not want to play bridge or turn over the pages of the *Tatler* at the Club. During that cold weather, I talked to her whenever I had the chance, but I did not see a great deal of her. I learnt that she read D. H. Lawrence, that she liked poetry, that she had once decided to be a Buddhist and had also been a vegetarian. It was an agreeable change to talk about such things.

The following summer, Hermione was at a cottage in the hill station of Naini Tal. At that time I imagined myself to be in love with a girl whom it was convenient to meet at Hermione's cottage, and she talked a great deal to us both, separately and together. She felt relaxed and safe, I suppose, because of our interest in each other. I learnt much that helped me to understand her husband. The thoughts that passed through her mind as she sat with her hands in her lap were far from demure. She was deeply but experimentally religious – that is to say, conscious of an Other, conscious of a world beyond the material one but far from sure how to formulate her beliefs. She was also capable of the most intense and passionate love and she had a will and a power of decision the equal of her husband's. She had fasted once for more than three weeks, as much to test her self-control as in any expectation of direct benefit. She made the most sudden and impulsive decisions.

There is a drawing by James Thurber of a woman who is in a rage because she has 'married below her emotional level'. This was true neither of Micky nor of Hermione Nethersole. They were evenly matched and both remarkable people. When I first knew her, she was proud that in spite of episodes in the past life of both, they were making a success of their marriage. But a disaster befell them, as a result of Hermione's readiness to experiment with religion. She was temporarily impressed by a disciple of the American Buchman, whose movement developed into Moral Rearmament. This person prevailed on her to make a public confession of all that had occurred in her life, a gruesome ordeal, which had to be carried through in the presence of at least some friends; it was not enough for her to mortify herself in the presence of strangers. It took place in England, where I was on leave at the time, but I was not there. I heard of this lapse from sanity through a mutual friend, who, deeply reluctant, had been persuaded to be present. Hermione must have felt it necessary to tell her husband what she had done and I suppose in such a mood of self-abasement she added that she had also told me a good deal of what she had confessed. Their marriage did not formally break up but it was never the same again. He could not bear the thought that anyone should know of what had happened; he would hardly speak to me. His black moods became more frequent; he tried to force her to his will in trivial things and she would not be forced. At least he did not smother her, though he was more like Othello than anyone else I have ever known.

2 A Fair Share of the Grain

I have said that our work was of such absorbing interest that it was easy to forget why we were in India, but I have said little about the most positive part of that work. The British Empire in India was the last of the old pre-industrial empires of the world and in some ways had more in common with the empires of the Mughals or of the Incas than with such vast agglomerations of people as Russia or the United States or China today. The most obvious function of the Government in these pre-industrial empires was to keep the peace. One part of that task was arresting criminals, preventing riots and the like. But there was also the less showy job of giving the cultivator some security for his land and enabling him to keep a reasonable share of the produce. More than four-fifths of the people made their living from the land and until about 1919 they lived in a society that was stable. It seemed permanent. It was possible to plan for the future. It provided the background for their 'pathetic contentment'. The physical force we had in India was tiny; bluff multiplied it by ten; stability by a hundred.

By ancient Indian custom, the land everywhere belonged to the sovereign and the sovereign was entitled to a share of the produce. But in the part of India I am talking about, the north-western corner of the United Provinces, there were people whom I have called landowners, because that is the nearest English equivalent. They had originally been courtiers, soldiers, advisers or favourites of the Mughal emperors, who had paid for their services by giving them the right to collect the King's Share of the produce of the soil. This was called by the British 'Land Revenue' and in this part of India the District Magistrate was also the Collector, who was ultimately responsible for seeing that the King's Share was collected, that it was not exorbitant, and that the rights of the cultivators were protected. The landowner might be responsible for several villages or for quite a small part of a village; he might have some land which he cultivated himself through his servants; he might have some hereditary tenants and some temporary tenants on short leases. The tendency of the Government had been to make it easier for tenants to get hereditary rights; they could then be dispossessed only if they obstinately and persistently refused to pay their rent.

Even when the system is described in the most simplified terms, it will be apparent that there was plenty of room for dispute. What kind of tenant was Loke Nath? Had his father paid rent for these fields and had the landowner accepted rent from him as his father's successor? In that case his right would pass to his son. That was the kind of thing that arose. But in practice it was much more complicated than this explanation suggests, because the rights of the landowner might be shared between a number of cousins, or some shares might have been sold to some outsider, or the original holding might have been divided long ago between brothers who could not get on together. Also, hereditary tenants might be combinations rather than individuals and might sublet part of their holdings.

Every thirty years or so, there would be a settlement. This meant that a settlement officer would be appointed for the district, with an army of soil-testers and surveyors; he would revise all the records and fix a fair rent which the tenant could pay. On that he would base the Land Revenue payable by the landowners. He would take into account prices, access to markets, the quality of the soil, everything. For the next thirty years it would be the business of the Collector and his staff to keep that record up to date. It was not spectacular work but of vital importance if the peasant was to feel secure. That was the essential condition for a stable countryside.

The records were based on a map, triangulated on points fixed by professional surveyors. It was on a scale of sixty-four inches to the mile – that is to say, one inch to rather more than twenty-five yards – so a field only ten yards square would appear on the map quite large enough for any encroachment to be checked. With the map went a field register. Every field was numbered on the map and in the register; the register showed the landowner, the tenant, the class of tenant, the crop – and there were two crops a year – and every conceivable detail. The map and the register were constantly checked; the supervisor immediately above the man who made the register was supposed to check one entry in four, taken at random, and the man above him one in twenty and so on up the scale.

This checking was indeed one of the first things I had done. You had to find where you were on the map; standing there, at the corner where three field boundaries met, you made sure by the shape of the fields and some natural feature that this really was, let us say, field 1138 at your feet. Then you checked the crop in the field with the crop in the register and questioned the circle of villagers about the other details. The records were quite remarkably accurate.

A settlement for thirty years implies a far more stable society than we live in today. Nonetheless, there was a very slow inflation operating throughout the seventy years before I came to India, and this gave the cultivator some advantage. He could usually sell his surplus grain or sugar at a better price towards the end than at the beginning of the thirty-year period. But his rent was fixed, so he had a bigger share for himself. There were however some parts of the Bareilly district which had to be treated differently. They lay along the banks of the Ramganga which was liable to change its course in the rains, sometimes washing away half a village, sometimes adding a stretch of waste sandy land; this would not be much good at first but could be ploughed and would give a light yield of some leguminous crop the first year and might do better the second. So these villages had a five-yearly settlement. If the village gained land, they used it free till the next five-yearly settlement; if they lost, the revenue would be remitted at once.

One of the first things I had to do in Bareilly was to go into tents early in March and look at some of these villages along the river. Most of the work had been done already by subordinates; my main duty was to check the new maps, making sure that half this village had really gone, while that one had a new hundred acres under peas or grain or sometimes a mixture of peas and barley reaped together as fodder. I would get up in the dark, shave by the yellow light of a hurricane lantern, and be off on Tessa with the first faint light of dawn in the east. In all that sandy ground by the river, the light seemed paler than elsewhere; the crying of the water-birds and the flight of that lovely creature, the Ganges tern, gave an illusion of being near the sea. The silvery light seemed to tremble upwards, reflected in liquid ripples from water and white sand, and the effect was enhanced by the white blossom of peas, ankle deep on pale grey tangled stems, scrambling for life in the sand.

Every evening I would summon to my tents the record-keeper – the *patwari* is his real name – for the nearest villages and two or three more from the neighbourhood, and a host of villagers would come in as well. The *patwari* was not allowed to alter the record himself; ordinarily there were many formalities to make sure that any change was justified, but here on the spot there would often be general agreement. Yes, it was true, Mannu had died and Gopal was his only son, and the leading landowner accepted him as his father's successor and the whole village acclaimed him as the man who drove the plough in his father's fields. So I would have the change made at once and Gopal would be saved journeys to Bareilly and stamps on his petitions and fees to many officials. Here by the river, everyone had heard I was there; the crowds would gather every evening in their coarse white robes and – once you were sure that everyone with an interest was agreed – you could do something for them, something positive, immediate, visible.

When that three weeks by the river came to an end, I rode Tessa along village tracks to the made road, gave her to the syce, who had gone ahead, and took my seat on a bus. For a moment, I caught a glimpse of my face in the driving mirror; how strange it seemed, with its cold glaucous eyes, its face, reddened no doubt by sun, but still unnaturally pale! Once before I had been conscious of two worlds, a world of warmth and love at home and the cold loveless world of my prep school. Now once again there were two worlds, but they differed in quite another dimension. In the fields, among the villagers, there was intense interest because the people who came to me were in deadly earnest about getting their names on the record or proving that they had paid their rent – but

I was always a figure of authority. In Bareilly, at the Club, at Nethersole's dinner table, at polo, I was among people over whom I had no authority, but on the other hand we were not concerned about anything that mattered very much. We were relaxing – and that is not always very interesting to remember.

I certainly did not stop to think about the corrupting influence of authority. After all, it was for exercising authority that I had been trained at school. But it is hard to convey the authoritarian atmosphere of India, the expectation that anyone would do whatever you told him. It was not an importation; it was native. Persian poetry, Indian folklore, Rajput legends, are full of tales of kings, and the good king is the strong king who will not suffer rebellion or anarchy, whom everyone obeys. At another level, the countryside in which I worked was steeped in the tradition of man's mastery over man. In the last chapter, I used the word 'henchman', a term both vague and archaic, but one that seems right because the idea for which it stands is foreign to Western society today. It was not only a matter of landlord and tenant; in every village, there would be people who owed someone else an allegiance, usually hereditary, which had little to do with land. It might be a professional allegiance; the priest and the barber and the washerman gave professional services to a patron, a protector, but they gave and received much more – total service on one side, total protection on the other. It was the same with landless labourers; each family had an overlord who gave them food, clothing and protection and in return they would turn out as ploughmen, messengers, beaters at a shoot, witnesses in a lawsuit, retainers in an affray – any task the protector thought suitable to their degree – again an archaic word but right because the idea is archaic. Master and man, protector and henchman, everyone you spoke to in a village fitted somewhere into this pattern. And it was not a relationship that could be casually dissolved but one that both parties were born into and would pass to their children.

It was impossible not to be affected by this network of hereditary authority, just as it was almost impossible not to be affected by the idea of caste. We – young men like myself, straight from Oxford or Cambridge – were superimposed on top of this system, like an additional caste, as patrons or protectors above the whole network. You would find that a junior official had mysteriously attached himself to you and become your henchman because you had given him a word of praise or encouragement; not only that, but everywhere, anywhere, at a word or a gesture, you could summon temporary henchmen who would do anything you told them.

It was not, in 1928, considered proper for a young British officer to have a car. A horse he must have, and that was the way to get about the district; with a horse you could go as far from your tents as you needed and anyone could stop you and speak to you. With a car you would sweep by in a cloud of dust. But in my third year in Bareilly, I was joined by a newcomer from England whose parents, still in India, gave him a very old two-seater open Morris, which we used sparingly, not in camp. Its self-starter did not work; it was almost impossible to start it with the handle. But this caused us no inconvenience; there was always someone within hailing distance who would muster a dozen men to push until it sprang into life. We were arrogant, unthinking, certain of obedience; it was part of the corruption bred by authority, somewhat redeemed by the discomforts of the life we led and by the responsibility for protection which we undertook as our part of the relationship.

It was hard though absorbing work. When I came back from my three weeks in camp by the river I settled down to deal with heavy arrears of work – and felt at first as bewildered as I had when I first embarked on the study of Kant. I was confronted with a flood of technical terms that had been learnt in the abstract but did not quickly penetrate to the toiling brain through rapid speech in a foreign language. It required determined concentration to seize quickly on the essential features of a dispute, cutting through the flowery formalities of the Persian tradition in the written matter and the rustic irrelevancies of the spoken.

I had succeeded an attractive and intelligent man, Bengali by origin but completely Anglicized. His father had been a Colonel in the Indian Medical Service who had decided to send his son to England when he was seven. He had been to an English prep school, to St Paul's, and to Oxford, never returning to India till he came out in the Indian Civil Service. His Urdu was no better than ours and – since he looked Indian – it was surprising to a villager to find him a foreigner. He was exact and meticulous in his work, so painstaking over every detail that he often did not finish his criminal work as a Magistrate till long after dark, when every other court was closed. There would be no time left for disputes about the nature of tenancies. There were more than three hundred such cases that were outstanding over three months and more than a hundred that were over a year old and in which the parties had been several times summoned to Bareilly, had been kept waiting all day to be told at evening that there was no time to hear them.

Mitter was charming in conversation but seemed constitutionally languid, lacking the resolution for simple personal decisions such as getting up in the morning or even calling for dinner. He was perhaps already unwell for he died early. He would argue that villagers did not mind this kind of thing, as they had no sense of urgency. I met a good deal of evidence to the contrary and it angered me that people should be treated with such lack of consideration. Better rough justice, I thought, than no justice, and in this outlook I had of course the support of Nethersole, who arrived soon after I did and would never have allowed Mitter's work to get so far behind. I determined to wipe off those arrears as quickly as I could. I introduced a number of highly arbitrary ways of speeding things up – methods that would have got me into serious trouble with the High Court if they had heard of them. But the Bareilly Bar were extraordinarily forbearing; not one of them complained to the Sessions Judge. I started work before the official time; I discouraged pleaders from calling unnecessary witnesses and told each side that I would allow the other no more witnesses than the first had called. I encouraged short brisk evidence, promising that cross-examination should take no longer than the examination by the pleader who called the witness.

These methods – shocking to a British lawyer – were based on a conviction that verbal evidence served little purpose but to stake out a claim. On one occasion there was a dispute in a certain village because the Hindus wished to take out a procession for one of their autumn festivals, while the Muslims said this was offensive to them and had never happened before. The Hindus maintained that it was a long-established custom. Someone told me that though the ordinary court oath was regarded as meaningless there were certain religious oaths that were binding. I procured a bottle of Ganges water and each Hindu put his hand on it and swore by the head of his son; each Muslim put his hand on the Qu'ran and swore by the beard of the Prophet. Forty Hindus swore that this procession was the immemorial custom of the village. Forty Muslims swore that it had never happened before. That was the kind of thing that made me take a somewhat cavalier attitude to oral evidence.

And I recall a man who claimed that he had succeeded to the leadership of a group of cousins who were the principal landowners in his area. All the tenants recognized him as leader; he was in possession and asked for his name to be entered in the record. He produced some forty or fifty tenants who swore that they had paid him rent and showed receipts for it, which he acknowledged as his. This was enough and his name was entered. Immediately one of his cousins sued him for his share of the rent. In this new suit, he pleaded that he had not yet collected any rent.

'But what about all those receipts?' I asked him sternly.

'Oh, those were fictitious,' he answered with complete innocence. 'They told me that was the only way to prove possession. No money changed hands.'

I told him he had committed perjury, which was a serious offence; could he give me any reason why he should not be prosecuted? But I could not be angry with him. He was so genuinely puzzled that I said I would accept a bribe; he must contribute a hundred rupees to my pet charity and I would forget the charge of perjury. It saved a great deal of time and trouble – but that too would not have pleased the High Court.

It was easy then – sitting long hours in court through the dry scorching heat of May and June, through the steamy saturated mugginess of July and August – to think of the people around me with, at best, an amused tolerance, at worst, with that irritated incomprehension that has so often marked the British in India. For my part I do not think I found the people I dealt with incomprehensible; their motives were usually only too clear. But the difficulty of being sure where the truth lay certainly caused irritation – and since you had to make up your mind, one way or the other, it encouraged any tendency you might harbour to be arbitrary and authoritarian.

The heat did not last for ever and by the end of September there would come towards dawn a touch of freshness in the air, and if you slept out of doors you might even draw up a blanket just before the sun rose. By November it was time to go into camp and then you would be out of doors all day, meeting people in their natural surroundings; rancour and irritation would blow away. Tessa would dance in the tingling cold when we started out at first light; fresh blood would sing in my veins too. Again in the evening it was blissful to go out from the tents and try to get a partridge for supper, to be aware of the man who had placed himself where he judged you would pass and who wanted you to look at that field on which his neighbour had encroached. But sometimes when the moment came and you said to him: 'Well, what is it?' he would be tongue-tied. 'Sit, brother,' I learnt to say; we would both sit and out it would pour. And it was blissful too to come back at last to the lamp-light in the tents, to smell the earthy, smoky, dusty smell of a village in the evening, when a whitish vapour lies in long straight lines level with the tops of the trees. In camp, you began at once to think more kindly of your fellow men.

I was lucky in my second year at Bareilly. There was the Census of 1931 and I was District Census Officer, so I could add a month's camping for the Census to my usual six weeks as SDO. The volumes of the Indian Census are a treasury of information for the anthropologist but at my level the main task was to train the enumerators to see that the returns were made correctly. There was an enumerator to every twenty households; he had to be literate, that was all. Some three weeks before the night of the Census, he went to each of the households and filled in the detailed information that was required; on the great night he simply checked that everyone was still there and added any new arrivals. I went round the district and tried to make sure that these enumerators – school teachers, students, shop-keepers – understood the questions they had to answer. For every so many enumerators there was a supervisor, usually the *patwari*. It was the usual Indian system – a pyramid with some work at each level checked by someone else.

My tents and bedding moved in bullock-carts. One evening I noticed the driver of one of these carts doing something unusual; one of his bullocks was lying on its side and he was standing on it, gently kneading its muscles with his bare feet. He had a vivacious face with a sparkle in his eye; I began to talk to him and found he belonged to the Arya Samaj, a reformed sect of Hindus, who reject division into castes as a corruption of the ancient scriptures. I asked him to come that evening to the gathering of enumerators and as a demonstration got one of them to fill in a specimen card for him. He gave his name and his father's name but protested at the next question – caste, sub-caste or clan. The enumerator had to decide what to write. The Arya Samajist entered wholly into the spirit of the thing, clowning a little and inventing difficulties for every question. He added something to his act every night and by the end of the tour he had been adopted and therefore had two fathers; he had two wives at least, several occupations and a variety of residences.

One other experience I treasure from that tour. At each day's camping-place a few local gentry would turn up, each with a marigold garland or perhaps a present of oranges or guavas. One of them told me that at my next halt I must visit the tomb of a Muslim holy man, who had been so holy that the scorpions which crawled about his tomb would not sting. You could safely take one in your hand.

'What would happen,' I asked, 'if you took it outside the sacred enclosure?'

'At once it would sting you,' he replied impressively.

Next day, having arrived near the sacred spot, one of my visitors began to tell me about the tomb and the scorpions and I went on to ask him the same question. Without a moment's hesitation, he replied:

'At once, it would vanish!'

'But I was told yesterday it would sting me.'

'Yes' – conceding a point – 'first it would sting you; then it would vanish.'

A trifle unfair, I thought, but next morning, at the tomb, with that curved vicious little creature crablike in the palm of my hand – not much less threatening for its magical quality – I put my question for the third time to the guardian of the tomb.

'Nothing whatever would happen,' he replied. But I did not quite like to make the experiment.

The reaction of my two visitors to the question seems to me characteristically Indian – but not in the least incomprehensible. Neither had thought before of the question I put to them but both wanted to make the most of the miraculous nature of the phenomenon and both had an amiable desire to please. They succeeded. I *was* pleased – and have been ever since.

3 The Murder of the Rajput's Daughter

Comment on the life of the British in India has usually concentrated on only one of the two worlds in which I now lived. This is understandable because, to a visitor, the British were usually only visible when they were away from the real business of their lives, which was urgent and sometimes dramatic. By contrast, life in the station, at the Club, seems in memory, as it is usually portrayed, insipid and uninteresting. But to picture only that part of the life is to produce something unreal. In Forster's *A Passage to India*, for example, though Aziz is sensitively drawn, the British officials are cardboard figures – surely because they have been wrenched from their context and no attempt made to understand their work.

In fact, our days were very full. I can describe only my own life, though some of it I shared with a succession of young men – younger even than I – who were sent to Bareilly to learn their profession from Nethersole and who lived in my bungalow. In my case, there was always the pressure of written work waiting for decision. Sometimes, in minor disputes, I could persuade the parties to reach an amicable agreement out of court and I would then record the result, but in most cases I would have to decide and this always meant writing a judgment. A judgment had to state clearly, fairly and concisely the facts and arguments on either side, the reasons for preferring one to the other, and the decision. This applied whether it was a criminal matter or a dispute about the land records; one must always suppose that there would be an appeal and the appellate court would have to understand one's reasons. So, at the end of a day in court, there would always be something to take home; I had to keep up with the criminal work and catch up with those dreadful arrears on the land records side. I would have to go through the written evidence and write my judgment. This I used to do for two hours before breakfast three days a week – that was on polo days – and in the evening before dinner on the other three days.

After a quick breakfast at about eight, there would be visitors –

officials or landowners who had come 'to pay their respects'. You had to listen politely and carefully, hoping for a hint about the inner story of the trouble between Rajputs and untouchables in this village, between landowner and tenants in that one, between Hindus and Muslims in another. How fatiguing these visitors were I did not realize until some years later, when I tried to deal with them while recovering from an appendix operation and became conscious of utter exhaustion. But at Bareilly I seemed tireless. I would walk to court – but often on the way I would be waylaid by someone who felt himself too humble to come to the bungalow. Five hours in court, of argument, of listening to witnesses, of hearing fresh petitions, of deciding, in a new case, what were the essential points to be proved. It made a great saving of time and effort, to me and still more to the parties, if, on the first occasion when a man put in his petition, one took the trouble to find out what it was all about and define exactly the points at issue. To scamp that would almost always mean adjournments later. Then, before the light failed, I would rush off to play polo or squash; it would be one or the other every evening.

It may come as a surprise to find that I, who had shown so little enthusiasm for games at school, should be so enthusiastic about polo. I can only say that I did find a thrill of achievement and mastery when I hit the ball clear and clean and Tessa went after it quick as a bolting rabbit – a pleasure like nothing else, though thirty years later sailing a fast racing dinghy in a stiff breeze came near it, and skating I am sure would give it too. It was a pleasure of utter absorption and release. Cricket and golf I found dull because there was so much time with nothing to do; it is admittedly gratifying to hit a golf ball a long way but in my case that rarely happened and, if it did, by the time I had walked after the ball and found it I was thinking of something else; I would much prefer to go for a walk. Polo was continual excitement and I even thought about it when I was not playing; you had to train the ponies as well as yourself and we would be knocking a ball about and reining back on the polo ground the three mornings when I was not writing judgments. I generally managed to have two ponies of my own and a third I was looking after for someone else who was on leave. In the Indian Civil Service we found it hard to compete with soldiers at polo because we never had four players in the same place who could practise together – but once, just once, in Lucknow, in the Low Handicap Tournament, we did field a team which beat four infantry regiments in succession and won the final! Do not fear; I have no other athletic triumphs to record.

Looking back, I feel that my time in Bareilly was an extension of boyhood – eager enjoyment and effort, not much thought of the future. There was hard work but it seemed worth doing; it was always concerned with people's lives. In the hot weather – when, as you shaved naked in the early light, the sweat dripped off your elbows and each drop vanished as it hit the brick floor of the bathroom – there was a feeling that you were in the front line; it was a braced, tense life in which there was the continual pleasure of responsible decision – and you never knew when drama would break out. There was the day when a woman was kidnapped on the steps of my court. I sprang from the dais, brushing pleaders and witnesses aside, and raced to the door in time to see her and her captors at full gallop in a tonga – a two-wheeled pony-trap – making for the city; I found a mounted policeman and sent him after them – lance in hand, the pennon a-flutter beside his scarlet turban – and I followed in another tonga, also at full gallop. We had a run of about two miles but they went to ground in a house in a narrow lane and barred the door; by the time we had broken in they were away on the other side. It made a change from routine. Next time I saw the woman she was firmly on the side of her captors; with Hindu village women, possession was usually nine-tenths of the law. Quite probably she had been kidnapped in the first place by those who brought her to court.

On three evenings a week, after polo, we would go to the Club and find ourselves in the bar, talking to subalterns about our ponies and how the game had gone, and usually staying too long and drinking too much. It was an undemanding interlude in a strenuous day, philistine no doubt by the standards of Sir Osbert Sitwell, but then a great part of the world is philistine. The mood of those days, it seems to me now, has been recorded as to externals by Kipling but best understood by Conrad in early sea stories such as *Youth* and *Lord Jim*, in which his young men are sustained in a life that is outwardly monotonous by responsibility, by mastery of their profession, by a sense that adventure, excitement, a testing experience, is always close at hand, by the play of light on water and the splendours of dawn and sunset and by moments of apparent understanding that are independent of their surroundings. Conrad writes, for instance, in *Lord Jim* of 'how we go through life with eyes half shut . . .' and adds that perhaps this is just as well and that perhaps

> . . . it is this very dullness that makes life to the incalculable majority so supportable and so welcome. Nevertheless [he goes on], there can be but few of us who have never known one of those rare moments of awakening when we see, hear, understand, ever so much – everything – in a flash – before we fall back again into our agreeable somnolence.

Or, to put it another way:

> For most of us, there is only the unattended
> Moment, the moment in and out of time,
> The wild thyme unseen, or the winter lightning . . .

Conventional pursuits might lead to moments that live in the memory for life. I was waiting one evening for a panther when the forest glade before me filled silently with living things. It was like a Mughal painting. The sun was sinking and its light had already taken on the warm golden colour of clear amber or honey. It fell in broken fragments on some forty or fifty spotted deer, does and stags together, the *chital*, *axis maculata*, very like the fallow deer of English parks. They were moving slowly towards the water where a bevy of wild peacocks, in the full brilliance of their spring plumage, were competing for the favours of a smaller number of females – strutting and turning in that golden light with their splendid tails in a full arch, pulsing and vibrating with desire. I held my breath. I was in time and out of time.

But the other, dramatic, world of Indian life would also suddenly intersect with conventional pursuits in which I took part with a certain lack of conviction, rather for what they might bring than for themselves. I was camping one day near a village called Aundh (rhyming very approximately with 'sound') when there called, 'to pay their respects', two Rajput landowners, father and son, whom I had known for some time. The village was dominated by a group of Thakurs or Rajputs, cousins and second cousins, who between them ruled not only that village but a galaxy of other villages near by. One of them, with his family, had declared himself wholly in the camp of the Khan Bahadur of Shahi, described earlier. Another was as firmly on the side of the Congress. My two visitors were playing safe and trying to keep in with everyone. They begged me to come and shoot snipe on a patch of marshy ground near their village. I could fit it in and said I would meet the younger man there at midday after looking at a *patwari*'s work and at some well near by, to which the right of access was disputed. The old man drove home in his pony-trap. The young man – tall, straight-backed, handsome, though rather weak of chin – met me as arranged. He showed me, rather shyly, like a boy, his gun, a far better gun than mine, a lovely piece of workmanship by Purdey or Manton or some other famous English firm. It was a special matter of pride to those Thakurs to have such guns. He had been to Agra University for a short time but had not finished his course. We chatted a little, then waded together into the mud and picked up a brace or two of snipe. I felt an interest in him, a certain liking, though something about him suggested a softness at the centre. A few weeks later I was told that he had shot his wife with that very gun.

It was an affair that roused intense interest. The wife's family were Rajput landowners with a good deal of property in a neighbouring district sixty miles away. They had been for some time on bad terms with the family at Aundh and were determined to make the charge of murder stick. The husband's family had burned the body of the wife the very evening she died, which was unusually hasty. They said she had died of pneumonia and then changed it to cholera – the haste had been to avoid infection; in any case, to have her body examined by a doctor would have been a great disgrace. They then admitted that she had died of a gunshot wound but said that it was suicide. The young man with whom I had shot snipe went into hiding but was persuaded to re-appear. He said he and his wife had had a violent quarrel; he had slapped her face and left her, then heard a shot, ran back and found her dying. All this was suspicious, but there was no proof of murder; it was true that they would have regarded suicide as a disgrace, still more a post-mortem. Whether it was suicide or murder, they would have wanted to cover up.

But three days later a woman went to the police-station near the wife's home in the next district and told a most detailed story; she was the wife's old nurse and had gone with her to Aundh when she married. She had been present at the quarrel and had heard the girl taunt her husband fiercely, accusing him of infidelity with low-caste servant-girls and ending with the savage words: 'Go on! Shoot me! If you were a true Rajput, you would shoot me for the things I've said to you!' The old nurse had seen him answer this provocation by going to fetch his gun, loading it, and shooting her. They had locked the nurse up but she had escaped and had managed to find her way to her old home, where she had come forward with her evidence.

I was intensely interested in this case, partly because I had been shooting with the young man, but more because everything I heard of the dead girl suggested a creature of high spirit, fierce and courageous, whose last years had been most unhappy. Her mother was as voluble and managing as Kim's old Maharani. But I was also intrigued by some extraordinary features of the case. In the husband's first statement to a magistrate he had said his wife had ended the quarrel with the same words which the nurse used in her story: 'Shoot me!' 'If you were a true Rajput, you would shoot me for the things I've said.'

I came in the end to the conclusion that the nurse's story was a fabrication, very cunningly composed, one in which she had been most carefully schooled. It stood up to long cross-examination but in the end she could not remember any details of the birth of her mistress's first child. This was hard to believe of an old and devoted nurse and suggested that the Aundh family were telling the truth when they said they

Our camp just below the Kuari Pass in Garhwal, at about 11,000 feet, looking northward: from this camp, there were snow peaks in a complete half-circle from west to east. The nearest peak, on the right of the photo, is Gauri Parbat.

The horns at a village dance near the Gauna Lake. The men in white turbans are our Muslim servants from the plains. The drums are on the other side of the dancers, outside the picture.

Terraced cultivation; this is near the plains where arable land is so valuable that hay is stored on top of poles.

Women cutting barley. It was women like this, working in isolated fields or cutting grass, who were killed by the man-eating panther as they came home in the evening.

Crossing the river. The river, a strong, brown god, is in spate. This is a Government bridge, very much better than the kind made of grass rope.

Below left A young man from the Tibetan border. His people lived in villages that were buried deep in snow all the winter. When the snow melted they sowed barley and a dwarf buckwheat called *ogil*; then they went over into Tibet, trading, carrying their goods on goats and hybrid yaks. They came back to harvest their barley and in winter went trading to the plains of India.

Below right Nisar on Lachman Pyari. He was a man who two hundred years earlier might have carved himself out a kingdom. He was a Muslim; the Garhwalis addressed him with great courtesy as *Faujdar* (leader of an army).

Kedarnath: this temple is a sacred place for Hindus who follow Siva. It stands at over 11,000′ altitude at the foot of a glacier and is buried in snow all the winter. Built in the Greco-Buddhist tradition, it is much more impressive than the more sacred temple at Badrinath, one of the four corners of the holy land of Hindus. The people in the foreground and at the top of the steps are pilgrims from the plains; the groups to left and right are Garhwalis.

had sent her away before the child was born and before her mistress's death. But in that case, how did she learn the words actually used in the quarrel? They were unusual words and it could not be coincidence that the nurse repeated them sixty miles away just when the husband was making his statement. Everyone in the neighbourhood of Aundh was a tenant or henchman of the family and everyone had a motive for keeping quiet. I was privately informed – but it was not evidence anyone would stand to in court – that the police had kidnapped a servant from the house, extorted with pressure all the details from him and sent the information secretly by word of mouth to the wife's family – who only then, and with the help of a barrister, had concocted the nurse's tale. But although I disbelieved the nurse's story I still thought it was probably murder. I was so sure the evidence was fabricated that I hesitated about committing the husband to the Court of Session for trial. But there was undoubtedly a case to answer so I sent him up – with a very long committal order expressing my doubts – and to my great surprise the Sessions Judge found him guilty.

Twenty-five years later, ten years after independence, I went back to Aundh; they brought me curdled milk and wheat cakes and oranges. We sat and talked about other things; after a little I said:

'It was about this time of day.'

'What was?' they asked.

'That that shot was fired – in that house there – twenty-five years ago.'

'Ahh!' they said. 'No, it was about two hours earlier than this!' But everyone was adamant that she had shot herself.

Some time after I left Bareilly I wrote a novel about the Aundh murder case. It was published as *Call the Next Witness* and I shall come back to how it came to be written and published. Here I want only to add that in the main story I stuck closely to what I believe happened, except that the husband was not hanged. He went to jail but was released before his time to die of tuberculosis.

I cannot end my time at Bareilly without recounting an occurrence which now makes me remember the events of those three crowded years in a different light. From what I have already written you might suppose that I would say in my haste: All men are liars. I certainly began to feel that I should not expect truth from an Indian witness, unless he was a doctor or some other expert. And then, in my last year in Bareilly, I had a serious case which involved British troops.

They were Irish, belonging to an Irish regiment, and had been temporarily attached to the Duke of Cornwall's Light Infantry for some specialized training to help them in civil life, carpentering or welding or something of the kind. On Christmas Eve, they had had a night out and towards midnight some soldiers had run amuck, breaking into several shops and looting the contents. In one case, the shop had sold alarm clocks, of which many had disappeared. The accused were charged with dacoity, that is gang robbery, theft with violence by five or more persons, punishable by ten years' imprisonment. Since the offence was against civilians, it could not be dealt with by court martial. I had to hold an enquiry and decide whether it should go to the Sessions Judge.

I found myself in an unusual position. The prosecutor was Indian; the accused had an Indian defence counsel, an able man, paid by the military authorities, but he, like the Crown Counsel, had difficulty in understanding what the accused and the witnesses said and was unfamiliar with their customs. I had to act as interpreter; usually of course it was the other way round and counsel would help me with obscure points of language and custom. One soldier witness had been in bed when the accused entered the barrack; counsel asked: 'Was your head covered?' and he stared in utter amazement. It was I who had to explain that Europeans do not usually draw the bed clothes over their heads as Indians do. One of the accused had to face the awkward fact that his kitbag was full of alarm clocks; in the thickest Irish brogue he said that before he went out he had asked the cook to leave him some sandwiches. When he came in, towards midnight, he went to the cookhouse and saw a tray covered with a white cloth. He took off the cloth and – lo and behold! – there were rows of alarm clocks.

'Nothing but clocks?' I asked him, with a smile which suggested that I found it hard to swallow.

'Nothing but clocks!' he replied, with a smile which suggested not much expectation that he would be believed. He thought they were a Christmas present, no doubt from the sergeant-major.

It was clear to me at the time that these men had no more respect for the truth than an Indian villager – though they were much less skilful at making up a convincing story. But it was only later that it occurred to me that, in their attitude to truth, Irish soldiers and Indian villagers had something in common; to both the court was alien, its procedure unfamiliar, its standards a matter of guesswork. Indian villagers, I know, have a different way of looking at truth among themselves, before their own caste-fellows, and I should be surprised if the same were not true in a barrack-room of Irish soldiers.

Once in camp they brought me a man whose back was a deep purple from shoulder to buttocks. He was a Chamar, one of the lowest of the servile castes, hereditary skinners of dead cattle and workers in leather. He had rebelled against the social system and refused to carry out one of the traditional services of his caste. Four Rajputs had held him down and two had hammered his back with shoes. I had his statement and that of his witnesses written down in Urdu and read over to him; we put their thumb-marks on it and I signed it. I wrote an English translation. I did all I could think of to make sure they had told me everything and to make sure it had all been recorded so that it could not be changed. I told them again and again that they must not alter their story. I think that at that stage they were telling the truth, but by the time they came to court in Bareilly they had made a far more serious case of it. Not only were several new people implicated but the Rajputs had broken into their houses, dragged out their sisters and wives, stripped them naked and struck them with shoes in the most intimate places. It was impossible to believe they would not have told me this when I had been just outside the village and the whole event was still fresh in mind. The surroundings of the lawcourts changed their approach altogether.

I must end my time in Bareilly – a kind of life I was never to encounter in quite the same form again – with the memory of one man whose face I still see clearly. He was charged with murder and he said as soon as he appeared in court: 'Yes, I did it. Take me and hang me.' I told him I should have to know what had happened and he explained. He was a little man with a sharp bird-like face, full of life and motion. His buffalo, he said, had broken loose and had gone into the sugar-cane of the man who was now dead. He had gone to look for the animal and met the other man, who had just driven it out of the sugar-cane. Soon they were hurling abuse at each other, both furious, blind with anger. The other man, a big burly fellow, ran at him and picked him up, lifting him right off the ground. The little man, though his arms were pinioned, did what he could – and with anger in his heart. He had a light stick in his hand which he had brought to drive the buffalo; he contrived to swing this round and strike the other's loins – and at the stroke his attacker fell dead.

'His hour had come and mine,' he said. 'Take me away and hang me.'

I asked for the medical report. It showed that the deceased had a condition of the heart which would have caused death at any sudden violent exertion. It was true that there was a very faint bruise on the loins which might have been caused by a feeble blow with a light stick but it could not have caused death; the deceased had a spleen enlarged by malaria, liable, as everyone in India knows, to be ruptured easily and cause death – but this blow had been too light to burst the spleen. He had killed himself by anger and sudden exertion. There was no case of murder or even manslaughter.

The relatives of the dead man were extremely dissatisfied; I explained and explained and explained – and sent them grumbling away. The little man I convicted of simple hurt and sentenced him to be confined till the rising of the court – which meant he must stand in the corner till tea-time. It gave the others time to get home. But I could not persuade him that it was a just verdict. 'My time had come,' he kept saying. 'His time had come. I did it.' Providence, he felt, had linked their two fates together. Perhaps they would have been reborn together, still tied in some mysterious bondage – but I had interfered and spoilt it. I hope he has forgiven me.

The time had come to leave Bareilly; I was going on leave to England. During those first years in India, I had never been far from the Himalayan snows. In the cold weather, from late October till early March, you could see them – enchanted in the northern sky, sharper and more serrated than any cloud, hard as diamond, bright, fixed and motionless; they were visible from most of Saharanpur district and from all the northern half of Bareilly. But as the days grew hotter, the dust of the plains hung suspended in the air and they became obscured until you could see them no longer. I have said nothing about the actual physical escape to the hills during these years, although it gave me intense pleasure and I was luckier than most in getting such opportunities. That does not really belong to the life I have been trying to draw. But in camp, in the winter, I did still sometimes raise my eyes to the hills, though not very often, because in this strangely extended boyhood I was too busy building sandcastles. I was often a long way from the still centre of my being, much further, it now seems, than I had been at Sedbergh or at Oxford. Now I was going back to England, from a life intensely different from anything my friends and family knew – a life against which I had not rebelled but in which I had found a place. I ought to have expected them to look at me with wide wondering eyes and ask whether this was the person they had known, but I took it for granted that we should go on just as we had before. I did not often stop to think when I was five and twenty.

VII

LUCKNOW AND DELHI

My parents were very forbearing. My father was forbearing by nature, my mother was not, but just as they were utterly confident about their relationship with each other, so they were certain of the permanence of my attachment to them. I see now that on that first leave from India I was immature, greedy and inconsiderate; as though I had been an adolescent of fifteen, I took it for granted that I was part of the family, entitled to a roof and a bed for as long as it suited me; but the moment my leave pay was lodged in the bank, I would be off to London, to theatres and lunches and dinners with my friends, or I would disappear on a round of visits, coming back when my pockets were empty.

I went back to Sedbergh, to Oxford, renewing my deeper friendships. But I was desperately hungry too for new experience, for a lasting love, ready also to engage in what I knew to be a passing flirtation. But it was permanence I sought. That however is too common a condition to be dwelt on here. Nor do I wish to dwell on the England of the early Thirties, to which I had come almost as a tourist. My work was else-where; the serious business of life was in India; this was a holiday from school and the troubles of the Thirties hardly seemed my affair. It was enough that I could get a second-hand car for £25.

There were changes at home, though they were not very sensational. The house was still the centre of a medical practice and the telephone had to be always manned; that law was sacred. My father continued to work long hours but he had now taken a partner whose headquarters were in a neighbouring village and that made it easier to have an occasional Sunday off. Maids were now more difficult to find and expected more time to themselves, but on the whole my mother was less cumbered with the house; for one thing, entertaining was less of a duty. Formal calls and 'At Homes' on second Wednesdays were things of the past and dinner parties much less frequent. 'But there is something called a sherry party,' said my mother, disapprovingly, because she felt there was some-thing rather rakish about drinking *before* a meal; she did however actually arrange such a party for me.

Though she spent less time on supervising household affairs, she was certainly not at this time less busy. She gave a great deal of energy to the Women's Institute and the Rural Community Council and still drove to outlying villages in Derbyshire, encouraging village communities and the revival of ancient practices such as well-dressing – when the well is framed in an elaborate picture made with the heads of thousands of flowers.

I have also the impression that my mother now spent more time on bridge, a game she had always greatly enjoyed, and in which she had tried in vain to interest me. None of her acquaintances disputed her supremacy at bridge; she read books about it and did problems. I suppose it was her mastery that gave me a distaste for it. It was not to me a relaxing way of passing the time, since when the hand had been played out she remembered where every card had been and explained how I should have finessed the knave or understood that my partner *must* have the king.

But a shadow had fallen across my parents' lives. My sister became suddenly blind and although that lasted only a few days it became clear that she was afflicted with a sclerosis for which no cure was known. For some years this sadness dominated their lives; there were no records of recovery from the disease but it had only lately been diagnosed, and my mother continually told herself that there might have been cases of recovery that no one had known about. It was admitted that there were intermissions, periods when the patient seemed to get no worse. My mother would not rest content with one opinion from Harley Street; she insisted on another. She had a vigorous Victorian feeling that the universe *must* be amenable to reason if only one could make it understand. The eminent authorities who were consulted expressed different philosophies of life rather than of medicine. One stressed the point so welcome to my mother about intermissions and failure to diagnose in the past; he advised that the patient should live as full and normal a life as possible. He believed that marriage and even child-bearing might be undertaken provided the risks were known; he thought that the happiness that might follow the birth of a child might help the mother's general health. He thought the risk worth taking; the disease was not hereditary and there would be no special danger to the child, but the mother's condition could possibly deteriorate after the birth and there should be no question of a second pregnancy. My parents, my sister and the man concerned accepted this advice and my sister married after I went back to India. Her child was born, a fine strong boy; he was about a year old and said to be forward for his age when he was found dead in his cot, having choked in his sleep. My father told me that in nearly forty years of practice he had never seen a case of this kind though he had read of it happening. 'That it should have happened to them!' he said. My sister's health began to deteriorate and she died about a year later, before she was thirty. 'She had been so full of promise and character!' said my mother but what strikes me in retrospect is how she had grown in loving affection during the years of her endurance, long years in which my parents too had endured their first real sorrow, a sorrow that lasted till death.

I travelled back to India with Raymond Vernède, a UP civilian of my year. Neither of us wanted another voyage by P & O liner, so we devised a more interesting journey, going by Messageries Maritimes from Marseille to Alexandria, spending a few days in Cairo and then going on by sea to Beirut. We drove to Baalbek, a place that fascinated me because it had been considered holy long before the Romans came to build the mighty ruins that remain. In those days, you had to take mules to cross the hills to the cedars of Lebanon and go on to the coast. We went on to Damascus, across the desert to Baghdad, spent a night at Ur of the Chaldees and so to Basra and down the Persian Gulf to Karachi. I shall say no more of that journey, since we were in effect tourists and my purpose is to describe ways of life in which I played a more intimate part.

On my return to India, I was posted to Lucknow, a city with a special atmosphere of its own which persisted from Mughal times through the British period. It was a city once famous throughout India for the pursuit of pleasure, for the politeness and wit of its courtiers and nobles, for the ingenuity of its poets, the skill of its painters, the extravagance and decadence of its rulers and, in British eyes, for the maladministration of the surrounding country. The province of Oudh – so our ancestors spelt Āwadh, rhyming it with 'proud' – had been governed on behalf of the Mughal Emperor by a Viceroy who made himself virtually independent and was at first a danger to the growing British power in Bengal; later he became an ally and was raised by the British to the dignity of King. For this title, he sold his independence. Oudh became a vassal state, surrounded by British territory on all sides. Deprived of the right to conduct external relations, the kings became increasingly frivolous and decadent, a scandal and a stumbling-block to the group of stern puritans who held the ascendancy in India under Lord Dalhousie. In their eyes, the nobles showed no glimmering of responsibility for the peasantry, the administration was corrupt, the King surrounded by dancing-girls, catamites and buffoons. He squandered his substance on firework displays, processions and fights between wild beasts, constantly made abject promises to reform and as constantly broke them. But since he never attempted any disloyalty to his masters, Dalhousie's annexation of Oudh appeared to Indians unjust and was one of the causes of the Mutiny.

It was in part a recognition of this injustice that, after the Mutiny, the great nobles were restored, with titles of Raja and Maharaja, to vast estates; they had no sovereignty but were feudal nobles with armies of henchmen. Each of them had a court in miniature; each had his palace in Lucknow as well as his country estate. The royal palaces were used by the British in a variety of ways; one was the Club, another was the Magistrates' Court. Everywhere in Lucknow there were buildings in the rococo style of the late Mughals and the tradition of wit, of pleasure, of raffishness, of formal courtesy, survived.

A traditional entertainment at Lucknow was the *mushā'ira*, a competition in impromptu verse-making. The master of ceremonies would give the assembled poets a line, and each of them would compose a verse ending with that line. You would see the face of each in turn lost in thought, suddenly lighting up as he saw his way through the difficulties, and then he would proclaim his verses, his head nodding to the heavy beat of the rhythm and the fingers of the outspread hand at last triumphantly extended to announce and display the climax. There are many stories of the habit of flowery compliment that survived, of which a typical example is that of two gentlemen of Lucknow who met by chance at the railway station, both meaning to take the train to Delhi. They were in good time but alas! – when the train steamed away, they were still exchanging politenesses on the platform. And one of the great nobles said to me of a senior Indian member of my service, whose manner was certainly brusque: 'He is discourteous – and to a man of Oudh that is the one offence which can never be forgiven!'

George Fisher had spoken to me with indignation about the British in Lucknow, isolated from the traditions of the city, going their way among the wedding-cake splendours of the past as though they did not exist. It was true of course, and yet, by some strange infection, British society in Lucknow assumed an air that was gay, light-hearted, frivolous, as it seemed to be nowhere else in India. Perhaps it was due not so much to the mysterious influence of the Kings of Oudh as to the presence of two cavalry regiments. Perhaps it was only a personal feeling, due to the restless and frivolous mood from which I had not yet emerged, and to the fact that at first I really had very little to do – something very unusual in my service. But the impression remains that between the palaces and the river at Lucknow there was something in the light of the moon that encouraged the heart to go a-roving.

While at Bareilly, I had been invited to go to Lucknow to write the annual administration report for the province. The invitation had been couched in amiable terms permitting me to refuse and I had pleaded that I must learn the groundwork of my profession as a sub-divisional officer.

Now I had been posted to Lucknow for that duty without the option of refusing. It was abysmally dull – statistics of crime and health and the output of crops – and the material came in from the various departments so slowly that I could seldom spend more than two hours a day on it. I could really have gone on three months' leave and done the whole job in a month. However, it was done at last and I became personal assistant to the District Magistrate and then for part of the summer I was City Magistrate. This was more the kind of work I had done in Bareilly – but it was concerned altogether with the great city of Lucknow; there was no camping.

The Hindus in Lucknow city were in a minority and had always taken second place. There was no danger of riots between Hindus and Muslims, but the Muslims themselves were fairly equally divided between the two sects, Sunnis and Shi'as. There was a long history of riots between these persuasions, to which Sir Harcourt Butler had brought a guarded lull some years before by persuading them to agree that each would abstain from certain named practices which the other regarded as provocative. In 1933 the District Magistrate left me for a fortnight in sole charge of Lucknow and no sooner had he gone than the Sunnis complained that the Shi'as were about to break the agreement by a provocative act. They had invited a well-known Maulvi to come and preach on 'The Tradition'. 'That does not sound provocative to me,' I said. 'But that man cannot preach on that subject without being provocative,' said a Sunni fiercely. There are many traditions in Islam but the Sunnis were sure that this Maulvi would preach on a tradition which they repudiate, that before his death the Prophet gave instructions that his son-in-law Ali should be his successor; these instructions were not observed – and this is the essence of the difference between the two sects. I spent a day in theological and philosophical argument, trying to bring them to an amicable agreement. Though at one stage, the leaders reluctantly agreed to a formula, their followers indignantly repudiated them, so I had to impose peaceful behaviour by a show of force. I banned public meetings over the critical few days, asked a battalion of British infantry to march through the city, and showed all the police we could muster as conspicuously as possible. Everything went off peacefully.

It was not very different from Bareilly – but as City Magistrate one was always meeting problems that seemed insoluble. What can you do when faced by more than a hundred cases in a morning in which a policeman says he caught a man riding a bicycle without a light and the man denies it? It is one man's word against another's; you have to back the police – and yet – and yet – you do know something of police methods. And the driver with the lame tonga pony! What do you do about that?

Send the brute to prison, says some fierce lady who is President of the RSPCA. But while he will be well-fed in prison, his wife and children, not to mention the pony, will starve. Fine him heavily? But he can only get the money to pay the fine by starving and overworking his pony. And the more you tighten inspection, the harder he must work his pony in order to appease the police. I would adjourn the case for a month and tell him to come back with the pony cured – taking very careful note of colour and markings to make sure it was the same pony.

Another problem was monkeys. They always hang round the office of the District Magistrate because litigants feed them; in Lucknow they used also to find their way mysteriously into the record room and it was surprising how often they would abstract the one document of importance from the file of some enduring dispute. Though they are too holy to be killed, monkeys may be discouraged and someone told me that if you caught a monkey and dyed it blue, its comrades would flee with horror from the spot where the outrage had occurred. There was never any difficulty in India about *how* to do anything; you just told someone to do it. There is a form of every Hindi verb which conveys that an order is to be passed on to someone else; I instructed the Nazir to cause this to be done. He found people of some aboriginal tribe; eight of them came into my court to show me two monkeys, each held by a limb, dripping with indigo. 'Release them,' I said, and sent an orderly to observe their companions scattering to other parts of Lucknow. He came back to report that on the contrary monkeys were coming from far and wide to admire the transformation.

Another absurdity from Lucknow days makes once more the point that the national struggle in which we were supposed to be taking part was not usually taken very seriously. When I first arrived, I stayed with the District Magistrate and found that he had been allotted a bodyguard, a police constable in plain clothes, generally known as the Orderly Pistōl – the accent being on the second syllable, to rhyme with goal. He sometimes accompanied the lady of the house on shopping expeditions and went to polo with the syces and ponies. Otherwise, he hung about rather aimlessly. I asked him once to show me his pistol. He was pleased and with a mysterious and secretive air drew out of his pocket a large-ish bundle. There was an oilskin bag carefully fastened; inside that were three yards of flannel which he unwound to reveal an automatic pistol; there was nothing in the chamber and the safety-catch was on. Later, when I became City Magistrate, I was gratified to find I had an Orderly Pistōl of my own. It seemed to raise one's status. But his case was different; he had been sent on a six-week course and trained to use the pistol and had passed out with very high marks, but when appointed Orderly

Pistōl he had not been given a weapon and no one had ever asked to see it before.

During that summer, I lived in one of the married-quarter bungalows of the 10th Royal Hussars and ate in their mess. They had a good many officers on leave and it helped them with their catering. I enjoyed their company; Charles Gairdner, who during the war commanded the Middle East staff college, was a man who had once been able to play any game he chose up to international standards and who, even after a shell fragment had shattered a femur, was an 8 handicap polo player. He had once been staying near Ostend when he heard that the Amateur Golf Championship of Belgium was about to take place; he borrowed a set of clubs and won it. He could give a game to top Wimbledon players at tennis, had played hockey for Ireland and was able to talk with distinction on any subject that anyone raised. Colin Davy worked away at his racing novels or read Byron in the afternoons when everyone else was asleep. Everyone in Lucknow read Byron, particularly *Don Juan*. Desmond Young, then editor of *The Pioneer*, later the author of a successful book on Rommel, was a frequent visitor. We talked of course about:

> Four things greater than all things are, –
> Women and Horses and Power and War

but mostly of the first two. The subalterns were charming and elegant young men; they pictured me riding about with a lasso and a six-shooter and called me the Sheriff. But they found it a problem to keep amused; there was morning parade before breakfast and then there would be stables and there might be an hour's work at the squadron office but, except for the orderly officer, work would be over before midday. They would sleep between lunch and polo – when I was in court listening to pleaders and witnesses – but after dinner they felt the need for amusement and I would usually join them. I have never known the agony of trying to keep awake so acutely as in the afternoons of that hot weather in Lucknow. There was one Major who had risen from the ranks; 'Nice young men,' he confided in me one day, 'but not very *serious*.' It was certainly not the thing to be serious. We used sometimes to play a mild form of poker – but nothing was paid for in cash in India and there was a rule against putting debts at cards on mess-bills, so we entered the results as 'Sale of polo-ponies', which was admissible. Each of them had a dressing-boy to put out his clothes and a bearer to supervise the work of the dressing-boy. Six years later they went to war in the desert and some of them survived.

In the autumn, I learnt that I had been recommended to the Government of India for the post of Under Secretary in what was then called the Army Department. Later, it became the War Department and later still the Defence Department; I shall call it the Defence Department. I was to spend ten years there, off and on, in various capacities. Colin Davy said to me: 'Well, I suppose you must better yourself, as the servants say – but I'm afraid that after us you will find real professional soldiers rather dull.'

In fact, I found many friends among the soldiers at Army Headquarters but it cannot be denied that a good deal of the work was dull at the time and still more dull in retrospect. I shall move on quickly to the next stage of my life, but it is worth making the point that it was incomparably easier to get anything done in Delhi than it appears to be in Whitehall. This was because there were so few of us. There were then less than a hundred ICS officers at the headquarters of the Government of India, in the capital city for four hundred million people. You could quickly learn who to speak to and everyone was used to taking responsibility. An incoming letter from a provincial government or from the India Office in London would be put up by excellent clerks – about twelve clerks to an officer – with a note drawing attention to precedents and suggesting a course of action and a draft reply. It was possible to get through a great many cases in a day, often merely polishing the English of the outgoing letter. Two matters, one important and one on a very small scale, will illustrate the sort of thing the Defence Department did.

Since Lord Kitchener's famous victory over Lord Curzon, the Commander-in-Chief in India had been also the Minister for War and the Viceroy's sole adviser on defence matters. This put a special responsibility on the Secretary to the Government of India in the Defence Department – a civilian – who had to make sure that the Commander-in-Chief as a soldier did nothing politically embarrassing. But Sir Philip Chetwode, who was then Commander-in-Chief, was aware of the political situation and was altogether at one with the rest of the Viceroy's Council in the matter which was at that time the most important issue that concerned the Defence Department.

There were about forty-five thousand British troops in India. They were supposed to be there for the defence and internal security of India, and India paid the cost of keeping them. But the War Office in London argued that we should also pay a share of the cost of training them in England. Our argument was that this should be set off against the fact that the training they received on the North-West Frontier – training with real bullets – was an imperial asset and also that they were a hidden imperial reserve. During World War I, British troops in India were reduced to seventeen thousand second-line troops and an Indian Army Corps went to France in 1914, forming a third of the total British force. The case seems to me now unanswerable but we were handicapped by the feebleness of the India Office, who took more notice of pressure from the War Office than of our lucid and convincing despatches. But we did in the end succeed in getting a tribunal appointed and our case was accepted in part. In this, of course, I as a newcomer played hardly any part, doing perhaps a little occasional drafting, but not expressing an opinion.

At the other end of the scale, I recall a morning when an unusually stout Major from the Royal Sussex Regiment came into my room with a ferocious letter he wanted me to send the UP Government. The Adjutant-General had received a complaint from a retired Jemadar – a Viceroy's commissioned officer – of Meerut District. His pension was twenty-five rupees a month, which does not sound much but was enough to make him a person of importance in his village. But the wicked Congress – the Jemadar assumed of course that the Adjutant-General would regard the Congress as an enemy – had a majority on the District Board – that is, more or less, the County Council – and they had clapped a five-rupee tax on Jemadars who had served the Government faithfully. Of course the Major was indignant; the letter was carefully worded to make this sound like a punitive tax of twenty per cent on the pension of Indian officers and no one else; he had drafted a stern letter reproving the UP Government for allowing such goings-on and the Deputy Adjutant-General, no less, had seen it – implying that it was not for a whipper-snapper like me to interfere with something approved by a Major-General.

It did not come naturally to a soldier to understand that the District Board was an elected body and not under the orders of the provincial Government in the same way that a brigade is under the orders of a division; nor did soldiers always realize that the provincial Government in its turn had some measure of autonomy. But I did not need to point that out. I knew that District Boards could not impose an Income Tax on anyone, still less on a specific class of person; it also occurred to me that 'a five-rupee tax' might be an annual tax – though the complaint was carefully worded to suggest it was monthly. Might I come with him to see the Deputy Adjutant-General?

So we went off, hand in hand, and I suggested that before writing a fierce official letter I should write a friendly personal letter asking the Commissioner of Meerut for the facts. He happened, I added, to be no desk-bound bureaucrat but a famous pig-sticker – Percy Marsh, well known to all gunners and most of the Indian Army. Of course the General agreed; I wrote my personal letter and was told, as I had expected, that it was a flat tax of five rupees a year on everyone above a certain level of property or income and that it had been held to be constitutional – and in the Commissioner's opinion was perfectly justified. It was a small matter, but it stuck in my memory as one of the first occasions when I was able to do just what I thought the Defence Department was supposed to do.

VIII

KINGDOM
IN THE MOUNTAINS

1 The Best Job in India

'What are they like?'

'They are like two children, laughing and playing!'

That, we learnt six months later, was how Mary and I appeared to the people of Garhwal when we made the three days' journey from Kotdwara, where the railway ended, to the headquarters of the district at Pauri. Three years with the Government of India had come to an end – and what I had wanted more than anything else had come true. I had the best job in India – and we were on our way to take over our kingdom.

Those three years had not been altogether wasted. I had been secretary to the Military Council, to which Sir Philip Chetwode used to summon his Principal Staff Officers, the Defence Secretary and the Financial Adviser for consultation on important matters, and I had learnt something of the considerations that influence decision. I had also learnt, incidentally, that it is a mere waste of time to take a stenographer to such meetings; if you want a good record quickly, you must rely on your own memory and your understanding of the arguments and go straight from the meeting to dictate the minutes. It should never take more than twenty-four hours but in Whitehall today they take months to produce minutes.

I had also spent a good deal of time adjudicating so far as I could between the soldiers and the outposts of the Finance Department who were allotted to Army Headquarters as watch-dogs. Since the soldiers usually wanted to do something positive, my sympathies tended to be with them – but I had a considerable admiration for one of the financial advisers, Chaudhri Mohammad Ali, later to be Prime Minister of Pakistan; he was imaginative and positive and would often suggest a better way of doing what was proposed. I had also kept up a constant struggle against the jargon which often appeared in the letters brought me to be signed. 'The greatcoat storage situation gives cause for grave anxiety' is one phrase out of hundreds that has stuck in my memory. It means that there are no proper arrangements for storing greatcoats.

Irritation at their misuse no doubt sharpened my sense of the right use of words but it was sometimes a rather weary apprenticeship. At the time, I was not sufficiently aware of the value of the lessons I was learning. I became very skilled in dealing with generals, mainly because I usually liked the general in question and admired his integrity. It was rare, at that stage, to meet a soldier who had got to the top by ruthless self-assertion, though I did meet one or two such men during the war – and I had no inhibitions about behaving with respect to high rank. On the whole, however, the attractive part of those three years had taken place outside the office.

To me the fact that we moved to Simla in the hot weather was always a joy. It was not fashionable to say so; in Delhi, successive Viceroys and their staffs lamented the hardness of the fate that sent them to Simla; they suffered from claustrophobia, they said, on the narrow ridges on which Simla sprawls; they could not sleep because of the height. Society was unreal and enclosed. To me it seemed that those who talked like that had either never endured a whole hot weather in the plains or they had forgotten it. How could anyone feel shut in on a mountain-top, I wondered. As for being cut off from the teeming millions – which had been a cry since the time at least of Lord Curzon – it required a nicer judgment than mine to distinguish between the degrees of isolation from the cultivators which afflicted the Viceroy's advisers in one place or in the other.

There was a keen positive pleasure in leaving Delhi in April, when it is beginning to get hot, when the grass is turning brown and the gardens are desolate, and going to a place where the flowers are coming out, where there are wild roses by the side of the paths and miniature torrents tumble down the mountain-sides from cold springs fringed with ferns, where by day there is the intoxicating scent of hot resinous pine-needles under foot and at night there are blazing log fires. From almost anywhere in Simla you had only to take an evening stroll to see the snows and even when the snows were invisible there was always the profile of Shali, a mere nine thousand foot, but a classical mountain shape, dark against a western sky. I used to leave Simla almost every Saturday after lunch – for in those far-off days we worked on Saturday mornings – and go out along one of the ridges that run north-eastward towards Tibet or west-ward to the sunset. I usually went in the company of two infantrymen, romantics like all soldiers, but admirers rather of the grim courage shown in sieges than of dashing cavalry charges, very different from the *beaux sabreurs* of the 10th Hussars. We would light a fire – picturing hostile eyes gazing at us from the surrounding dark – and cook something in a frying pan; then we would settle down in our sleeping bags under the stars and next day cross some stupendous valley – where a stream would run through boulders that burnt the hand – and toil slowly up the thousands of feet to Simla. To rest after physical exhaustion, to satisfy extreme thirst, were pleasures of the body in those days; the mind was stilled, the eye could again recall the pond with the willow trees, the patch of shade where goats rested beneath a rock, the isolated cottage with its patch of maize or potatoes.

'There will be enough about mountains later,' I wrote as I remembered walking with Sligger up the zig-zag path to the Châlet. I had moved away from the mountains during my first five years in India, from Saharanpur to Bareilly and then to Lucknow. Now the mountains had come closer and were to fill my life until the outbreak of war in 1939.

In Delhi, I had met Mary Hayes, who had come to India for the winter to stay with her uncle, General Twiss, at that time Military Secretary. We became engaged. I suddenly realized that I must clear up the debts which used to accumulate so easily in India, where everyone was eager to give credit. I sold my ponies – but something more positive was needed. I had written some stories; I wrote some more – before breakfast, in the evening. One of them was the story of the Aundh murder, in which I had been so interested in Bareilly. I sent these to my brother, then a medical student at St George's; he showed them to Thornton Butterworth, a publisher whose son had been a friend of his at school. He picked out that story: 'If your brother will write a novel anything like as good as that, I will publish it,' he wrote. I had always felt it was much too condensed, so I set to work, at odd times, when I could get a moment.

I wrote Mary long letters about those expeditions from Simla and wove something of one rather longer journey in the hills into my novel. It was still half finished when I went home in 1935. I finished it in Dorset, after we were married, and took it to Thornton Butterworth. He promised to read it quickly – which he did – but he came back with the verdict that it would not sell without a handsome English hero and a beautiful girl who fell into his arms on the last page. This seemed to me very silly – but I recognized that it might need revision. So I put it aside – as it turned out, for several years.

Mary and I came back to India overland by the Orient Express leaving the train at Innsbrück and walking through the mountains to Salzburg; the train ran twice a week and we left it again for three or four days to explore in succession Vienna, Buda Pesth, Istanbul and Aleppo, staying with friends in Baghdad, and going by sea from Basra to Karachi. There was another year in Delhi and Simla and our first sorrow – we lost our first child. The servants stood round with tears in their eyes. 'Do not grieve,' they said; 'God will send other children.' In Simla, we explored the hills at weekends and Mary loved as much as I did the distant snow mountains, the forest tracks chequered with patterns of leaf and sun, nights under the stars.

My three years as Under Secretary came to an end. I was asked if I would like to stay another year but I said I wanted to hold charge of a district, as I should if I went back to the UP. We were encouraged to state preferences and I wrote to the Chief Secretary giving mine; my first choice was Garhwal. He wrote back, kindly but rather drily; unfortunately, everyone wanted the three districts I had mentioned and they were all occupied. He offered three which would be fairly low in most people's preference. I chose one in Oudh, to the west of Lucknow, and tried to become enthusiastic about it. I was posted there; it was published in the *Gazette*. Then at the last minute, the telegram came: Garhwal! The best job in India.

There were several reasons why at thirty it seemed the best job in India. The railway had put a timid foot into the district at Kotdwara, about a mile over the boundary, and then stopped. There were twenty miles of motorable road up to Lansdowne, at about six thousand feet, the permanent headquarters of the Royal Garhwal Rifles, of whom there were usually two battalions present, and the 2/3rd Queen Alexandra's Own Gurkhas. But apart from that twenty miles, there were only mule paths and paths from village to village which were sometimes negotiable by mules and sometimes not. A normal day's journey for a traveller with any baggage – which would include a roll of bedding as well as food and cooking utensils – was about ten or twelve miles. Mules and porters could do a double march but not too often. Along the main mule paths, there were bungalows at the end of a day's march where a traveller could stay the night; they usually had two rooms and a verandah with a row of three or four little rooms for servants. But there were not many of these main routes. In such steep country, and with heavy rainfall all packed into three months, even a mule track needs quite a lot of maintenance.

To see the country you had to use tents, and it was essential for me to see the country very thoroughly indeed. It was normally provided that the Deputy Commissioner of Garhwal should spend half the year travelling about the district, but in my case there were maps to be made of the cultivation in every village, and this would mean nine months of the year travelling. Walking among mountains was what Mary and I liked better than anything else – but there was much more to it than that. To be inaccessible is to be independent; instructions from the Government arrive late and are often so quaintly out of the question that they can be disregarded. Ministers do not come to see you. And in Garhwal, just because it was remote, power had so long been centred in the District Officer's hands that he had a prestige that in the rest of India was a thing of the past. For most of the district he was policeman and civil judge as well as magistrate. He was even a forest officer in large stretches.

From Kotdwara to Pauri, the headquarters of the district, was three days' normal march. From Pauri, it was fifteen days to the Mana Pass into Tibet; eighteen to the Niti pass, a little further to the east. The Mana Pass lay between two great peaks, Kamet and Chaukamba. Kamet was the first peak of over twenty-five thousand feet to be climbed by man and the highest peak in the British Empire, but from the point of view of a traveller Kamet was usually hidden. Chaukamba was more impressive, a home of the gods to Hindus, a great square block of a mountain, four-square, 'like a crown', said the Garhwalis, though to a Western eye its fluted walls looked more like a distant view of some great Norman cathedral, with no central spire but a pinnacle at either end. Beneath Chaukamba lay on one side Badrinath, one of the four holy places at the four corners of India, and on the other side Kedarnath, less holy to Vaishnavite Hindus, but far more rewarding to the visitor, its Greco-Buddhist temple standing within a few hundred yards of the foot of a glacier within a semi-circle of twenty-thousand-foot peaks.

From the high waste snows, you came down to the first villages, half the year deserted and deep under snows and then to steep villages clinging to the almost precipitous sides of narrow valleys; then there was country not so bleak, thickly forested, where there were clearings along the banks of the streams and a village wherever a terrace could be built and a plough be made to go, and at last, towards the plains, you came to hills below six thousand feet, where the forests had been destroyed and every inch of land was used, and then right down to the foothills, where the district proper was separated from the plains by a belt of broken jungle, once too malarial for habitation and even now frequented chiefly by tigers, elephants and forest officers.

I have left the people till the last because it took longer to get to know them. But, even from the start, what I did know about the people of this rugged country was a part of the attraction. It was a land of villages; Pauri, the headquarters of the district had barely two thousand inhabitants; there might have been a few more at Srinagar, in the valley below, the old capital of the Kings of Garhwal, but not many; there was no place in the whole district that could be called a town. The people had the virtues of peasants: simplicity, fidelity, courage, power to endure. They got their living from the narrow fields, often no more than two or three yards wide, often faced laboriously with stone. Traditionally, every two or three years a cultivator would go to the plains to buy iron and salt. He might be away six weeks or two months but he would not lock up his house when he went. The village brotherhood would look after it while he was away. I must let them appear, stage by stage, as I got to know them; it is enough here to say that from the start I felt committed to liking the Garhwalis and being on their side as against that outer world to which they looked, from their remote and isolated haunts, with diffidence and distrust.

On the third day, we came to Pauri and met my predecessor, Duncan Coghill. It was a long-standing ICS tradition to waste no time on ✓ handing-over; everyone had his own way of doing things and it was useless to tell the new man how to run his district; he would do it his own way whatever you told him. Duncan was leaving next morning; still, during that one afternoon and evening he tried to tell me a good deal. There was a touch of embarrassment on my side, because I had only the sketchiest idea of why there had been this sudden change; Duncan was going to the district in Oudh which had been allotted to me. He was a man whom I had known slightly before and whom I liked; he had been happy in Garhwal and was sad to be going but he showed no sign of resentment towards his supplanter. He went on talking till far into the night; towards the end, I became drowsy with the fresh mountain air, the day's walk and the log fire, but I struggled against sleep and tried to piece together what had happened.

Duncan was about two years older than myself, unmarried, a solitary by inclination, and extremely interested in agriculture; after the independence of India he took up farming in Herefordshire. He was a man of a deep, almost obsessional honesty; at some stage he had had contact ✓ with the Moral Rearmament movement, whose dangerous insistence on telling everything that is in the heart had reinforced a natural characteristic. He impressed me as a sensitive and lonely figure, who expected perhaps too much in a world of fallen men. He was severe with any subordinate official he suspected of any degree of corruption. It appeared to me, as the evening wore on, that with every new subordinate he assumed an attitude so guarded that the man was bound to feel suspected. But in Garhwal everything depended on mutual confidence, on bluff if ✓ you like. That was true of the British everywhere in India but in Garhwal there was really nothing else. I should think it incredible if I had not been there.

Everywhere in India, the pay of subordinates was far too low for their responsibilities. The *patwari* – the village record-keeper – in the plains received twelve rupees a month for long hours of difficult work, and his evidence was the deciding factor in most disputes. It was utterly absurd. In practice an honest *patwari* would accept presents in kind and take what were really fees for appearances in court. It was illegal – but everyone knew and a wise man took no notice unless he found the record falsified.

But in Garhwal this disproportion was even more ludicrous. The *patwari* WAS the administration; he kept the records and reported on disputes; he collected the Land Revenue as in the plains; but over and above all that, he was the police. In practically the whole district, there were no regular police with uniforms; the *patwari* was the only police officer in his area, which on an average contained sixty villages. He had the powers of a sub-inspector – and to enforce them a pair of handcuffs, a shotgun, and a servant. He might have to investigate a murder. He was on his own; it might take days for his report to reach a superior. He was paid fourteen rupees a month – rising to eighteen after twenty years' service – and his servant had less than half as much. Traditionally everyone gave the *patwari* a present of grain, according to the size of his holding, and I was told confidentially that for a reasonably honest *patwari* the job was worth at least two hundred rupees, more than twelve times the pay. It was a very loose administration, but such as it was it depended on things left unsaid, on recognizing that there is no absolute virtue, but that there are degrees of honesty. The system would work if the peasants had some confidence in the *patwari* and if the *patwari* believed he had the support of the Deputy Commissioner so long as he kept within bounds.

It was only a hint, that impression I had of an attitude on Duncan's part that might easily defeat its own ends. I learnt later that Ibbotson, the Commissioner for the three hill districts, had been worried by a similar impression and that he had been afraid this might interfere with making new cultivation maps, a project that was very near to his heart, in which indeed he felt that his personal honour and good faith were involved. This map-making was a matter of which Duncan said very little to me that night; what really interested him was agricultural improvement. The Village Uplift of which George Fisher had talked had become more respectable in the course of seven years but it was still a very poor little Cinderella. For Garhwal there was an allotment of five thousand rupees a year held at the Deputy Commissioner's discretion. Duncan had used a good deal of it that year on bulls, to improve the yield of milk, but he had many other schemes in mind.

It was later that I learnt the significance of all this. Ibbotson had been Deputy Commissioner at Garhwal more than ten years earlier. He was a man of great energy and a simple direct outlook, a Cambridge mathematician, one of the last I believe to win the strange distinction of Senior Wrangler. He was struck by the great extension of cultivation in Garhwal since the last settlement in 1896. The ploughed land was always on terraces, made wherever the slope was least severe, but as the pressure on the land increased it became worth while to undertake the labour of lengthening the terraces into land that had once seemed too steep.

Ibbotson judged that the rewards of cultivation were more than they had been; it was still basically subsistence farming but the rupee was not the rare object it once was and the district was really under-taxed. New maps which would show the extensions were badly needed. The essence of good administration was to settle disputes fairly and this was very hard if the maps were out of date, so he proposed a settlement – new maps and a new assessment of the Revenue.

The Government said no. They did not question that new maps were needed, but it would be an expensive business and even if the Revenue were doubled, as Ibbotson hoped, it would still be tiny. The extra money would not pay back the cost of the maps for years and years. Ibbotson seized on the last point and put up a new suggestion: let him do a sample revision of the maps in a limited area to test his ideas about the cost and to train some Assistant Record Officers. Let him also, in the rest of the district, do scattered samples to get an approximate idea of the extra cultivation in different parts. And then let him increase the Revenue as fairly as he could, using his judgment and his extensive knowledge. Let the Government postpone the new maps for ten years, by which time they would be half paid for. They took the bait – he did his samples and increased the Revenue.

But, of course, in ten years time, when he came back as Commissioner and asked for the maps, he had to start the battle again. Costs had gone up and times were hard, said the Government; they really could not see their way to spending so much on a district which paid so little in Land Revenue. But you promised! said Ibbotson – and anyhow I will reduce the cost. He consulted the Assistant Record Officers – whom he had trained himself – and decided he could safely undertake to speed up the pace and cover the district in less time than he had originally estimated, but it would need ruthless pressure on the survey parties. In the end, by twice cutting the costs, he got his way. Part of the expense was the appointment of a senior officer of the provincial Civil Service who would be an Additional District Magistrate at Pauri and would leave the Deputy Commissioner time to inspect these survey parties in the field. They were going to need a lot of inspection if their work was to be accurate, because they must work fast.

The operations began. Forty-eight survey parties under four Assistant Record Officers started work in the late summer in the highest villages and were sweeping down the district trying to get as much outdoor work as possible finished before the snow. Of course unexpected questions of principle cropped up; this kind of work on this scale had not been done since 1896 and Ibbotson could not foresee everything. It was essential to visit them and settle these points before the snow came down.

And at this juncture, demented by the gods, Duncan had written to Ibbotson to say he was not interested in making maps and he suggested that the extra officer should do that, while he looked after the district in the usual way. Hence all these telegrams; wiser to get between a bear and his line of retreat than between Ibbotson and the project he had cherished for ten years and felt he owed as a personal debt to the people of Garhwal!

Most of this Ibbotson told me later. It had to be the Deputy Commissioner who did the maps. He was still virtually king of the district, usually referred to as the Zillah Sahib, which means simply The District – as it were personified; the survey parties must have all possible help from the *patwaris* and they must all, *patwaris* and survey men alike, be confident of backing and support from the top. They would need drive, enthusiasm, pressure. But all I knew at the time was that I had to see them before the snow came and that I must leave the day after tomorrow.

I said good-bye to Duncan next day, sadly, for I felt I had turned him out of paradise. And then Mary and I began to get ready for our first working trip – up the district to visit the survey parties. It would be nearly three months before we were back again at the house which for the next three years was the nearest thing we had to a home.

2 *Look at my Field*

Whatever I might have persuaded myself about the task of leading a new dominion to independence, it had really been the spicy smells and bright colours of the bazaar that had drawn me to India. And yet here I was, only eight years later, taking refuge with enthusiasm in a country utterly different, a country where the evocative scents were of fern and rotting leaves and where one of the attractions of the people was that in so many ways they were so different from the Indians of the plains. To see Garhwali children coming out of school was to be aware of the difference at once. They might have walked five miles to get there and have five miles to walk home, but they would tumble out of school like puppies tipped from a basket, wrestling and chasing each other, uproarious with chatter and laughter. Or shake hands with the retired Subedar who came to meet you as you came near his village, and you met a hard firm grip from a square hand like a sailor's. In diet, physique, temperament, the Garhwalis seemed a nation apart.

In the last years of the eighteenth century, Garhwal had been overrun by the expanding empire of Nepal. They had fought the Gurkhas, and 'Gurkhali' was still the word they used to express the ultimate in tyranny and violence. Nevertheless, there had been many Garhwalis in the Gurkha armies which gave so good an account of themselves against the British, and in many ways the two peoples resembled each other. When the war was over, in 1817, most of Garhwal became British, the King expressing himself – or so the current myth had it – only too glad to give up the greater part of his territory to make sure that his boundaries should be a long way from Nepal. Even before the war was over, the British were enlisting soldiers from Garhwal as well as from Nepal. For many years, no distinction was made between them and it was not till 1887 that the Garhwalis' own regiment was formed. Even after that, some were recruited to Gurkha regiments. One of my visitors in Upper Garhwal had risen from the ranks in a Gurkha regiment and had ended as Subedar-Major, the highest rank he could hold, the Colonel's right-hand man. Everywhere in the district there were soldiers, but the Royal Garhwal Rifles, who in peace could pick and choose, preferred the men from the higher hills. Nearer the plains the soldiers were more likely to have served in the Supply Corps or the Indian Hospital Corps.

I always found it moving to meet the men who had gone to France in the chaos of 1914, men who in their own homes had never seen even a bullock-cart, who had suddenly found themselves facing machine guns and shell-fire in unspeakable conditions of cold and mud. Cold they had certainly known but not, as a rule, mud. I have seen men in Upper Garhwal whose toes had come away with their boots when they came out of the line. But they had cleared German trenches with bayonet and kukri, they had won VCs, they had left France with a reputation second to none.

They would appear, as we started out on that first journey towards the higher hills and the survey parties, suddenly and mysteriously, by the side of the rocky path, at a corner where it emerged from the forest and gave a clear view across a valley. There would be old soldiers in tattered uniforms that now hung rather loose or villagers in shapeless coats and trousers of woollen stuff spun and woven from their own sheep; further north, more and more of them would wear a folded blanket secured with two long iron pins. Their cry was always the same: 'Come and look at my field!'

The word does not really mean 'field' but the place where something happened, the scene of an occurrence. But there is no single word for it in English and it was usually a field.

'Come and look!' they would say. 'Only ten steps!'

I would pace out ten steps – if there was room on that high eyrie – counting them aloud.

'No, no,' they would say indulgently, as to a child: 'Not *that* kind of step. Over there!'

And after much pointing and questioning we would identify the scene of the dispute, perhaps beneath a tongue of forest, on the opposite hill-side, three or four miles away as a bullet might fly, but twice as far on the ground, with a drop of three or four thousand feet to be climbed up and down.

'But what would it say to me if I got there?' I would ask. 'Would the earth open its mouth and tell me who ploughs it?' But it would be no use. They would go on pleading. More than a century ago, in Central India, Sir John Malcolm – Boy Malcolm – would say: 'Why did God give me two ears?' to make villagers understand that he must hear both sides of the case. It was no use going to 'the spot' unless the other party was there too. And even one such deviation from the route would mean you disappointed someone else. There might be a dozen waiting at similar vantage-points along the expected path, and at the end of the march, where the tents would be going up, there would usually be another dozen or more with petitions and sometimes as many again asking for medicine. It was really important to get there before dark.

The difficulty about two ears always remained. By the time both parties to the dispute could be collected, you would be three days' march away. Nonetheless, they were right; it would be better to see the spot if you could, but that could happen only occasionally. The orthodox thing to do was to pass the petition down to one of the sub-divisional officers, but the people had such faith in the personal power and the personal goodwill of the District Officer that it was hard to do that; they felt it was rejection. Every man in Garhwal was convinced that his cause was just and that its justice must be immediately apparent to me if only I could be enticed to the spot.

But we are on our way to the survey parties – whose work I should have to learn by making decisions about it. The first step was to understand how land was held and a good deal about this had been lovingly recorded by great men of the past. The core of the business was the village brotherhood. It was a communal system, very ancient indeed and once widespread, but in the plains almost entirely vanished. The characteristic village was an island of cultivation surrounded by country too difficult to plough. The sea surrounding the island would often be forest, but sometimes steep ridges where nothing grew but coarse grass. All this encircling country was held in common; on the maps it was marked, rather romantically I thought, K-i-H, Kaisar-i-Hind, Emperor of India, because in the end the soil of India belonged to the Sovereign. But the village community had the right to take their cattle to graze there, to cut wood, to cut grass for thatching. Within the cultivated island, where the slopes were not so steep, terraces had been built and often faced with stone, and the narrow fields, winding like snakes along the contours of the hillside, were ploughed and sometimes irrigated. These ploughed fields were not held in common but were cultivated as separate holdings, by families – in practice usually by the eldest of several brothers, one or two of whom would perhaps have gone away to the army or to some other employment. These separate blocks of cultivation differed a good deal in size, because all the sons were entitled in theory to a share in the father's holding and in the past some had been divided. They could not be sold except by agreement between the shareholders. 'Shareholder' is the literal meaning of the word that was used.

The system had worked beautifully when the population was smaller; then the holdings in the cultivated land were enough and so was the grazing land and the forest. But by 1936, there was pressure on the land almost everywhere, severe near the plains where hardly any grazing or forest remained, and beginning to be felt even in the highest villages – thus a clash of interests would develop. Every shareholder was entitled to extend his holding wherever his terraces could be stretched out into the common land without interruption. But many terraces could be extended no further; sooner or later they would come up against a rocky crag or something impossibly steep. If there was a break, it was new cultivation. No one could start new cultivation on common land without the consent of all the shareholders. Once, long ago, that had been easily obtained; a man would sometimes find a comparatively level place in the forest far from the village and no one would mind if he made a clearing and started a new plot. But now, in almost every village, any new cultivation would meet opposition because the rest of the village thought that the grazing and forest areas were already insufficient.

That was the basis of half the disputes in Garhwal. Another fruitful cause of trouble was the exact line of the boundary between the common land of one village and the next. When the first records were made, very roughly indeed and almost immediately after annexation in 1817, the men sent for the job were told to note down the four cardinal points of the common land that each village claimed. There was plenty of land in those days and plenty of forest; everyone knew where the cattle grazed and where each village went to cut wood. They would write: North, Goat Peak: West, Bhim Sen's Ridge: East, Blue pine where vultures sit: South, Pebbly Stream. This was some evidence of ancient custom but sometimes very difficult to interpret a hundred and twenty years later. For one thing, Garhwalis never speak of north and south, but always of up and down; even in what seemed to me perfectly flat country near Delhi, a Garhwali soldier guiding me to the battalion lines did not say: 'Turn left' (as a European would) or 'Turn south' (as a plainsman would) but: 'Turn up' or 'Turn down'. So Goat Peak might well be east of the village or west. The blue pine where the vultures used to sit would have almost certainly disappeared and it would sometimes happen that two villages would identify two different valleys as Pebbly Stream.

About thirty years later, there was another attempt at mapping the cultivation, still very rough but measured with ropes. This time, the village boundary was described as a continuous line: 'Along Bhim Sen's Ridge by the crest of the ridge to Goat Peak; then down the Rocky Ridge to the rock like a panther; then straight down to the blue pine where the vultures sit; then to Thorny Valley and down Thorny Stream to the main stream; across the main stream and up Pebbly Stream to Bhim Sen's Ridge.' That was the kind of thing, rather better than before, but it was still open to a wide range of interpretation. What we meant to do in 1936 was to go right round the village and mark the boundary by a line of numbered concrete blocks corresponding to numbers on the map. It would – we hoped – prevent a great many disputes in the future. In the settlement, anyone could raise an issue of any kind without payment of court fees and it would be settled on the spot by the Assistant Record Officer. There were thirty thousand such issues raised and settled in a year; anyone who was dissatisfied could appeal to me but very few did – except about boundaries. There was no doubt in my mind that Ibbotson had done the district a great service by his fight to get the map-making approved.

Each Assistant Record Officer had twelve survey parties. On one visit I would check the work of four or five parties under each ARO. I would look at the map – it was thirty-two inches to the mile in the hills – and see how much of this village was old cultivation, printed in black in 1896, and how much was new – extensions of old terraces and patches of newly broken ground – all drawn in red in the last two or three days. Then we would go to some point where we could look over a fair stretch of hillside with a good deal of new terracing and I would choose two points on the map which could be identified on the ground. I would draw a line in pencil on the map joining the two points – perhaps two inches long, which would make five chains. Then the chainman would measure along that line. The ground was sloping and broken by terraces. How do you measure sloping ground and transfer it to a map? He would keep the chain level till he was holding it about a man's height from the ground. Then he would drop a pebble and go on measuring from where the pebble hit the ground. It was rough and ready but surprisingly accurate. When he reached a terrace wall which was also the boundary of a holding he would shout: 'Eighty-three links!' and I would measure on the map with dividers and find that on the map it was perhaps eighty or eighty-five. And at the end of five or six chains, he would not be out by more than five or six links, and often not by half so much (a link is eight inches).

Years later in Kikuyu country in Kenya I expressed surprise to an officer of the Colonial Service that they should attempt to run the country without detailed maps. He told me crushingly that I had no idea of the cost. You had to have aeroplanes, special cameras, elaborate equipment; the cost was fantastic. This was in country which in Garhwal we should have called 'just like a parade-ground'. Perhaps they did not yet need maps as much as we did; that would have been an answer I could have respected. But aeroplanes and cameras! Our maps were made with a plane-table, a spirit-level, a compass, a chain and the instruments a child uses for elementary geometry – but then we had evolved our own methods before we were tied to London by a telegraph line. The villagers fed and housed the survey parties; they were most of them young men from school, or even from a university, who hoped to win eventually some permanent employment with the Government. They toiled in the fields from first light till darkness fell; long after that, when the lamps were lighted in the smoky thatched huts, they worked on at the share-holders' record, asking how many sons had been born to Autar Singh and how many to Kedar Singh, and how many to each of *their* sons, calculating the fractions due to each brother and uncle and grandson. I suppose one in ten of them won the reward of permanent service.

When I had checked the maps in the field, I would go to a threshing-floor – a little circle paved with mortared stone, with a low wall, where the cattle could be driven round to beat out the corn. Most of the share-holders would gather there. I would go through the shareholders' record, repeating all those questions and making sure that each of Autar Singh's grandsons and great-grandsons had been entered with the right share, and that all the shares added up to the right number. By the time you came to great-grandchildren, you might find there were more than sixteen hundred shares and that one cousin had four hundred or more, while another might have only fifteen or twenty because he came of a more fruitful line with several sons in each generation.

When the maps and the record were finished, they must be available in the village for anyone to read; all the battalions knew the dates and soldiers were given special leave to come home to look at the maps and record. Anyone could lodge an objection and when all these were settled, the papers were 'attested' by the Assistant Record Officer. For the next forty years, that system held good and to change it would have been as difficult as upsetting the finding of a judge and jury.

The boundary disputes were the most difficult and the most interesting. There was almost always an appeal to me from the decision of the

Assistant Record Officer and often an appeal from mine to Ibbotson. By the time they had got so far as that, the honour of the village was involved; it was no longer a matter just of that one scrubby little ridge between the two tributary becks that were claimed as the original Pebbly Brook of 1817. It was like the Cup Final, like the last charge at Waterloo. Very soon I decided that when a boundary was in question I must *always* see the place and write down what I found while it was fresh in the mind. And what a wealth of information emerged! If it had not been for a boundary dispute, I should never have known that near every village there is a glen or corrie – the cup round one little streamlet – haunted by the ghosts of dead children. Grown people are burned when they die; children – esteemed perhaps 'too tender a morsel for the fire' – are buried. And between that sepulchral glen and the inhabited village, the apprehensive parents plant a thick hedge of thorns, so that the spirits of the children shall not follow them wailing home. Guilt, remorse, sorrow – these as well as fear seemed to me expressed in that hedge of thorns. By chance an example of just those emotions, expressed in much the same way, turned up in my reading at just that moment. Eskimos, I read, used to build the last snow house for a person too old to walk any longer with the sledges; they would go away, leaving the failing old man alive, breathing slowly and more slowly, alone in the icy dark. But before they went, they would build a wall of snow across their tracks to deflect his reproachful ghost.

Whether I was going to spend the day with the survey parties or whether we were moving camp, we would be out of the tents by eight o'clock. The light would be fresh and sparkling, glistening in sharp points among the pines, reflected from wet rock or tumbling stream in a thousand tiny glints, but a bluish smoke would be rising from the villages and often there would be a light mist in the next valley bottom, marking the line of a ridge so that it stood out dark and strongly drawn against the faint opacity beyond. Or we would climb in shade through forest on some western slope, and turn a corner as the path reached a shoulder, bursting out into sunshine – and there before us the lovely fluted peak of a great snow mountain, faint blue and silver edged with fire, Nilkanta or Dunagiri. In spring the buds of the rough contorted oak trees would be bursting, pink edged, from little bundles of pale yellow; or the path might lie through high forest and on the northern slope you might find pale blue primroses. Mary would utter little cries of joy at the sight of a flower not found before or when a turn in the path disclosed some new opening between the dark forested slopes. And almost everywhere the blanket-clad figures would scramble to their feet as we drew near and the cry would go up: 'Come and see my field!'

We used to have a good breakfast before we started – porridge made from wheat, almost unground, like frumenty, and eggs; then we could last till evening if there was no time for sandwiches. We were so fit that we hardly felt hunger till we saw food and then were ravenous. At night we ate mutton; we bought a sheep every fourth day and it was killed in the camp by beheading. We had mixed grill the first night, stewed mutton the second, roast leg of mutton the third and roast saddle of mutton the fourth. On our first journey Mary came to me with tears in her eyes: 'They've brought me a sheep and if I say it's all right they will take the poor thing away and kill it!' But to that aspect of reality she became accustomed. A sheep cost two rupees in the higher part of the district (then about three shillings or fifty cents) but three rupees nearer the plains. It fed the clerks and messengers and servants as well as us.

There were two clerks as a rule, four messengers, the cook and two or three other personal servants from the plains, the syce for the Tibetan pony which Mary rode uphill, and various local officials, the *patwari* and his immediate supervisor. It was reckoned that forty-five porters could move our camp, but this number might vary. One mule would carry a little more than two porters and cost the same, so we would usually have ten mules instead of twenty porters for some sections of the journey. But there would be bridges that mules could not cross and paths too steep and narrow and then we would switch back to porters. There were porters from Nepal who carried heavier loads than Garhwalis but were slower. The whole expedition was organized by a Superintendent from the Government Transport Agency; it was an established convention that he was always given the head of our sheep.

One of my predecessors had been accompanied in camp by small children, and he took along goats to supply them with approved milk. I do not think he moved as often as we did and he certainly did not go into such inaccessible villages. The children must have taken up most of his wife's time. In memory, it seems as though for us almost every day was a marching day and on such days Mary walked with me, except on very long ascents, and would never have time to put up her easel. But when I was looking at survey parties, she would be sketching. In camp, there was not much she could do for the women of Garhwal unless they came to us for medicine; they were more shy and backward even than the women of villages in the plains. We were firmly back in the Victorian era when a wife was utterly involved in her husband's work and I find it hard to imagine how I should have lived this life without Mary's company.

When we reached the camping place, there would always be a gathering of people with requests, petitions, disputes. The *patwari* would be there and sometimes we could settle something on the spot, as I always longed to do. Sometimes we could arrange to visit 'the spot' and settle it next day. But often the difficulty of 'two ears' prevented it. Meanwhile Mary would be busy with the first-aid box. Sometimes a medical crisis would be dramatic. Once one of the porters had a swelling; one side of his belly was inflated to the size of a football and it had happened only that day. It was clear something must be done quickly; I gave him a brass tumbler containing three fingers of castor oil and three fingers of proof rum. He drank it all. Two hours later they came to tell me it had worked vigorously; the swelling was gone; he was weak but had recovered; I had saved his life. When I next saw a doctor, I was told my treatment was a gamble, kill or cure, even chances. I had been lucky – but something had had to be done.

Once when we were on the pilgrim route in May – down at about three thousand feet, in the valley of the Ganges, stifling between the high hills at midday – we started at four in the morning to get our march done before the heat. Nothing would persuade the camp staff to eat before starting, as we did; after twelve miles on a rough path in that heat, one of the minor officials who was with us was exhausted and in his hunger he ate raw some leaves of a wild plant often cooked and eaten as spinach. Within fifteen or twenty minutes he was sinking into a coma and his hands and feet were turning cold. They rushed to us; hastily we thumbed through the first-aid book and diagnosed narcotic poisoning. We made him drink salt and water, hot tea and I think castor oil as well; we slapped his hands and feet; we dragged him upright and knocked him about till he took a few steps; we kept him moving, in spite of his piteous pleading and that of all his friends. They begged us to stop being so brutal and let him lie down. In the end we saved him; he thanked us next day and was sure he would have died – but again, what luck! So hasty and ignorant a diagnosis!

And I remember a woman who had somehow tipped a boiling pot over her leg. The burn had suppurated and from thigh to ankle there was a thick crust of stiff yellowish jelly. We cleaned it a little but there was not much we could do. She would not go to hospital; hospital was a place where people died. I put her under arrest and told the *patwari* to take her to hospital. I had no right, but they often told me I was a king in Garhwal and it is no use being a king if you do not sometimes break the law.

But as a rule our medical practice was fairly humdrum – castor-oil, aspirin, tannofax, quinine, plaster and cough-drops. By the time our surgery was over, the stars would be coming out and sometimes there would be a touch of frost. Perhaps that peak we had seen in the morning against the east would now hang above our heads, a shadowy mysterious bulk, faintly grey, but the highest point still touched with rosy pink. Then that too would fade. I would call for my bath; in the back of our sleeping tent was a tiny bathroom, not big enough to stand in. I would hear the clang-clang of the tin tub being pushed in through the back of the tent and the sound of pouring water. It had been heated on a wood fire in a five-gallon kerosene oil tin and was nearly boiling; I must rush to get my clothes off and – pimple skinned and trembling – creep into the bathroom and add cold till the water was just bearable; it got cold very quickly. The water and the cans smelt of wood-smoke and the whole cramped pocket of canvas smelt of damp straw. There was no lingering; it was a matter of washing off the sweat of the day and then huddling on all the jerseys you had, thick knitted stockings and long felt boots up to the knees over the trousers. And then, glowing from scalding water and freezing air, settling down to deal with the files sent from Pauri by the two head clerks, one for the district and one for the settlement. But sometimes the fatigue of the body was too much for the brain and the words of some carefully drafted instruction from the Government had no meaning; there was nothing for it but to give way to delicious languor, eat our mutton and crawl into the sleeping-bags.

3 Politics and the Road

It was so full a life that I did not often stop to think. Today, if I am questioned by someone under thirty, brought up with a different set of prejudices and assumptions, I will agree at once that I was highly 'paternalist', a word he does not much like. But I am not ashamed of that. Take the woman with the putrefying leg. She would not go to hospital and her leg was beyond any help we could give. If I had sat and argued for three days, I should not have persuaded her – and many other things would have been left undone. In that district and at that time, paternalism was what was needed. Indeed, the Garhwalis would have preferred it if I had given them a more directly personal rule than I did, disregarding Lucknow and its cautious prohibitions. It was the stage the district had reached and it suited the stage I had reached. Sometimes, as I sweated up some steep hillside, I would indulge in childish fantasy and picture a Garhwal that was independent – with myself, need it be said, as Raja. At Lucknow, they never *could* understand how different everything was with us! But we should have had to find a gold mine.

But did you not perceive – my youthful questioner might go on to ask – that you liked these people so much because they were obedient to you and useful for your imperial purposes? To that the answer must be

below Mary with Sundari Devi, who was given this name by the Garhwali officers of the regiment at the party after her christening.

above 'Playing like two children . . .': it was when we had been in the district about a year that an official of the United Provinces Civil Service – a Rajput with landed property near Delhi – told me that when Mary and I first arrived this had been the description of us passed through the district by word of mouth.

The view from our drawing-room window at Pauri. But we were not there very often.

A survey party in the field making maps. With the simplest instruments, they achieved astonishingly accurate results, mapping the fields to a scale of 32″ to the mile.

A King's Indian Orderly Officer. The finished product, shining with health and confidence. But old soldiers sometimes became very discouraged by the jealousy and conservatism of the villagers.

A villager from Upper Garhwal. Such men often believed they would die if they went to the plains in summer but in fact they stood the heat very well when trained as soldiers.

Tea-party for old soldiers. We gave parties for old soldiers both at Pauri and Chamoli. One was to commemorate the fiftieth anniversary of the formation of the Royal Garhwal Rifles as a separate regiment, distinct from the Gurkhas. In the top picture in the centre, the man with his cap at a rakish angle is Lieutenant and Subedar-Major Makar Singh Kunwar, who commanded a platoon at Neuve Chapelle in 1915.

above left Mary with garlands. Garlands might be a problem when one was walking twenty miles a day; it seemed impolite to tear them off at once. On the route followed by pilgrims from the plains on their way to Badrinath, there would be pipal trees, which have some degree of sanctity, and it seemed proper to hang them in a pipal tree. But when there were no pipal trees?

above right Amateur barber.

below Reconciliation: the opening of the motor road, March 1939. The Premier of the UP Pandit Govind Ballabhe Pant is in the middle, the Chairman of the District Board, Thakur Harendra Singh Rawat, on his right and P.M. on his left. The Chairman does not look wholly reconciled and I do not think he was.

an emphatic no. I thought I liked them because they were simple and brave and had a sense of humour. I certainly enjoyed responsibility and power. I liked being in a position where I was sometimes able to help people and I was flattered when they implied that they knew I wanted to help them. I would certainly have indignantly repudiated any idea that I was the unconscious instrument of some impersonal force whose object was economic exploitation, but I would have agreed that in a general sense I had been trained for just the kind of leadership I was exercising and enjoying so much. I was the product of an imperial society.

Looking back, nearly forty years later, it does seem to me that I was trying to have it both ways. I did up to a point identify myself with the people of the district – but it could be only up to a point. I did not live in the cottages through whose thatch the blue smoke could be seen percolating in the early morning nor labour to repair the terrace walls when six inches of rain washed down stones and soil together. Nor did I mean to stay there for ever. But it was not, for example, out of policy that I wanted to show that I felt some understanding of Hinduism.

When you have toiled up three or four thousand feet to a place where the path crosses a ridge and begins to descend – plunging perhaps from scorched grass, bare rocks and brilliant sun on the south side to shade and trees and water and damp ferny smells on the north – you will often find a tiny grotto built of unshaped stones with a roughly carved wooden figure inside and perhaps some minute offering, a pinch of rice or a few nuts or a rag tied to a bush. Or, on one of the lower peaks, you might find a wooden temple with a sharp curved roof. From all over India pilgrims came to the snow hills which are the home of gods and where the Ganges rises. A peak, a pass, the meeting-place of two streams, all such places are holy. Since something in me responds to this symbolic recognition of the forces of nature, I bathed with the pilgrims at Kedarnath at over eleven thousand feet, in water straight from the great bowl of glacier and snow that surrounds the temple. It was like fire. I dipped myself more deeply than the pilgrims – but then waiting for me were warm clothes, hot tea and a charcoal brazier. This was in a bungalow that was being prepared for the visit of a Maharani of the ruling house of Nepal. I had been put there for the sake of grandeur, but it was a good deal less comfortable than our tents as it was still half finished, the windows unglazed and the walls lined with fresh cowdung; light a fire in any fireplace and smoke poured into every room.

The Garhwalis knew that I thought of them as friends. For five years after I left the district, there would be one or two waiting by the gate in Delhi every morning asking for help of some kind. They felt they had been neglected by 'the Government'. It was hard for them to understand this new business of politics which was coming into their lives. They knew there was a legislative council in Lucknow to which they could send two representatives but they did not yet entirely grasp that in 1937 this body would provide a Government for the UP. They thought of their representatives as spokesmen who would express their grievances to an undefined, everlasting, remote 'Government'. They did not want a spokesman who was a pensioner or one whom they thought a toady but someone who would not hesitate to speak up. They elected two Congressmen.

Even after the election few of them understood. In Lower Garhwal, the defeated candidate was a barrister, the only barrister we had in the district, a man who had eaten his dinners at Lincoln's Inn. He came to me one morning and said at once:

'I hear the Government is very displeased with the Cabinet.'

'What *do* you mean, Barrister Sahib?' I asked. 'The Cabinet *is* the Government. Or do you mean the Government of India?'

'No, no,' he replied. 'Who cares for the Government of India?'

'Can you mean His Majesty's Government in London?' I asked.

But that was not what he meant either. He fell back on the Indian word *sarkar* – which literally means 'The Head of the Work' and was often used as a term of address to me; but I think that what he really meant was an abiding British presence – the Governor, the Viceroy and the King all rolled into one. There was no doubt that those who voted for the Congress meant to express dissatisfaction and felt they were being daring – but very few pictured a possibility that the British presence might end.

Politics disclosed many curious attitudes. Just before the election, one of my subordinates came to me; he was the head of the Government Transport Agency which arranged for the supply of mules and porters. He began confidently:

'Sir, we all want the Government to win the election.'

'Oh, no, we don't,' I said. 'I am a civil servant and as far as I am concerned, there is an election between two candidates in which I am impartial.'

'But you don't want the Congress to win!' he said, as though I had said the earth was flat. We went on like this for some time. He clearly thought I was being tiresome and I decided to help him.

'Let us put it that you – very naturally – want your uncle to beat the Congress,' I said. His uncle was a pensioner of the Forest Department who had been awarded the title of Rai Sahib and would certainly not have expressed the grievances of the district. His nephew was happy to accept this starting-point and went on to explain that the shareholders of a certain large village, very influential in the neighbourhood because of marriages and clan connexions, had decided to vote as one man for one candidate and put all they had behind him. But they had not decided which candidate it should be. It was a matter of bargaining and they had entrusted one man with the delicate negotiations. That man was employed in the Government Transport Agency and one of his conditions was that he should be recommended for promotion.

'I am bound to help my uncle and so I have to recommend this man to you, sir, for promotion, and this I have done,' he concluded. 'But, sir, I am in duty bound to tell you privately that I do not think he is fit for it.'

I told him I quite understood and he went away happy. If I had been a Moral Rearmament man I should not have heard the story. But who was I to scold him? It seemed to me that on the whole we in Garhwal conducted our election in a more civilized way than the free and independent voters of Eatanswill in England a hundred years earlier.

Some of the consequences of the election were odd too. Before the election, the Congress had raised an outcry against the revision of maps. It had been a feeble and ill-informed agitation and had never come to much. After the election they realized that the maps were valued by the villagers, so they changed their song – like a cuckoo at the end of June – and said the principle was sound but great injustices were being committed. I suggested that someone should come and see how the work was carried out and how it was checked. The Premier of the UP, Pandit Govind Ballabh Pant, sent instructions to the Captain of Congress Volunteers to come and inspect our work. The Congress Volunteers – of whom there were about twenty in Garhwal – though supposed to be a peaceful body, had a vaguely military style. Their Captain wore riding breeches and a khaki shirt and carried a cane. He was a young man of about twenty-three who had failed to pass examinations or get a job. He had hung about without employment round our one railway station until this chance came along. I cannot pretend that I was pleased that he should inspect our work but for me it was easy to make light of it. It was much more difficult for the Assistant Record Officer, Kundan Singh Mall, whose work he came to inspect. Kundan Singh had passed the examinations the Congress Captain had failed; he had won a clerkship against stiff opposition and had been confidential clerk and stenographer to Ibbotson who had promoted him to executive rank. He had done outstandingly well and was proud of it. He came from Upper Garhwal. He was very short but strongly built, highly intelligent, with a quick alert look that reminded me of a terrier who is sure you are just going to take him for a walk. Ibbotson had trusted him and so had I; his judgments in boundary disputes were most painstaking and capable and his survey parties were accurate and quick. He had worked hard and had every reason to think he was on the way to further promotion. It is easy to imagine his feelings at being inspected by this swaggering, useless cornerboy, ten years his junior.

We proceeded much as usual. I drew two or three lines and measured them; we questioned the shareholders about the boundaries of plots. The Captain did not seem to think he needed instruction; he was too proud to ask questions and merely stood about. Then we moved to a level place to check the register of shares. The villagers had placed a table there, with two chairs, one for me and one for Kundan Singh. I saw Kundan Singh make a lightning appraisal of the implications; he sat down on the ground with the register in his hands, just the right distance from the two places of honour. The Captain flung himself into one chair, lounging carelessly with one arm over the back. The villagers of course crowded round Kundan Singh to make sure the shares were right; they sat round him in a circle on the ground. I sat for a minute or two on the other chair – not to appear rude; then I moved closer to take part in the questioning, sitting on a rock by Kundan Singh. The Captain was left in lonely grandeur, while we got on with the job. I suppose I should have laid myself out patiently to explain things, but the combination of arrogance and ignorance was hard to bear. I was in touch for a long time with Kundan Singh; his career was one of the tragedies of independence. He had been far too single-minded to win any further promotion.

It was also hard to explain politics to such a man as Makru – Honorary Lieutenant and Subedar-Major Makar Singh Kunwar – who had led a platoon at Neuve Chapelle, when the Germans had been driven out of their trenches and the Garhwal Brigade had reached their objective. It had seemed for a while as though we had really broken the line but there had been no one to exploit their success. What was it all about? he asked me. Why had we made a Government of these 'bad characters' of the Congress? To him they were simply rascals, enemies of the King, on a par with robbers or gangsters. I told him there had been a Labour Government in England. The Labour Party had learnt a lot in office; it was a good way of dealing with critics. They found they really had to do things much as they had been done before. He shook his head: 'I don't like it,' he said; 'I don't like it.' I had not the heart to say more and I still do not know what else I could have said to that simple courageous old man.

For me too the right course was not always easy. Before the election, the two principal planks in the Congress platform had been a motor road to the top of the district and reduced taxation. Once in office of course they perceived the difficulties. To make a motorable road in country like

Garhwal would be extremely expensive. After much delay they announced that they would not build a road to the standard of the Public Works Department but would make an annual grant to the District Board towards the cost of a cheaper road. The amount proposed was ludicrous; it would take two years of the grant to pay the fee for making the estimate; it would take fifty years for the road to reach even Pauri. The District Board announced that they would declare civil disobedience against the Congress Government.

The Premier asked my advice. I told him his party had made promises and they really ought to make a better offer. Yes, he said, that was probably right, but the District Board had been rebellious and must submit; they must ask permission to see him; they must come to Lucknow and plead for a better offer. I said I would ask them to meet me and advise them accordingly but he said I must take no open initiative. I must let my advice seep through to them unofficially. Those instructions I had to disobey. Some members of the District Board took a week to reach Pauri – at that time of year, walking through snow – and I had to see them all. I made my initiative personal. I invited them to come to Pauri to see me, not as District Officer but as a friend, to talk over the difficulty we were in. They came – and I went to *their* office to meet *them*. I told them I was trying to find a way to get them what they wanted; my advice – and I emphasized that it was purely personal – was to ask to see the Premier; if they did, I thought they might be given something; they had waved a formidable weapon, because the whole of India would laugh if someone declared civil disobedience against a Congress Government. Very well, they said, they were ready to go, but only if the Premier made the first move and invited them. After all, it was he who had been in the wrong. It was an impasse. I sent a cipher telegram to the Premier saying that they had agreed to come and I asked him to suggest a date, and would he make sure to reply in cipher? He gave me a date and I told them he had invited them. Each side went to the meeting believing that the other had made the first move. The District Board came back as though they had won the Cup Final. The irony was that I could not help feeling that a motor road would prove a snake in the garden of Eden. But they believed it would solve all their problems – just as many people thought independence would solve the problems of India. My efforts to get the Garhwalis a road seem to me now symbolic of much effort in India.

To write as much as I should like about Garhwal would spoil the plan of this book. The episode of the road and the District Board I have to tell – though I have told it before – because it is so essential a part of the political scene and of my involvement. Many of the most dramatic stories that I heard were embodied in a novel, *The Wild Sweet Witch*, published in 1946. I heard most of them from Kalyan Singh who, though not the senior of my orderlies, was always the leader. He was a capable, practical man; Mary noticed that he was curiously like a sailor in his movements as he set about pitching the tents; he had a blunt round face like a Gurkha. He was not very articulate and had to be cross-questioned.

'It was that house,' he said once, at Rudraprayag, and I had to drag out of him, sentence by sentence, that it was on the upper-floor veranda of 'that house' that the famous man-eating panther of Rudraprayag had attacked a man. And it was from that tree, after killing over four hundred people, that the panther had at last been shot by Jim Corbett, who wrote a whole book about it. And it was Kalyan Singh who told me how the people of the district thought there was a man who turned into a panther at night and how, to prove his innocence, one of my predecessors put that man under arrest and had him watched at night till the panther killed again. And he told me how five brothers killed a bear with sticks alone, and in their triumph thought bears were easy and tried again but met disaster. But his stories came as bird-lime comes from frieze; only once do I remember Kalyan Singh being fluent. That was just before sunset one evening in the belt of jungle at the foot of the mountains, when a tiger followed him for half a mile, keeping just behind him on a ridge above the path, till he was quite near the camp. Kalyan Singh had not dared to hurry. He rushed straight to my tent to tell me about it and that time the words tumbled out.

Tigers are rare now and it is thought a crime to have shot one – but it was not so then. Everyone rejoiced if you shot a tiger or a panther. Panthers were a pest throughout the district, very bold and cunning, taking sheep, goats, dogs, ponies, cows and sometimes, like the famous man-eater, killing people, usually women coming home from cutting grass. Tigers usually kept to the belt of thick jungle that bordered the plains; outside that, anyone could shoot a tiger if he had a heavy rifle, but inside that belt of 'reserved' jungle they were protected; you had to have a permit and there were limits on the number you might shoot. For four months of the year and for half of every month shooting was forbidden and shooting of any species of animal would be forbidden if it became scarce. This was meant to preserve a balance between tigers and deer; a tiger will kill a hundred deer in a year; a tigress with big cubs will kill every night. If there were too many tigers they would come out of the forest and take the villagers' cattle; if there were too many deer, they would destroy the villagers' crops. And yet most Englishmen felt that it would be a sad day if there were neither. So we tried to keep a balance. The Premier, in passing as it were, once reproached me with being too careful to preserve wild life.

One tiger will for me always be *the* tiger. We were in the thick belt of tiger jungle – tall trees and open glades and patches of thicker cover – moving from one camp to another. Instead of walking, as we did in the hills, we rode on Pyari, an exceptionally well-trained she-elephant who was really meant for the inspection during the rains of a Government estate at the foot of the hills. Nisar, her driver, was a most accomplished tracker and a great character, a man who at an earlier period might have carved out a kingdom for himself like Haidar Ali of Mysore. Suddenly Pyari let out a sort of muted hoot, a breach of discipline for which she at once received a crack on the skull from the heavy iron ankus. There was a tiger near us. There were also a great many deer. Nisar made a long detour round the deer; sitting on the elephant's neck, he moved through the jungle like a man walking on stilts, the elephant's forelegs moving like his legs to the sway of his body, each step controlled, unbelievably quiet. We went round the main body of the deer but they were everywhere. A fawn bolted from a couch in the grass almost at our feet and Pyari flinched, as even the best elephant will at anything small underfoot. Suddenly the long grass ahead stirred and we saw the ridge of a great striped back, showing for a moment like the back of a dolphin, going away in a swirl of tall dusty stalks. The jungle fowl clattered into life with squawks of horror; the grey monkeys leaned down and shouted their fear and hate; the deer with their silvery calls spirted in every direction. We went a few steps forward and there lay the deer which he had just killed, the back broken, the neck twisted back, the body torn apart.

'He must be very hungry to kill at midday,' said Nisar. 'He will come back soon.' So we came back too. They put me in a tree – a very unsatisfactory tree, much too slender, a tree which rustled at every movement and was full of ants into the bargain. I knew I should have to keep perfectly still and might have to wait some time so I determined to make myself as comfortable as I could and began to experiment with various positions, while Kalyan Singh and Nisar and the elephant were still moving away and purposely making a good deal of noise. I took up a trial position but it was thoroughly uncomfortable and I could not use the rifle. At that moment, before I could move, the tiger roared. It was unbelievably close, unbelievably loud. I froze. I dared not complete my settling down. The outraged cries of jungle fowl and monkeys were growing closer – and then I saw him, enormous in the golden light of evening, striding purposefully towards his quarry. He prowled round it, his great paws reaching out left and right, circling his kill; he was directly beneath me, only a few feet away. He came on to the kill and began to lick it and I could see his great amber eyes, but the rifle was pointing at heaven and there was a branch in the way. I could not move without making a hideous noise.

He escaped – but he had made me feel part of the processes of nature. I had heard the fear and anger of the other creatures of the jungle, who in their turn preyed on life, as all life does. I had wanted to kill him; the tiger was a killer – an immensely powerful killing machine – and there would be a kind of justice in killing him. But Nisar and Kalyan Singh did not feel any need for such thoughts; they were simply and unashamedly glad when a tiger was shot.

My happiest memory of Nisar was one cold morning in December. We had evolved in that part of India a method of dealing with a tiger which involved a good deal of skill, which I was at that stage still learning. The essence was to locate the tiger exactly, in a place previously chosen, a thick piece of cover where he would lie by day and from which he could be guided gently along a route also previously chosen. It needed careful consideration of the ground and understanding of a tiger's habits. That morning we had climbed on Pyari when she was still only a dark shape against the stars; you could smell her before you could see her. We were trying to find places where a bait might be tied and a tiger would lie. Every time I found a spot that I thought would do, Nisar would shake his head. That place would be all right in March, when the sun was getting hot, but for this time of year it was the wrong kind of grass.

I became a little petulant when this had happened several times; I thought Nisar was being fussy about his kinds of grass. About nine o'clock, I found once again the perfect place for a tiger to lie up; again Nisar insisted that it wouldn't do and I uttered some sound of irritation. I was cold and cramped and had been a long time on that elephant. I climbed down and told Nisar to go on; I would step into the grass and follow him. I took two paces into that grass, which was about eight feet high – and I was soaked, as though I had been in a shower bath. Every stalk was loaded with ice-cold dew. I looked up at Nisar, still on his elephant. He was shaking with laughter. 'Now you understand,' he said, 'why a tiger won't lie in that kind of grass at this time of year.'

Nisar had not enough to do in April, May and June, and it was rumoured that, instead of soaking in opium, as most mahawats do at that time of year, he kept his wits in good shape by organizing petty burglary over the area near our railway station, where the elephant was stabled – but he was much too cunning to be caught. It was nonetheless a scandal and Ibbotson, when he was District Officer, decided that, in spite of his quite extraordinary skill as a tracker, Nisar must be dismissed. A new mahawat was installed, but after a week he reported sadly that he had lost the elephant. He could not think where it could be. Ibbotson sent for Nisar. Did he think he could find the elephant? Well, he did know its habits. If he could find it, it would be just that he should be reinstated, said Ibbotson thoughtfully – but the petty burglary must stop. Nisar admitted nothing and promised nothing but he did find the elephant and the burglary stopped. It started again in my time; I told Nisar that story – gazing at the sky – and again he admitted nothing but again the burglary stopped. He was an expert fisherman with rod and line and also kept the best fighting quails for miles.

I wish I could say more of Garhwal. I despair of conveying the flavour of a life in which everything depended on the length of a day's march, in which Mary never wore a skirt nor I a tie, in which for months on end we were out of doors all day, moving from snow to tropical heat and back again, never seeing another European. I should like to write of the house at Pauri where we sometimes spent two or three months, a house set in its own private forest with a vista cut through the pines direct to the great square snowy block of Chaukamba thirty miles away, a house round which panthers prowled at night and where in winter you could hear the crack of boughs breaking beneath the weight of snow, a house with a billiard room complete with billiard table, brought up, it was said, by a hundred porters in 1896 – but with no safe. (I was looking once for the key of the confidential cupboard when Kalyan Singh kindly pointed out that I need not bother; all you had to do was to move it away from the wall – there was no back to it.) I should also like to say something of the hermit I found naked on the Satopanth glacier, fifteen thousand feet above sea level; and I should like to tell how Duncan's bulls proved unaccountably shy with the little mountain cows; how we tried to persuade people to grow fruit – but they wouldn't because they hadn't enough land for grain; but how we did make some progress over the use of common land. Near the plains, the villagers were eager for help in that and it was quite easy to persuade them to agree that they should set aside an area for the growth of young trees, another for this year's thatching grass, another for this year's grazing.

But what could be done for the Doms, the aboriginal outcasts, untouchable serfs who lived down the hill outside the village? They had been conquered two thousand years ago and ever since they had been serfs – not legally, but by custom. It was a matter, it seemed to me, for education, for public opinion, certainly not for me. It was a job for a national Government, I felt. Just before I left, the Congress tried to force the issue, proclaiming the right of a Dom bridegroom to ride on a horse to his wedding. But it provoked minor riots; the opposition was so fierce that they gave it up.

Once again I had to move on – with grief and a sense of the inevitable. I had hoped to lead this gipsy life in Garhwal for five years till the settlement was finished, but the world was moving towards war and in the summer of 1939 I was nominated by the Commander-in-Chief to a year at the Imperial Defence College in London. I could not refuse and we booked air passages for October, when we hoped our expected baby would be a month old. But, on 1 September 1939 two days before our daughter was due, a telegram told us the IDC course was cancelled and I was summoned to Delhi to the Defence Co-ordination Department.

It was not a final good-bye to the mountains but I would never again be a part of them as I had been in Garhwal. One mountain memory belongs here – not in time, for I am not quite sure when it took place, but because it may stand for many others less intense. It was a clear day, an hour or two before sunset, and I was alone, at a height of between nine and ten thousand feet, gazing through thirty or forty miles of sun-drenched space to a group of fluted icy peaks, scarped and chiselled, the carving of the eastern slopes and gullies already marked by shadow, faint blue against the bright silver. The certainty of something infinitely greater than myself was never far away in the mountains; at that moment it was overpowering. But could that something greater have anything to do with me? I felt like Blake looking at the tiger. Could He who made the lamb make thee? What had those remote and terrible peaks to do with human warmth and love and the toil of these simple people in their narrow stony terraces? My eye fell to a blade of grass, to the tip of which hung a drop of dew, made up, I knew, of molecules and atoms like solar systems. That too – the infinity of tiny cells that make up the body, no less frightening than the silence of infinite space and the vastness of the mountains – that too must in the end be at one with the human spirit that could comprehend and suffer. But how? I knew only that I was overwhelmed.

I did not go on puzzling about it, there was too much to do. But the memory was one of the unassailable facts of experience.

Part Three

WAR AND
THE AFTERMATH

IX

PLANNING FOR VICTORY

1 Blindness

France was falling. Each telegram was more dreadful than the last. The impregnable Maginot Line had been turned. The German tanks were climbing over piles of dead. The British army in France had been hunted to Dunkirk and had left its equipment behind. France had surrendered. There was a numb ache at the pit of the stomach, a numb refusal to believe; everything we had taken for granted was falling to bits – and there was so much we had taken for granted! But in Simla there was to be a Viceregal garden-party and the band would play soft music while tea and ices were consumed. It was confirmed by the Military Secretary to the Viceroy that the party was to go ahead as arranged. Morning coats and grey top hats would be worn and ladies in summer frocks and Ascot hats would be propelled along the Mall by sweating rickshaw coolies.

This was deliberate policy, the policy of the stiff upper lip. Lord Linlithgow had decided that we should show the natives of India that the imperial machine was still in being and the rulers of the Empire were confident of victory. He put it himself in more negative terms: 'I think there is probably a good deal of importance in retaining even in times of stress such as these a sufficient degree of public appearance to indicate that we have not retired into our shell and sunk into the depths of depression.' For the first Christmas of the war, a special train took the Viceroy's Bodyguard to Calcutta so that the Viceroy could drive on to the race-course in state with a sovereign's escort of lancers in scarlet coats. I do not know whether this impressed the people of Calcutta; among the British of whom I saw most, mainly staff officers at Army Headquarters, there was a strong feeling that it would have been better to give an impression of being stripped for action, of taking the war seriously. There is a certain magnificence about the stiff upper lip and it is undoubtedly preferable to panic; I was aware of admiration on the afternoon of the garden-party. But it can look very like a complacent indifference to reality.

My arrival in Simla ten months earlier had certainly been a shock.

In Garhwal it often took a week before the newspaper reached us. Runners would pant after us, moving twice as fast as we did, and then suddenly, when we had turned in a long circle, we would find a runner coming to meet us with news a week younger. We had learnt in that way of the abdication of Edward VIII, with none of the week's discussion that had prepared most people. It made world events strangely remote, and as for being 'in the know' – something that gave people in Delhi a glow of satisfaction – that was a sensation that we had altogether forgotten. I had continued to hope, quite irrationally, that somehow the threat of war would go away. When war did come, I had supposed, with equal naïveté, that everyone would boil into frenzied activity.

I arrived in Simla after travelling all night; I had left Mary waiting for the baby to be born and I had marched out of Lansdowne with the pipe band of the Royal Garhwal Rifles playing me good-bye. We expected at every minute to hear of a bombing attack on London and already Mahatma Gandhi was weeping at the thought of Westminster Abbey razed to the ground. I had gone straight to the office of the Department for Defence Co-ordination, where I found a Staff Captain – no one else.

He told me that for at least a year Delhi had been preparing the War Book. Everything that would have to be done to make a peaceful organization suddenly war-like had been considered by a variety of authorities and the results embodied by the Staff Captain in this tome. The Secretary of the Department and an Under Secretary had drafted the sheaf of Ordinances putting these decisions into effect. War was declared on Sunday morning 3 September 1939; this was Monday the 4th and the Ordinances had all been promulgated. The War Book was finished and in operation. The Secretary to Government – corresponding to the Permanent Under Secretary in England – might be expected in the office soon after midday. That was his usual time. Then why, I wondered, had I been sent for in such a hurry? The Staff Captain thought it was something to do with Manpower.

When at last the Secretary did appear, I found him a man of agreeable personality. He had gone up to Balliol just fifteen years before I had; he had a distinguished record as a classical scholar, and considerable personal charm; he was quite free from pomposity. But he valued his leisure more than anyone else I ever met in the Indian Civil Service. His province was Bengal and he had at an early stage chosen to leave the rough-and-tumble of the executive branch for the judicial, where hours are regular and life less hectic; he had served as a judge in Assam and with the Law Department of the Government of India. He was a brilliant draftsman and had cast the Ordinances required for defence into clear legal language which I never heard criticized. But while most able men –

in a position such as his, with the label 'Co-ordination of Defence' – would have sought power and influence, he was indomitably determined to avoid any such commitment. Traps might be laid, but no bait would tempt him. Once a conspiracy of generals was formed with the object of involving him more directly in that mysterious abstraction the War Effort – but he emerged unscathed, blandly unaware of his victory, and with his already nebulous responsibilities somewhat reduced. What he did find fascinating was taking clocks to pieces. But I had nothing to complain of; for me his habit of mind was convenient since he allowed me to go my own way about my own task.

There was a group of problems loosely called Manpower which had been of importance in the preparations for war in Britain but to which no one in India had had time to give much thought. Both the Adjutant-General and the Master-General of the Ordnance were concerned that someone should now take these matters in hand and, since my year at the Imperial Defence College had been cancelled, I had been suggested. As it might mean holding the balance between the defence services and industry, it had seemed best that I should not be in the Defence Department proper, under the Commander-in-Chief, and so I had been attached to this strange new department of Defence Co-ordination.

It did not take long to find out that one aspect of all this, though important in Britain, hardly raised problems in India – this was the distribution of skilled technical artisans. I was supplied with an immense list of trades I had never heard of, sandblasters and cupola men, men employed in the great steelworks of Tatanagar, welders and boilermakers and sub-divisions of their crafts, men who made the breech in guns and rifles accurate to a thousandth of a centimetre. In India the factories which made guns and rifles actually belonged to the Defence Department; their output was to be increased and so there could be no question of taking men from them. The steelworks was privately owned by Tata, but there too an immense expansion was clearly coming. Every factory that employed men of this kind would be engaged on war work. The defence services had to train young soldiers in the use of electronic equipment and in the maintenance of petrol engines but they would take them raw and start from scratch; there was no general competition for the kind of highly skilled men on my list. Every one of them was needed on the workbench where he was already.

The other matter was simpler, but there was a real clash of interests. There were many British firms in India which employed young Englishmen of good education, sometimes with university degrees, who were what were known to the army as good officer material. Many of these had joined territorial units in peace; tea-planters might belong to the

Assam Valley Light Horse and there was the Calcutta Light Horse for the great commercial and shipping and industrial firms of Calcutta. Many high-spirited young men were eager to be commissioned in the Indian Army – usually in the cavalry – and they had two advantages over any men of similar age who could be obtained from England; they had some knowledge of Hindustani and they were physically acclimatized. But the firms which employed them did not want to lose them and in most cases it seemed essential that the firm should continue to do business as usual. Most companies employed more men of this kind than they needed at a given moment, in order to permit leave to England; clearly leave would stop and so they could spare some of their people. A generous firm might agree to spare more than those who made up the leave reserve; they would keep places open and take men back after war service – but a firm which took that attitude ran risks; they knew they would get no fresh blood while the war lasted and middle-aged men cannot work beyond their strength indefinitely in such a climate as Calcutta. Also, they wanted to make sure the load was spread evenly; they did not want unfair competition from firms who took a more selfish view.

It seemed to me from the first essential that we should have conscription for Europeans in India. In the First World War, before there was conscription, officious ladies would sometimes present a white feather to a young man in civilian clothes. If a man was required to stay with his firm in the general interest, everyone should know that an independent authority had made the decision. Similarly, it should not rest with a firm to decide in its own case how many should be allowed to go. And if a man did join the armed forces, his right to return to his old firm should not depend on the firm's generosity.

Every argument seemed to lead the same way, provided only that the decision rested with a body that knew the circumstances of the different firms. Local bodies at the big commercial centres seemed to be the answer; they would approve the lists that each firm would draw up and settle any disputes between a firm and its employees or between two firms. The army would call up men from these lists as they needed them. I discussed my ideas with the small group of Europeans who represented commercial and industrial interests in the Assembly; there was no difficulty about getting their agreement nor that of the generals. I did receive a sharp public snub from a member of my own service, because I sent these agreed proposals simultaneously to all the civil departments which were in any way concerned and said I should assume they agreed if I had no answer in a week. This was high-handed and impatient, I was told; the proper thing was to let each in turn pore over the proposals, giving each in turn every opportunity to think of objections.

Objections however were not what I wanted – and as I was reading this rebuke the telephone rang and I heard the voice of the Master-General of the Ordnance, who said he was disgusted by these remarks and that he on the contrary wished to congratulate me personally on my breach of procedure. My critic became the Governor of two Provinces in succession and a fruitful Chairman of Royal Commissions; he was wise in his generation and I was not – but I am unrepentant.

It did not take long to decide what needed doing, nor to get the agreement of the people most concerned. It required more patience to get the arrangements put into legal language and made law, but even that was accomplished within about three months. I had not then quite worked myself out of a job; there was still a flow of 'volunteers' offering their services for 'war work'. We made lists and circulated them, but by March of 1940 the job was finished. The Deputy Secretary in the Defence Department proper was at that time Godfrey Hind, a Brigadier who had been an Assistant Secretary to the Chiefs of Staff Committee in London; he was suddenly appointed to command a brigade and I moved over to take his place. This was pleasing in several ways; I had relieved a soldier, I was certain of plenty to do, and the Defence Secretary – though I disagreed with him on a great deal – was temperamentally more congenial to work with than the urbane and charming amateur of clockwork.

Certainly, Charles Ogilvie was very different. He was warm, impulsive, emotional and inconsistent; his essentially affectionate nature was sharply at variance with his professed philosophy. He had the distinction of having scored a First in history both at Oxford and at Cambridge. After about twenty years' service he had decided to be a headmaster and had taken two years' leave in order to re-qualify as a Cambridge historian. But he had changed his mind, come back to India and had then done a course at the Imperial Defence College. He was an admirer of Hobbes, believing that anarchy was as terrible a disaster as could befall mankind and that one man was far more likely to act wisely than a number. To avoid anarchy, members of a civilized state surrendered their right of individual action to a ruler, who used force in the general interest. If political institutions did not correspond with the control of force, they were futile. He therefore expressed contempt for any international body which equated the vote of Nicaragua with that of the United States. He had no sympathy with any idea of helping India to independence and combined a low opinion of Indians in general – and particularly of politicians – with affection and admiration for those he knew. He had spent most of his time in the Punjab and, if I was a Garhwali, he was a Sikh. I once heard him answer a telephone call from a Sikh; it was a wrong number but the caller without hesitation began to talk in Punjabi and Charles kept up the conversation for some time. 'He thought I was a Sikh!' he said, chuckling with delight. For members of the Legislative Assembly his most frequently used term was 'apes'.

He was not, therefore, in my view, a good political adviser for Sir Robert Cassels, now Commander-in-Chief, a frontier soldier, a soldier's soldier, who took little interest in politics. More than one General remarked to me in an aside that Charles was really too much of a Blimp. But within Army Headquarters he was a force for peace. At that stage of the war, the Chief of the General Staff – who ranked first among the four Principal Staff Officers – was kindly and conscientious but somewhat indecisive while the Adjutant-General, who ranked second, was forceful and hard to move. Discussions of high policy often reached the conclusion that the real difficulty would be getting the Adjutant-General's approval, which could usually best be done by persuading him that the proposal was his own idea and that to bring it off would be a victory over the Chief of the General Staff. 'At A-G-management, I am *facile princeps*,' Charles Ogilvie told me with engaging triumph.

I was his Deputy and at that time I really *was* the Deputy. Later there was an Additional Secretary, two Joint Secretaries and I don't know how many Deputies – almost like Whitehall; but at that stage everything but the highest policy came through me. I conceived it my task to keep the Secretary as free as possible from everything that was not important. There were five Under Secretaries or Assistant Secretaries putting up their more difficult cases to me and I would deal with seventy or eighty of them a day; next morning I would go in to the Secretary as soon as he arrived, tell him what I had done on a few of the more important matters and ask for his decision on two or three more. He was decisive and quick and we used to get through a great deal.

Sadly, he could not allow himself to rest. He would come into the office on Saturday afternoon and Sunday morning when no one else was there, except his stenographer, a British soldier clerk. I once commiserated with this man, who said: ''T isn't as though he *did* anything; he just turns over the files and messes about.' Charles felt that for him to take time off would be a betrayal of trust. Sleep will revive the tired brain after long hours of arduous work, restoring the power to assimilate and arrange information. The power of decision appears to be controlled by some slightly different faculty and is eroded more gradually – but almost irrevocably. It is inseparably associated with confidence, and once it begins to go rest alone will hardly restore it. Charles not only grew tired; he realized that his Hobbesian politics were not those of Auchinleck, who became Commander-in-Chief in 1941. I saw that twin erosion gnaw month by month at a will that had once been prompt and resolute.

For my part, I was glad to have long hours and work to take home but I was determined to take time off if I could. The sections below sent up only the more important cases, so that the main work of the department was more interesting than it had been when I had been an Under Secretary. The Military Council, of which I had been Secretary in Sir Philip Chetwode's time, had died away because Sir Robert Cassels did not like discussing things with all his advisers together, but I had inherited the Chiefs of Staff Committee. This was meant to discuss matters such as Coast Defence, which affected air, land and sea forces. All three services came under the Commander-in-Chief but he sometimes needed advice which combined the experience of them all. In the early stages of the war, this body did not meet very often – but I felt it would develop.

Some of the work still induced in me that sensation which Mary summed up as 'swimming in treacle', an irritated frustration from which I had been quite free in Garhwal. Whereas in my first spell in Delhi, it had been the pettiness and triviality of interpreting regulations that had brought on these attacks, now it was the phoniness of the phoney war. This was worse, I should imagine, in India than in Britain. It had been agreed that the United Kingdom should pay for all India's defence expenditure in excess of what was spent in peace and the Military Finance Department had been appointed watch-dog to prevent our squandering the British tax-payer's money. In London it was held that India would not be seriously involved in this war. Our offers to raise additional troops for service outside India met chilling negatives. No more would be needed; it would be a European war. The staff officers of whom I saw most fumed at the senile inactivity of their elders. Indeed, I made a collection of the repressive sayings of our elders during those first eight months of the war. I put them in a file cover which I labelled 'Guilty Men'. I had no clear idea what I should do with them – but there they were, in the secret safe in my office, when the bolt struck and I was blinded. It was two and a half years before I was back in that office and by then of course someone more discreet than I had removed my seditious portfolio of quotations. I see now that it was unfair to hold the Financial Adviser and the Adjutant-General responsible for a view of the war dictated by Mr Chamberlain's Government, but they did appear to accept it with enthusiasm.

Things quickened after the fall of France. The burden of long hours mounted. Policy changed in England and we were expected to finish in a moment what we had been forbidden to begin. Auchinleck arrived and a staff officer said to me: 'Isn't it grand to have the impetus coming down to us instead of pushing up at an immovable weight?' I was, nonetheless, still determined to take time off when I could.

There are, I suppose, men who are self-sufficient, or at least who think they are. I am not. I need a hinge on which to swing, a still point at the centre of the dance. Indeed, to follow the more prosaic metaphor of the two, my gate swings the better when there are more hinges than one, certainties of human relationship and certainties of metaphysical conviction. I had never had a moment of doubt about the certainty of love and support on which I could count from my parents; another certainty had now been added:

> Where either I must live or bear no life,
> The fountain from the which my current runs,

and after the years of companionship in Garhwal it was unshakable. I had gone back to Lansdowne to fetch Mary and our daughter; she was christened Susan Janie and we had had a party afterwards for British and Garhwali officers, at which the Garhwalis had given her a second name in Hindi, Sundari Devi – the beautiful goddess – because she lay there so bright and shining in her cot. But pleasure in the birth of a first child is a human experience that has befallen others and I shall not dwell on it.

In the last days of 1941, the pace of disaster grew more rapid. Pearl Harbor was a shattering blow – but to an Englishman in India it brought at least a feeling that we saw a little more clearly where we stood. America was in the war at last and in the long run that must outweigh the addition of Japan on the German side. But it was going to be a long war and I strengthened my resolve to seize a day off when I could. In 1941, I decided to add Sunday to Christmas Day. We could go by the night train from Delhi to Hardwar and cross the Ganges in the early morning to join my successor in Garhwal – Raymond Vernède, with whom I had gone to Baalbek and Damascus nine years before. His camp was in the jungle at the south-western corner of the district.

For two days we were going to forget the news, the steady flow of paperwork in the office, the telephones, the locked boxes of files that followed me home in the evening. Our hearts leapt up as we crossed the river and found ourselves back in the jungle, in the sparkling early morning of December when the blood tingles and the nostrils snuff the sharp scent of bruised leaves and dust and dewy grass. It was as though time had turned back to the gipsy life we had enjoyed so carelessly and rapturously – but not quite, for we knew it hadn't; it was a heart-shaking pleasure, with a pang in the pit of the stomach, like dreaming of a happiness that you know is lost – like going out with your parents at half-term, almost sick with the expectation of bliss and the knowledge that it cannot last. But there they were, Kalyan Singh and Nisar and the elephant and the tents we knew so well, and our hosts, Raymond and Nancy, and other friends too.

It was a holiday. We were in the jungle. We followed the tradition of our kind and went shooting. There was no news of tiger so we pursued the little red jungle cock, the ancestor of all the domestic chickens in the world. He looks like a bantam and is very good to eat, like chicken with a flavour of pheasant, but he is inclined to fly low, skimming over the top of long tiger grass. It is therefore important to keep most strictly in line. I suppose I must have edged forward as we went through a patch of such tall grass. I remember a vivid flight of little green parrots which fled before us screaming – the last thing I saw for some time. Then I felt something like a violent punch on the nose and could see nothing but whirling scarlet circles. Mary was kneeling beside me and I was quite blind in both eyes.

I was afraid there might be another accident and I remember asking if everyone had unloaded – and I remember a distinct consciousness that this was putting on a rather impressive act, which I followed up by apologizing to Kalyan Singh for spoiling the shooting. But – the act over – the overwhelming thought in my mind was that before I recovered – and I was quite sure I should recover – I should have time to think things out. By this I meant that I should be able to reflect on that contrast, of which I wrote at the end of the last chapter, between the remote and terrible beauty of icy mountains and the warmth of human love and suffering. I was as sure that there was some means of reconciling all that these stood for as I was that sight would be restored. It is surprising that this should have been the dominant thought in my mind, because I had not been conscious of puzzling over it lately. It was Christmas morning but until a few moments before it happened my thoughts had been altogether set on the physical pleasures of sun and air and movement, on temporary release from slavery in the office. But it was of that reconciliation that I thought as they led me away in that whirling scarlet darkness.

2 The Worst Possible Case

I knew how lucky I was. In Europe and North Africa, in Burma and Malaya, there were men, horribly wounded, left lying where they fell, often without help till death came. Here was I, with Mary by my side, surrounded by friends who were attentive to my least wish. I was hardly at all in pain, though I shivered and could not get warm.

They took me back across the Ganges to Hardwar, where an Assistant Surgeon put some dressing on my eyes but was positive that there was nothing else to be done except get me to Delhi, which was a night's train journey. I was taken to the Hindu Rao's House, on the Ridge above Delhi, a famous defensive position in the Mutiny, at this time a nursing home. From there, I was taken at once to some other hospital for X-Rays and examination. I was wheeled along many passages, remembering the adventure stories of my boyhood, in which the hero, gagged and blind-folded, but already planning his escape, is carried along underground tunnels and counts the paces of his captors and their turns to left and right. Quite impossible, I concluded.

I was full of shot in face, chest and fingers – and still have to explain this if I have an X-ray of any kind. For a fraction of a second, as they tenderly pried open my right eye, I saw a light and part of the ceiling. I had known I would be all right; I was even more sure then. The left eye had a pellet through the retina and a hole in the surface of the eye had to be sewn up; the IMS eye specialist told me that Dr Sukh Deo was a more skilful surgeon than himself and would repair the puncture. I heard Dr Sukh Deo say to the orderly: 'Suy lao!' 'Bring a needle' – just as the dressmaker on the veranda might – and with incredible skill he drew the edges of the hole together. Not long afterwards I was back at the Hindu Rao, made warm at last with hot-water bottles, put to sleep.

When I came to myself, I thought again of those men wounded in the field and my own good fortune. There was really nothing to be done but lie still and have soothing drops put in my eyes; the shot would take care of itself. The specialist admitted, when I pressed him, that he did not expect I should ever see again with my left eye; the right eye had not actually been touched though some of the pellets had been very close and it was simply a matter of gradually restoring the surrounding muscles and tissues, which were so much inflamed that I could not open the eye. It would be a long wait.

There were only a few beds at the Hindu Rao and, as the place was barely half full, they allowed Mary to stay in the room next to mine. I could not have been more spoilt. Our little girls – two of them now – had a Swiss nurse and there were friends sharing the house with us. Mary went to see them every day but spent nearly all the day with me. I did not then know the history of the Mutiny as I do now; perhaps if I had I should have felt – as Thomas Hardy would certainly have expected to feel – something of the pain and fatigue endured by the men who held that post for over three months in the worst of the Indian heat, losing three men out of four in killed and wounded. It was the Sirmoor Regi-ment, later the Second Goorkhas, who bore the brunt of that defence, but it was not till much later that I learnt that many, if not most, of the men in that regiment at that time were Garhwalis. But no ghosts disturbed me, no consciousness of death and pain. On the contrary, I felt it was a miracle that shot should have passed so close to that right eye without doing lasting damage. I was at peace, hushed and calm, altogether at peace. More than thirty years later, the peace of early morning in the Hindu Rao's House comes back almost physically. No one disturbed me; I lay still and listened to the black partridges calling, very clear and loud, in the scrub that used then to run along that stony ridge; the room would be fresh with the early morning air of winter, sweet and cold as though distilled from spring water.

For much of the day Mary read to me. We read from all kinds of books, usually keeping a biography going – we went through the three volumes of Trevelyan on Garibaldi I remember – picking and choosing here and there, according to mood, from ghost stories, from children's stories about wolves and moose, from W. H. Hudson and from Cobbett's *Rural Rides*, from Carroll and Lear, from all kinds of poetry. We learnt by heart, so that we could say them in alternate lines, *Lepanto* and *The Hunting of the Snark* and other things I have forgotten. But also, and from the beginning, we read slowly and carefully through the four gospels. There I found what I had hoped to find.

Those words are carefully chosen. Modern man, and particularly a modern man in whose life words have played an important part, can pick holes in the gospels easily enough, but he must have hope – as a beginning – if he is to find there what he is looking for. I was looking for the reconciliation between two vivid aspects of reality – to me the two most vivid – human love, suffering and endurance and the frightening silence of eternity. The Christian answer to that is the Incarnation, the incredible statement that Almighty Power and Love became flesh. I had believed that once because I wanted to believe it; for some years now I had not been sure that I did. I had intermittently reflected on intellectual difficulties – as an excuse, I now think, for not accepting the implications of that incredible statement. I had picked holes. I had thought about the readiness of man to construct for himself the myth of a dying god – I knew something of Adonis, Osiris, Mithras – but that did not worry me unduly. To say that men have repeatedly shown a desire for something that resembles the Christian understanding of certain events is a good reason for meticulous examination, not only of those events but of the interpretation put upon them; it is no reason for rejecting either.

There was one aspect of the events presented in the gospels which I had picked as for me decisive. I do not now regard it in quite the same way; I suspect that for me at that time it was merely an attempt to find a reason for evasion, but since it seemed decisive at the time, it would be another evasion to omit it here. It was a difficulty about humility, a mark of all the great saints. The figure at the centre of the gospels had lived, had healed, had taught; his teaching, but far more his death and continued presence with his followers, had transformed the Western world. Was it possible that he had been a good man and humble and a saint until the last weeks of his life, when he had fallen into the sin of pride and supposed himself to be something more than a man? It is a view expressed with fastidious delicacy by George Moore in *The Brook Kerith*, a book I had read at Oxford.

Now as I lay blinded and Mary read those four short biographies through to me, I became entirely convinced that it was not so, that the power, the certainty of a dual nature, the understanding of the purpose of his life and death – and of all life and death – had been there throughout. It was impossible to think him a deluded saint; he was either not a saint at all or much more. This was truly the reconciliation of power with love that I had hoped to find. Since then, though I have often been weak, silly and self-indulgent in my conduct, I have never seriously doubted that there is unity between almighty purpose and the best part of the spirit of man. I used to think about this particularly in the afternoon when I was left alone and told to sleep. I lay still on my back, thinking of these things, and saw strange shapes and colours, mountainous compositions of angular forms, squares and triangles and prisms, in scarlet, brown, crimson and a reddish orange, shifting like the patterns in a kaleidoscope, but always building up again, with architectural precision, into shapes like the west front of a great cathedral or the gateway of some gigantic mosque, with steps leading up to it and dim vistas beyond. Then I would doze and wake to renewed peace.

It was perhaps six weeks or two months before I was first allowed to move about, though with spectacles of which the left eye was blacked out altogether, while the right had no light except through a tiny hole in the centre, so that the whole head must be turned, not the eye. I had to grope and feel for things and then turn my head towards them when they were located. The hole was enlarged week by week until the black spectacles were done with. There was a day of bliss when I saw flowers – little heartsease pansies and many-coloured nemesias – and could hardly believe that they could be so lovely. As things grew more normal, there was a new difficulty; strangers did not understand what was wrong with me. For a long time, I could not move with confidence and felt so different from before that it was hard not to be apologetic with anyone but close friends. People could not be expected to know that I felt like a grown person suddenly new born, as Lazarus might have felt when he came out of the tomb, like someone who has worn a mask all his life and has had it suddenly stripped from his face.

I cannot explain my confidence that I should recover. Once before I had been just as calmly certain that I should die. It was in Garhwal and we had been making plans to go into Tibet and perhaps close the correspondence with my neighbour there, the Daba Djong-pen, who was alleged to have tied up and threatened some traders from Garhwal. It was a slow correspondence, since I could never expect an answer in less than a year. But that expedition never came off. One day I had a pain in exactly the spot which the first-aid book allotted to appendicitis, and it would not go away. I had known two people who had died because of an appendix when in camp. So I knew I should die. For some time I said nothing and we went on as planned, moving away from help; I looked at the sky and the mountains all that day with a resigned poignancy, sure I should not see them often again. On the third day I woke to the conviction that this was madness; we should be going the other way. So we put everything into reverse and with every step we took towards a hospital I felt better. The pain, the nausea, the conviction of imminent death all passed away – and a part of me was *annoyed* – a trivial word, but it was a trivial feeling. No doubt the certainty of death was part of the physical condition – but it is hard to suppose that certainty of recovery can be part of blindness.

One anxiety that I had felt was that I might lose my Chiefs of Staff job. The expansion of that work which was so obviously coming might easily have taken place while I was blind. But it happened that it came just as I was ready to go back. I was told I must not attempt the amount of paperwork I had been doing before the accident and it was settled that I should give up my job as Deputy Secretary in the Defence Department but go on as Secretary to the Chiefs of Staff Committee, which would soon take up all my time. This was what I preferred; there would be far less reading and more listening, and I should be closer to the war.

In fact, it was an entirely new job. There had been no planning staff in India. Now there was to be a staff from all three services which would be responsible for thinking what offensive operations against the Japanese could be mounted from India and what defensive preparations should be made against what contingencies. There were to be three Directors of Plans – army, navy and air force – and the three, operating together, would have a joint responsibility to the Chiefs of Staff, who advised the Commander-in-Chief. But each of the three would keep his personal responsibility to his own service Commander. He must let him know what plans were being made and warn him if he thought there was danger of his forces being asked to do what was impossible. That double responsibility was an essential element in the British method of planning and is important in what followed.

My own responsibility – in a formal sense – was to the Chiefs of Staff Committee as a whole. I had to submit to them the plans prepared by the Joint Planning Staff, record their views and pass them, if they were approved, to the Commander-in-Chief; also, and increasingly, to draft telegrams to the Chiefs of Staff in London. In practice, it was essential to know as far as possible what the Directors of Plans and the Chiefs of Staff were thinking, where misunderstandings were taking place, where there were differences of approach and emphasis. Most of my usefulness, if I had any, lay in informal consultation. I had also a kind of residual responsibility through being more aware of the political and financial background than most of the people I worked with. Later, there were various highly secret inter-service organizations – the cloak-and-dagger folk – who dealt direct with the Chiefs of Staff; the Special Intelligence Service, the Special Operations Executive, and the Combined Operations Directorate brought their proposals to me for the Chiefs of Staff to approve.

The first task for me was to understand how plans were made. As far as I could, I sat in with the Joint Planners and watched them at work. Their secretary was my assistant. They would start with an outline – the bare bones of something that looked at first sight as though it might be possible. I remember sitting down, very soon after I began, to think of how we could get back into Burma. George Still was the army Director of Plans. I had known him when he was ADC to Lord Willingdon as Viceroy, in that first winter in Delhi nine years before; we had gone to the same parties and flirted with the same girls; we had both become engaged that winter and had been married a year later, by an odd chance, on the same day; he in Hanover Square and I in the west of Dorset. Now we sat round a table and gazed at maps and studied what Intelligence Reports we had, about where the Japanese were and about what trails there were through mountain and jungle into Burma.

Once the outline of a plan was formed, the details would have to be checked. The Planners would consult the Director of Staff Duties in the General Staff as to what forces were available; they would see the Quartermaster General about supplies and their movement; the air force must consider landing grounds and their maintenance – and here the Engineer-in-Chief came in; calculations must be made about the weather and the moon and, if it was on the coast, the tides. Sometimes there would be only a limited period in which the thing could be done – and it might be a race to make preparations in time. It was a world in which every proposal was desperately urgent and yet not one plan in fifty would come to fruition. The Planners would sit up all night putting the last touches to a plan; the Directors of Plans would reel to their beds

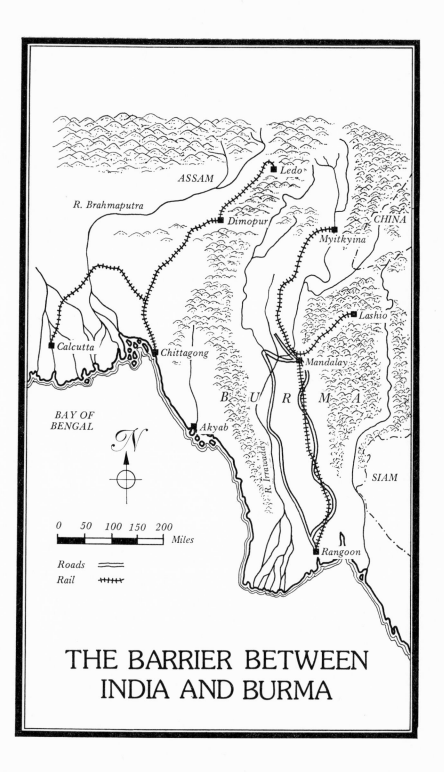

THE BARRIER BETWEEN
INDIA AND BURMA

in the dawn and at breakfast-time the last tired typist would creep home – and then, as the Chiefs of Staff were meeting, someone from Ciphers would hurry in with a signal, just decoded, to say that shipping and vital equipment had been deflected to another theatre of war and everything was upset. In London, there was a Strategic Planning Staff, a Forward Operational Planning Staff and an Economic and Logistical Planning Staff. We did as much as we could of all three jobs, severely hampered from the start by the almost complete lack of trained troops, equipment and aircraft.

This is not a history of the war nor of India's part in it, on which I have touched in *A Matter of Honour* – an account of the Indian Army which I wrote thirty years later. But let me recall one or two memories with a personal bearing. There was a week in April 1942 when the Japanese navy came into the Bay of Bengal and sank over a hundred ships. Japanese carrier-borne aircraft bombed Trincomalee and the RAF Commander in Ceylon told me that at the end of that day he had not a single fighter that would fly. Ralph Edwards, then a Commodore and Chief of Staff to Admiral Sir James Somerville – a fighting sailor if ever there was one – told me in the most vivid terms how he had stood with the Admiral on the bridge of their slow obsolete flagship, knowing they were outgunned and outpaced, hunted from the sea, wondering where they could hide. There was not a division in India fit to fight. We had an army in Africa; we had lost an army in Malaya; we had lost another in Burma. We had nothing in India. It was a maxim of the Joint Planners that we should have plans ready for the moment when it would be possible to take the offensive – 'and so far,' said George Still, 'this war's been nothing but dentistry' – but also for the Worst Possible Case. We looked again at the Worst Possible Case; it had never seemed so relevant as that April. There was no reason we could see why the Japanese should not land troops in India – only the blind hope that they must be getting rather tired and might have bitten off all they could manage. We had relied in peace on the active co-operation of two or three million Indians and the passive tolerance of about four hundred million more; the active critics were about as many as the co-operators and so far less effective. But no one could suppose that the balance would be maintained if there was an enemy landing.

Mary had taken the two little girls, now aged three and one, to Wildflower Hall, once the weekend retreat of Lord Kitchener, six miles beyond Simla on the road to Tibet. I went to see them in May, travelling all night, as always in India. Of course I could say nothing about the Worst Possible Case; I could not dwell even in thought on the possibility of their escape into the mountains towards Tibet. Should I ever see them again? Could they possibly get to Garhwal? I must not think of it. I could only live in the moment, rejoicing in the children's red cheeks, watching them on a swing, and being happy that I could see the pines and the snows.

There was another unforgettable memory, some weeks later. I was in Cairo. I had gone to learn how the Chiefs of Staff and the Joint Planners worked in the Middle East Headquarters. Except for the Minister of State and the Ambassador I seemed to be the only civilian in Cairo – and a very strange one I must have seemed, doing a military job of the highest secrecy, still peering and groping as though blind and feeling as though just out of a chrysalis. I had been out to General Auchinleck's desert mess and slept at the foot of the Great Pyramid with the sand beneath and the stars above. It was the week when the great retreat began. We had been moving pins on the map, counting the tank losses reported. We had begun to realize how bad it was on the very day when I was due to go back to India. I found an ADC and told him I did not expect to see General Auchinleck at such a time but I should like him to know I was flying to India that evening in case he wanted me to take a letter. He was back in ten minutes; the Commander-in-Chief would see me at five o'clock that evening.

I have often admired Auchinleck but never so much as then. He was alone, unhurried, sitting at an uncluttered desk. He told me simply and clearly what had happened and why. He told me that he would stop the German advance at El Alamein. They were burning papers in the Embassy in Cairo that night. In Basra, people anxiously asked us whether the Germans were in Cairo. In Delhi, I was sent straight in to tell Field-Marshal Wavell. 'Not till Alamein!' he repeated. 'Not till there!'

Later in that summer General Stilwell – 'Vinegar Joe', the President's military representative in China – flew from Chungking to Delhi with a Chinese–American plan for driving the Japanese out of Burma from the north. American planes would bring three Chinese divisions to the north of Burma and they would drive the Japanese back to Rangoon. But a Chinese division was equivalent in strength to a Japanese brigade; they would be outnumbered by at least six to one and their equipment was rudimentary. Their supplies would have to come from Calcutta up the Assam railway, a line of very limited capacity. India was not ready for the effort that would be needed to support anything the Chinese could do. Between India and Burma lay a wall of mountain and forest six hundred miles long and two hundred miles wide, without roads, swept for half the year by the heaviest rainfall in the world. Some two hundred airfields would in the end have to be built to give aircover to the kind of operations that would be needed. The Japanese forces were well equipped, confident, victorious.

All this we knew – and some of it General Stilwell knew. It could hardly be doubted that his mission was more diplomatic than military. Field-Marshal Wavell did not comment on the General's outline plan but suggested that he should depute a staff officer to sit with the Joint Planning Staff and examine it. We spent several days going through it; the American staff officer did not take much convincing. At the end of those days there was a meeting at which Wavell presided. George Still gave the planners' conclusions; one after another specialists got up and added chapter and verse – the Quartermaster General, the Director of Movements, the Engineer-in-Chief, the sailors, the airmen. It was devastating.

'Are you satisfied that your plan will not work?' Wavell asked Stilwell.

'I am,' in the grimmest voice, was the reply. A pause.

'Are you satisfied on purely military grounds?'

'I am.' A pause.

'And what shall you say to Chiang-kai-shek?'

'I shall tell him the bloody British wouldn't fight!' The words were spat out with all the vinegary directness of a vinegary character. There was a stunned silence. Then Wavell said:

'I see.' And the meeting broke up.

I do not know what he said to Stilwell afterwards. But, though I am a Wavell man – a point to which I shall return – that was a moment when Mountbatten's qualities were needed. He would have burst out: 'You can't say that. If you're going to say that I'm going to signal the President and the Prime Minister at once!' At the least he would have made it clear to all present that he was not going to let Stilwell get away with that. Yet in a curious way that quality in Wavell – the quality of holding his fire, of controlling immense reserves of inner strength – appealed to most Englishmen who knew him. We were left wondering what he *would* do – and that speculation about what he had up his sleeve was something he wished to encourage. In our minds, it somehow contributed to his stature but, in spite of the fact that poker is an American game, it appealed much less often to Americans.

At about this time Peter Fleming arrived in Delhi, where it was his task to deceive the enemy as to our intentions. He found two serious difficulties. We were ourselves still far from clear what we meant to do and in any case the Japanese were not particularly interested. They made their own plans and carried them out with rigid and unalterable determination. Deceiving the Germans had been very different; they wanted to know our plans and expected us to try to deceive them. That had been like playing chess with someone not quite so good as oneself; with the Japanese, it was like setting up the chess-board against an adversary whose one idea is to punch you on the nose. Nonetheless, Peter contrived to get a good deal of amusement from his own efforts and contributed a touch of gaiety to the whole headquarters. He asked me to write letters from a fictitious Indian clerk who professed to be anti-British on patriotic grounds, but whose main object was money. His first letter would enclose some genuine but quite uninformative papers from my office – giving the time of a Chiefs of Staff meeting or correcting a typing error. Then, if this packet reached the Japanese mission in Kabul, we would send some documents from the same typewriter that would lead them to some wrong conclusion. It would be difficult to think of anything at all plausible that we might not one day mean to do – but we could try.

Peter also persuaded me to start playing squash again. This was a kind act because squash is a dull game if your opponent is no good, and at first, with one eye, I could not hit the ball at all. But he persevered and I soon discovered that it was possible to play quite reasonably again. I then asked him to read a story I had written about a murder in an Indian village. He looked gloomy and said he had a prejudice against that kind of story – however he would. He did and sent Jonathan Cape a recommendation to publish it.

Towards the end of that year, 1942, the tide imperceptibly turned and began to flow. Roosevelt and Churchill met at Casablanca with the Combined Chiefs of Staff – that is, British and American – and sent us instructions in the broadest terms for large-scale operations against the Japanese in Burma in the winter of 1943–44, a year earlier than anyone in India had supposed possible. They would give us all the equipment we needed. No one representing India had been at Casablanca and it did not sound as though anyone there had understood the difficulties. There was the geographical barrier between India and Burma; there was the climate, which limited much activity to half the year; there would have to be lines of communication which ran from Calcutta some seven hundred miles to the north-east, made two right angle turns and then would become longer as the Japanese lines grew shorter – a Staff College nightmare. But there was something else that neither London nor Washington seemed able to assimilate. India was practically a continent, with over four hundred million inhabitants; its industrial development was only just beginning and its railway system was designed to haul very large numbers of people – slowly and with a minimum of comfort – long distances for very low fares. This it did most efficiently; it worked at a profit – but it was not designed for vast movements of stores and equipment to the north-east. To turn this land into a base for operations on the scale proposed meant that a great deal of work had to be done not only on railways and docks but on roads and, above all, airfields. All this would require equipment; time; shipping.

We sent London an encyclopaedic signal. It pointed out the difficulties in broad outline. These however could be overcome if London or Washington would send us the supplies and equipment we needed – but they must start arriving at once and continue at monthly intervals. The first shipment must arrive in February 1943. It would be no use sending six months' supplies all together in June; the docks and railways would not be able to handle such a consignment, and the monsoon would begin in Burma in May.

And things must come in the right order. Railway track, for instance, must be laid before locomotives can run on it. We sent them a list, worked out month by month for a year; it ranged from pierced steel plates for airfields to toothpaste and bandages for hospitals, but the emphasis was much more on engineering than on what the troops would need for the battle. And work must start *at once*. It was an enormous telegram, minutely detailed. Sometimes one despairs of making a point strongly enough. 'I said it very loud and clear, I went and shouted in his ear.'

Nothing happened. February came, March came – but nothing else came. Early in April we said it again. We could not see how we could meet their dates. Owing to this business of the monsoon it would now have to be a year later – as, secretly, we had always supposed. This time they did answer. 'We think you had better come to London to discuss.' I had an unfair advantage. It was I who took that signal to the Chief of the General Staff and I said: 'I suppose the Field-Marshal wouldn't think it useful to take me?' But he did.

3 London and Washington

We had been in London a few days when a dinner took place at which Churchill and Eden met Wavell and Sir James Somerville. I heard of it from Ralph Edwards who heard from Admiral Somerville; prodigious quantities of champagne and brandy disappeared and the talk flashed from one segment of the spinning globe to another. By this time the London Directors of Plans and the London Chiefs of Staff had accepted our argument that really decisive operations against Burma could not take place till a year later than had been supposed at Casablanca. By the end of the dinner, the Prime Minister had accepted it too and about two in the morning he had suddenly decided that he must go to Washington to discuss this and other things with President Roosevelt. He would go in the *Queen Mary*, at that time chiefly engaged in ferrying prisoners of war to Canada and bringing back Canadian troops. His personal staff immediately began to telephone dazed and sleepy folk and give orders.

The *Queen Mary* had been stripped but the peacetime fittings would be restored within twenty-four hours to part of the 'sun deck' and there would be a guard of Marines to seal off that part of the ship for a hundred passengers. These would include the British Chiefs of Staff and selected Joint Planners, one or two Cabinet Ministers, and our little party from India, now reduced to seven. The *Queen Mary* would keep wireless silence, zig-zagging across the Atlantic and sending any message which *had* to go to the outer world by one of the escorting cruisers, which would sail to a discreet distance before despatching it. Of course it was all as secret as the grave and those who were to go had only a few hours' notice. I was able to tell my parents by telephone only that there was no chance of coming to see them as I had hoped. I had time to rush round to Jonathan Cape, to whom I had just given the typescript of *Call the Next Witness*. Now I asked to have it back; I told him I was sure it must need some revision and I foresaw six or seven days in which I might have periods of hectic activity but some days of absolute leisure – and that was something that might not happen again for years. Jonathan said he had only read a few pages but he would publish it.

That was stimulating – my first published book! But the situation was stimulating enough anyhow. We went by train to Glasgow to embark and as soon as I had settled into my cabin I began to read once more the tale written eight years before about the Aundh murder, smelling the dust and spices and dung of the Indian countryside, strong enough in memory to drown the antiseptic smell of a modern ship, and hearing the creaking of bullock-carts louder than the throb of the engines or the stamp and rattle of the Marine sentries. As I had expected, I had little official work except for two sharp bursts. One night in the small hours the Prime Minister dictated a minute of some twenty pages which was handed to us next morning. It began with a good deal of rhetoric. I remember one passage to the following effect: 'If you wish to bring a shark to book, you do not grapple with him in mid-ocean but lure him into the shallows where you have him at a disadvantage.' Or was it the other way round? He continued: 'And so with the Japanese. We must not become entangled in the swamps and jungles of Burma but attack the enemy where they do not expect us, at points which they must summon all their forces to defend.' 'That part,' we said 'is for the book.' But there followed two paragraphs to which we gave minute attention. One began: 'Pray let me know by this time tomorrow the exact state of every formation in India, specifying the number of . . .' and here followed a list of everything – fighting vehicles, guns, machine guns, rifles, bicycles, typewriters and paper-clips. The next asked in the same courteous terms to be told at once what forces would be required for no less than twenty operations. I do not remember them all but they included amphibious operations against the Andaman Islands, Akyab, the Kra Isthmus, the Sunda Straits, the northern tip of Sumatra, the southern tip of Sumatra, various points in the Strait of Malacca, Singapore and Rangoon as well as land operations against various parts of Burma.

Fortunately we had with us Major-General S. W. Kirby, later one of the official historians of the war against Japan, who had an unrivalled grasp of detail and could answer as nearly as anyone the first question. For the second, there was only Ralph Edwards and myself – no soldier, no airman. We sat on the bunk in my cabin and concocted an answer. The Joint Planners in Delhi had made plans for just this kind of thing whenever they had a moment to spare and I had about ten in my briefcase; each had taken about a fortnight to prepare, by a considerable staff. We extracted from these the 'forces required'. But about half remained, which were new; these we did as best we could. 'One assault brigade, two follow-up brigades,' we wrote. So many landing craft (assault), so many landing craft (tank); so many short-range fighter aircraft, so many long-range; so many Dakotas, so many Mosquitoes. It was all guesswork, but it was good enough for the purpose; it provided a basis for some kind of comparison and we knew that long before anything happened, there would be endless planning of every detail. I do not remember when we finished but it was ready within twenty-four hours.

Back to Northern India and the village murder; I found that very little change was needed. Then, about two days out from New York, General Ismay stopped me in a companion-way. The Prime Minister had in mind a possibility which would have certain consequences. There might be a Supreme Allied Commander, South East Asia. How would the structure of command look? He would like suggestions. We should have to consider land, sea and air forces, the various Allies, India as a base, the position of the Viceroy and the Commander-in-Chief and so on. I asked him some guarded questions about the Viceroy and he gave me guarded answers – but it would be a different Viceroy – a Viceroy with a military background. So again Ralph Edwards and I sat down on my bunk; we did a very short report with diagrams – and of course no names in it. We learnt much later that our proposals had been accepted by the Chiefs of Staff and the Prime Minister but changed at the request of the India Office in London. We had put the C-in-C India under the orders of the Supreme Allied Commander, level with the three operational and inter-allied Commanders-in-Chief, naval, land and air. The India Office said this was not in accordance with the constitution of

India, which said: 'There shall be a Commander-in-Chief India'; I have never understood why this prevented his coming under the orders of a Supreme Allied Commander – and in theory I still think it would have been better if he had been. It was surely right that troops should be under the same command when they were being trained for fighting in Burma and when they were actually fighting. In practice no difficulty arose, and indeed, in view of the personalities, it may have been better that the C-in-C India was independent. But if so, that was due to the magnanimity of Field-Marshal Auchinleck, whose nature was singularly free from self-seeking.

We arrived in New York – where those from rationed Britain gasped at the lavish helpings of food – and travelled to Washington. We were most hospitably looked after but there can be no doubt in my mind that American opinion – I do not mean public opinion so much as military and political – at this stage of the war looked on us just as we looked on the Dutch in the time of the great Duke of Marlborough. In both cases, a small power had been facing a formidable antagonist for a long time without support; the Dutch had learnt to face Louis XIV's armies with caution; they could not afford to lose men or guns, and to the British – who were new to the war, had far greater resources, and who had a convenient sea-barrier between themselves and the enemy – they seemed negative in outlook, far too conservative, too pusillanimous to take a risk. That was how we seemed to the Americans; Vinegar Joe Stilwell had put it in characteristic language when he said: 'The bloody British wouldn't fight.' What astonished me – and I see now how naive I was – was to discover that American officers, to whom we had explained the situation in Delhi, did not support us. They had apparently accepted our analysis then, but to say so in Washington would have been professional suicide. I do not think I had any success at putting our main thesis to the American Joint Planners, but before we left Washington the President and the American Chiefs of Staff had reluctantly accepted it.

There was a fundamental difference of spirit between the approach of American planners and ours. The British planners would calculate the stores needed for a particular task and *add* a margin for error; they would consider how many tons a day the railway could carry and *deduct* a margin for error – and if there was a gap between the two results they would be likely to consider a modification or a postponement of the scheme, or propose a different plan. The Americans – with a justified confidence in their immense resources and robust memories of taming the prairies and conquering the West – would say: 'Hell, we'll get the stuff there somehow!' There was some justice in the criticisms each directed at the other; if we were cautious, they were sometimes reckless; but in the end

I believe that the extremely fierce fighting of the Burma campaign and the stubbornness of Japanese resistance justified the British insistence on intensive preparation and the postponement of the campaign till full air cover could be provided.

Wavell was instructed to stay longer in Washington and then in London, ostensibly to talk about the new post of Supreme Allied Commander, South East Asia. He did not know he was to be Viceroy, although Ismay's remark on the *Queen Mary* about a military Viceroy shows that this was already in the Prime Minister's mind. I was told to go back to India as quickly as possible and since Sir Richard Peirse, the Air C-in-C, was in a hurry, it was arranged that I should go with him in a bomber. It was a strange journey – in memory like a dream. Europe was in enemy hands and to avoid enemy patrols we flew, mostly at night, across the Atlantic by the northern route to Scotland, then far out to sea and round to West Africa, thence across North Africa to Cairo and the Persian Gulf, outlining – as a cartoonist might in a diagram – one half of the world front against Germany and Japan. Washington in May was hot, damp, sticky, almost tropical; a few hours later we came down somewhere in Canada where there was deep snow; there were log cabins and I expected bears. About midnight we were in Newfoundland, where we spent most of the next day waiting for dark. Someone took us to a little harbour, smelling of fish, tar, salt and seaweed. The skies were cold and bleak and there was a lot of snow about. Later that day we flew over Newfoundland, which seemed to be all creeks and lakes and snowy forest, looking from above like deep moss and grey lichen on a frozen rock. At nightfall we took off for the Atlantic crossing, flew all night and spent a poignant day at Prestwick on the Ayrshire coast. The gorse was in bloom, there were gilly-flowers in the flower-beds and the sun was shining; the sea air was cold and fresh, kissing the face with a salutation very sweet to one who had lived many years in a hot and dusty land. I telephoned to my parents; it was five years since I had seen them but there was no way of getting home without missing the AOC-in-C's bomber. I could not say much. I posted my novel to Jonathan Cape. Then at dusk far out to sea; Casablanca, Cairo, Delhi; thousands of miles; at some point – but it must have been going the other way across North Africa because it was in a Flying Fortress, not a Lancaster – someone told me there was a possibility of attack by enemy fighters and asked me to stand at a gunport where there was a heavy machine gun. If I saw an enemy fighter, I was to swing at it, as with a shotgun at a bird, and press the button. But I saw none and did not render myself liable to be shot for firing at the enemy without wearing uniform.

We came into Delhi in the morning, having beaten some kind of wartime record. I went to the office but found my mind quite incapable of taking anything in. Later, when I had rested, I went to see Lady Wavell. 'You had the wonderful experience of hearing the Prime Minister address the Congress of the United States,' she exclaimed. I had to explain that I had not. 'Then what *were* you doing that afternoon?' 'I was playing squash with Peter Fleming.' 'But you can do that every day in Delhi!' It was true and I could not explain my blockish lack of interest in being present at a historic occasion. I saw its importance, of course; I was aware of the symbolic implications. I was full of admiration for the Prime Minister – but I seem to have little of the itch to be present at great events.

There followed a difficult period in Delhi. For the second time, Auchinleck became Commander-in-Chief; he was in a trying situation. He was the Indian Army's own man; his reputation in India at the beginning of the war had been immensely high; he had been picked by the Prime Minister; he had been Commander in Norway, then had come to India as Commander-in-Chief. Suddenly he had been transferred to the Middle East where he succeeded Wavell. That was his time of glory, from the autumn of 1941 to the summer of 1942. He had stopped the Germans at Alamein, as he had told me he would that day in Cairo. He was preparing his counter-attack when he was replaced – and I do not wish here to enlarge on that; justice is hardly a relevant consideration and perhaps it is best that in war a Prime Minister should ruthlessly discard generals whose chance has been thrust upon them before they had the resources needed to make the most of it. A general needs luck, and without luck his troops will lose confidence in him; perhaps the supreme manifestation of luck lies in the moment when the opportunity of high command occurs. If it comes too early in the war, he is likely to be under-equipped.

That is by the way; my purpose is to underline the effect of supersession. For nearly a year Auchinleck had been unemployed – and he was absorbed in his profession. He was a man of strong emotions, deeply loyal to his friends – and indeed it was a weakness that he sometimes supposed that his friends had qualities in which they were lacking; he had the quality of inspiring immense loyalty in troops and this was partly because they sensed in him an equal loyalty to them. He was also sensitive to Indian middle-class and nationalist opinion, to a degree unusual in British officials who had reached positions of power. He understood how humiliating to Indians had been some aspects of British behaviour in India which were relics of Victorian supremacy – and how irritating was the cautiousness of the advance towards a relationship more like that of Canada with Britain. To such a man those months of unemployment must have been wounding; to many they would have been destructive.

Now he was recalled as Commander-in-Chief and Wavell was to be Viceroy. But a Supreme Allied Commander was soon to be in charge of operations; the Commander-in-Chief India would be responsible only for training and supplies and preparations for the great offensive. Until he came, Auchinleck had the whole responsibility that Wavell had held, current operations as well as the invidious task of planning for operations he would not direct. It was a trying period for us all, much worse of course for him. 'George Still has turned a fish-belly white,' I remember his noticing. It was long hours and exhaustion. Signals flew to and fro as we did what we could with what we had against the Japanese and at the same time did our best to prepare for the new era.

The arrival of Lord Louis Mountbatten as Supreme Allied Commander was clouded by a misunderstanding which had deep roots and of which the effects persisted for some time. We in India had taken it for granted that the arrangements for planning would follow the usual British pattern. We pictured a Supreme Allied Commander with a small personal staff, whose planning would be done by joint planners jointly responsible to him, but each separately responsible also to his own Commander-in-Chief. We thought the three Commanders-in-Chief would probably meet to discuss plans and then put them up to the Supremo, as he came to be called. Perhaps he would then wish to discuss them with the Commanders-in-Chief. We understood, of course, that all the way through his ideas would inform and guide the whole and that, in the end, he would give the orders, yes or no. In short, we had supposed that there would be friendly consultation all the way up the line and one common allegiance. We arranged accommodation with this in mind, supposing that the Supreme Commander would wish to have the three Commanders-in-Chief near him, their staffs radiating outwards.

In all this we were quite wrong, but we did not learn that till his arrival. The Prime Minister had told Lord Louis that he was to be a Commander, not the Chairman of a Committee. He had spoken favourably of American methods of command; he had also given him the impression that he would find the British in India sluggish and apathetic and the Indian Army unreliable. At this stage of his life, Churchill remembered his days as a subaltern with a British cavalry regiment in South India and forgot what he had written of the Indian Army when he was a war correspondent in the Malakand Campaign. Lord Louis expected to find the Commanders-in-Chief over-cautious and had accordingly decided that he must have his own planners, responsible to himself and to no one else. He brought them with him, so that they should be uncontaminated by previous Indian experience. He would consult his own planners and they would construct plans in accordance with his general instructions; these would be handed down to the C-in-Cs' planners for the detailed work of checking requirements in stores and the capacity of lines of communication.

The British method of planning involved dual responsibility, to which Lord Louis was temperamentally averse; he wanted his advice to come from men altogether his own. At the root of the whole trouble was the distrust sown in his mind by the Prime Minister, magnified perhaps by his own ardent temperament and vivid imagination, so that it is perhaps only a slight exaggeration to say that he felt like Prince Rupert of the Rhine bursting into the deliberations of a parochial church council considering whether they could afford to re-hang the bells. We, on our part, were altogether unprepared, not only for his views but for the passion with which they were held. We were also unprepared for a staff who seemed to expect to leave the office sharp at six o'clock in the evening. The Americans were full of goodwill but naturally quite inexperienced in Indian conditions; some of the British gave an impression of having been picked for elegance rather than efficiency and contrived to invest the opening scenes with a faint air of musical comedy.

Lord Louis repudiated the arrangement by which the Commanders-in-Chief would have offices near his. Had he not said that he wanted his own staff near him? We had taken this to mean that he wanted the whole operational group of South East Asia Command to be together, and separate from the Commander-in-Chief India. No, the Commanders-in-Chief must be separate; his own planners must surround him. There would be no Chiefs of Staff Committee or Commanders-in-Chief Committee making recommendations to him. He said once that it would be mutiny if the three Commanders-in-Chief met to discuss plans in his absence. I do not suppose this was a judgment that he would have put in writing but it indicates the tension of those superheated days.

No one could help falling under Lord Louis's spell. Dazzling good looks, a superb presence, royal birth, indomitable energy, a quick mind, rapid decision, fertile imagination – Rose Aylmer, all were thine! Of course I was under that spell and I do not doubt that I would fall under it again tomorrow if exposed to the full blaze of its splendour. But, when I was not in his presence, that system of planning seemed to me designed to increase mistrust and cause friction. And in the first months it certainly did. All three Commanders-in-Chief disliked it, and particularly Sir James Somerville, the Naval C-in-C. The two planning staffs soon came to be known as the Sacks and the Sinks. The Sacks produced outline plans which took little account of what used to be called the Q or quartermaster's aspect (which we were now learning to call logistical); the Sinks proceeded to point out objections and finally justify their name by a well-aimed torpedo.

> Oh, Sinks are Sinks and Sacks are Sacks,
> And each of the other must think
> That they ought to be ruthlessly pruned with an axe
> Or be drowned in an ocean of ink

wrote one of them in a ballad which at least conveys the atmosphere of the early days.

It was taken for granted, so far as I recall, that I should go over to the Supreme Allied Commander's staff. I was no longer called Secretary, Chiefs of Staff Committee but Head of the Conference Secretariat; I had with me a British Major, who had been Secretary to the old Joint Planners – who now became C-in-C's planners – and I was joined by two American Majors. Between us we looked after the documents of all the planning committees. My special task was to be present at the Supreme Commander's daily meeting, at which all the leading members of his staff were present as well as the Commanders-in-Chief. These meetings might go on for two or three hours after which it was for me to record the decisions and the essence of the discussion. But usually, before anything else, I had to draft the signals that came out of the meeting, sometimes to London, sometimes to Delhi, Chungking or Ceylon. These signals would have to be taken round by hand and shown to two or three people – to check figures about movements and stores, to make sure that a point about airfields or air cover was right – before being finally approved by the Supreme Commander or his Chief of Staff. It was for me to record the essential, to clarify the issues, to draft results, to prevent misunderstanding – never to express views of my own. A distinguished General once said as we came out of a meeting: 'I have no idea what we have decided – but Philip will tell us.' It meant paying sharp attention, particularly to what Lord Louis was saying. But sometimes the course of the discussion for the next few minutes and the inevitable outcome could be foreseen and it would be possible to relax.

So far as I remember, my minutes were only once amended; that was on grounds political rather than military. An American General sent for me; he had made a point in discussion which I had not recorded. 'I remember it, of course, but it was overruled and did not affect the decisions.' 'Right,' he said, 'but I must have it on record that I made that point and that it was overruled.'

Misunderstandings on the personal level were more easily removed.

When the Conference Secretariat began, there was a discussion about what we should need – typists, typewriters, and the like. Archie Dunbar, my British colleague, and I did most of the talking. Jimmy Muir, the first American to join us, listened for a long time and then said: 'I can't see why you guys are so keen to know the time.' We gaped – but in the end puzzled it out. The word we both spelled 'clerks' he pronounced 'clurks' but we called it 'clarks', which to him sounded very like 'clocks'. But in the nine or ten months when I was part of this inter-allied unit, I remember only one moment of real embarrassment; this was imposed on me from London. I was handed a long signal from the British Government about the future of Ceylon. It was marked with a code-word which meant 'not to be shown to Americans'. What was I to do? I believed we had, between the four of us, established a fund of personal confidence. We had one safe, one set of keys. Was I to start a new secret depository with a separate key? They would be bound to know – and how could they fail to suppose I was holding back from them some vital instructions about the conduct of the war? I decided that the only thing was to be quite frank. I told them I had this signal, which was about the constitutional development of Ceylon after the war, that it was nothing to do with them, or with the war, and that I had put it in a separate file cover, in our common safe, and I asked them not to look at it. I do not think they did.

When I was recalled to the Defence Department, from Ceylon, in the late summer of 1944, one of these two met the news with the comment: 'Do you mean to say that, just when we've turned you into a decent American citizen, we've got to start work on another goddamn Britisher?'

But that is to run ahead. I must first say something of Ceylon.

> X <

BEGINNING
OF THE AFTERMATH

1 Wavell

There was something unreal about Ceylon. The grass was too green, the air too moist and too warm. Fruit grew on every tree. The people of Kandy laughed and smiled but in spite of their look of plump good nature they killed more people in a year by murder or manslaughter – so we were told – than any population in the world except Chicago's. It was hard to see why. They seemed kindly, gentle, hospitable folk and would crack a coconut and give you the milk if you went into one of their villages in the course of a Sunday walk. But of course we did not know them; we were utterly remote from the people of the island. On me at least the effect of all this lushness and softness, the bright colours, the smiling people, was to relax tension, to make it easy to be idle. I felt physically well – but there was no desire for exertion. It would be a good place to come for a holiday, I decided.

The air of unreality was accentuated by the stately palms, the wealth of tropical flowers, all the botanical splendours of the Peradeniya Gardens, where the Supreme Allied Commander had set up his headquarters. Many of us took sandwiches and picnicked in the spicy shade of some exotic tree – clove or cinnamon or nutmeg. In my case the dreamlike quality of the island was varied, but also accentuated, by the monotonous twilight among the tall straight stems in the rubber plantation where I lived, in a private mess with one of the cloak-and-dagger organizations, so secret that we never breathed a word in that mess of what they did. The grey cathedral gloom among the rubber trees merges in memory with the sunshine and bright flowers of Peradeniya and then fades away as though a wisp of cloud had blown across one's face on a high mountain.

War depends on destroying a sense of common humanity. We could not wage war if we thought of our adversaries as actual men; the enemy has to become a generalization – the Hun, the Jap – a monster made up of faceless automata. War may add a poignancy to love or friendship because death and parting are so common, but the general effect is to deaden emotion and to make most relationships superficial. The dream-like artificiality of the Peradeniya Gardens added to this effect and made it hard to believe that our activities had much bearing on human affairs. In Delhi, we had seemed closer to wounds and battle. George Still, whom I had known best of the planners there, had always at the back of his mind the thought that a bad plan might mean that some of our friends would hang on the wire, riddled with bullets. To remember the realities of blood and death was more difficult in Kandy, where the spotless white uniforms and gay three-cornered hats of the Wren officers flitted between the tree-ferns and the orchid-house, where Noël Coward came and sang to us, where the atmosphere of a large-scale *fête champêtre* could never quite be banished. Passion-fruit cocktails seemed the proper drink, sweet and exotic, slightly cloying. We had moved to Ceylon because it was desirable to be away from the fettering presence of the Viceroy and the Commander-in-Chief India and – added Lord Louis – because anyone who wasn't crackers would prefer Ceylon to Delhi.

I was not many months in Ceylon, because the Government of India asked for my return, but before I left, one episode contributes in memory to the slightly fantastic effect. I was summoned late at night to the Supreme Commander's lodging. A new Naval Commander-in-Chief was coming and Lord Louis had decided that he must make his peace with the Admiralty; it would not do to have a sharp difference of opinion with two Admirals in succession. He had never concealed his ambition to be First Sea Lord and thus put right the wrong that had been done when his father had felt he must resign from that post in the Kaiser's war. He had therefore decided to adopt the British system of planning after all. He had sent for me as the only member of his staff who believed in the British method and also because he knew that I got on well with Sir James Somerville. I was to go down from Kandy to Colombo next day to make sure that Sir James would agree to the change. I was astonished.

'But of course he will agree, sir,' I said. 'It is what he has always wanted.'

But Lord Louis thought he might now raise some objection and I must go and make sure. It seemed to me a misreading of Sir James Somerville's character. However, off I went to Naval Headquarters in Colombo, where I was to stay the night. I was taken to the Commander-in-Chief as soon as I arrived. I explained.

'Well, of course I agree,' said Sir James. 'It's what I've always wanted.'

'That's what I told him you'd say, sir.'

'Well, now I've said it. Now we can settle down to enjoy ourselves.' He paused and went on. 'Wanted to help him. Young naval officer.

Always anxious to help a young naval officer. Very promising young naval officer. Full of energy. But then he got these ridiculous ideas which wouldn't work. Anyhow, it's all over now and I'm glad.'

Sir James had been in Delhi when our son George was born. He adored babies and told me he was coming to see Mary in hospital. 'Just after feeding-time,' he said. 'That'll be six o'clock, I suppose. I'll be there six-twenty. Don't bother to bring up his wind. I'll do that.' And at George's christening, he said he was senior godfather and led the responses. We had not suggested that he should be a godfather, having a reluctance to inflict that responsibility on anyone older and more eminent than ourselves. But he had so many godchildren that he must have thought he had been asked and had forgotten; a silver porridge-bowl arrived next day.

There are so many stories about James Somerville that I am reluctant to add to them. But it strikes me that while many of his sayings were meant to appeal – as they certainly did – to those under his command and to spread his own confidence and courage, there were others, of his own special brand, which brought a crisis to the point where it had to be resolved. He would lance the boil by a remark of devastating candour – like Vinegar Joe Stilwell's, but, unlike Vinegar Joe's, accompanied by such an air of fundamental good humour that it ended by establishing good relations. When he left command of the Eastern Fleet for Washington, where he was British naval representative, there was an inter-allied dispute about the Bofors gun, a light anti-aircraft gun of which there were never enough. His staff briefed him on the British case; the essence of it was that the Americans had agreed to give us a share of these guns which Admiral King was keeping for the US Navy. A meeting was arranged; the two Admirals met, each with a staff of experts. Sir James stated the British case; Admiral King replied. There was a pause. Then, without malice, indeed with a touch of admiration, as of one making a discovery, James said:

'Christ, you *are* a bastard!'

Admiral King replied:

'Admiral, I guess you and I had better go and have a cup of coffee.'

It worked. He got the guns; they became friends.

But, as I have said, I was recalled. The decision had been made, at the beginning of the war, that members of the Indian Civil Service would not be allowed to go in to the armed forces; because of my blindness, my case had been exceptional, but it had always been temporary. My right eye was now recovered and able to take the strain of more paper-work. Lord Louis did his best for me but Delhi was adamant. I asked to see the Viceroy.

'I can't let you go, Philip,' he said. 'There are so few of the ICS. You must come back.'

It is hard to convey the affection that we felt for Lord Wavell – I and others of my age, Peter Fleming, Bernard Fergusson and many more. It was an affection with an element in it of something more than respect, something more like veneration. None of us, I think, could talk to him quite as an equal; he was a being of a different and higher grade. My first encounter was terrifying. He had just come to India from the Middle East; Bernard Fergusson was with him as Private Secretary and I had soon found a link with Bernard because he was the brother of James Fergusson, the Heptarch of Valentia. It happened one evening that the Commander-in-Chief was leaving Army Headquarters in Simla just when I was; it was dark, about seven o'clock, and we were both about to walk home – over three miles in my case, not quite so far in his. Bernard, an experienced ADC, fell us in, side-by-side, and pushed us off into the darkness. I made no progress at all with attempts at small talk and I was relieved when our ways parted and I turned down into the Lakkar Bazaar – just past the place where Kim met Lurgan Sahib. Later, when I came to know Lord Wavell better, I learnt to take the initiative in conversation and hold it till he began to spark. When he was Viceroy, the ADC at an informal party would often fetch me to talk to him, and as we threaded our way through the crowd I would choose my opening and start talking at once, perhaps about something I had read the night before. His face would light up and he would start to talk himself. I could be confident that he would respond to almost anything that interested me – biography, poetry, novels – or some thought or happening. I would not choose politics or topics of the day.

His silences, I have since come to think, were of two kinds: professional and social. Sometimes he would deliberately cultivate what at other times he regarded as a social handicap. A friend of mine who had recently joined his staff had to explain to him long and complicated proposals which he as Viceroy would have to put to his Executive Council next day. Lord Wavell did not appear to be attending to the exposition; he pulled out an album and began sticking photographs in it. My friend's heart sank; he asked to be present at the Council meeting next day, feeling sure that he would have to come to the rescue. But not at all; every word had been remembered and the mass of detail was rehearsed with improvements. His son, Archie John, told me that this was a deliberate ploy; in the Middle East, he would stroll round the room looking at bookshelves while high plenipotentiaries held forth, coming back to his desk to astonish them by his mastery of the points they had made. It was a development of something he had learnt in the First

World War from Wully Robertson and from Allenby. It was effective. The air of inattention, the secrecy, the silence, combined to make his subordinates regard him as primitive people regard a force of nature, something beyond their calculations, something liable at any moment to surprise them.

Lord Wavell's social silences were not meant to impress. On the way to Washington, we were held up by engine trouble and had to spend a night in Karachi; without warning, the Commander-in-Chief and three staff officers were catapulted on to the Brigadier commanding the area as overnight guests. It was Sunday afternoon and the Brigadier's wife was in the midst of a tea party for the ladies of Karachi, who were planning something to do with the Red Cross or entertaining the troops. The Commander-in-Chief, a square sturdy figure in bush shirt and shorts, established himself on a round stool in the middle of the vast drawing-room. The ladies sat round in a circle; they did not feel it proper to go on with their business nor to start any topic of their own. There was a long dreadful silence. I watched Wavell carefully, not – as I should have been – wondering how to end the embarrassment but puzzling about him. It seemed to me that he wanted to end it, but that he felt it would be discourteous to talk about the things that filled his own mind at that moment and that he really could not be satisfied that anything that did occur to him would really be of interest to them. He sat there like a new boy at tea with his housemaster's wife. It was humility not arrogance; he did not despise their interests.

His journal makes it clear that he really did regard this lack of small talk as a handicap. He thought it over and at last hit on a gambit that he could play at the dinner table. He would turn to the lady on his right and ask what would be her choice if in another life she had to be an animal. Of course the confidence must be returned and reasons given on both sides, so that the slightly absurd game could last a little time. Everybody knew about this – but when I told him of the man-eating panther in Garhwal who was supposed to be a man by day, he explained his dinner-party game as though it would be news to me and went on to tell me how once in Assam he sat next to a lady who said she had no choice; in her tribe they *must* turn into panthers.

Our affection easily overrode this eccentricity. There was so much to admire. 'You can never send him a draft that he will not improve,' his private secretary told me; his own notes came from his hand in beautiful writing, legible and pleasant to the eye, masterly in their lucidity and concentration on the essential. Long before he was Viceroy, in that tangled period when nothing was going right, the planners, after long and tortured thought, decided that we must try to make the Chiefs of

Staff in London understand our situation by a paper which would set out all the possibilities, all the assets we could muster, all the shortages that afflicted us. We began the laborious accumulation of data; Majors went scurrying off to the Quartermaster General and the Engineer-in-Chief and we groaned at the thought of the long session when all this mass of material would have to be hammered into shape. Suddenly down came a draft signal from Wavell setting out with limpid precision and balance all that we were hoping to say. There were blanks to be filled; there were figures to be brought up to date. But the whole thing was there, presented with shapely elegance.

Others have written on his sense of history. It marked him off from most men; his mind would turn always to historical reasons and precedents. 'How did we get into Burma the first time?' he enquired early in 1942 and we supplied him with books about the campaign of 1823. It cropped up in the most trivial conversation. I said once that I began to feel I was back in Europe on arriving at the Dead Sea, then a staging-post on the way to Cairo. I suppose this was probably because one saw holiday-makers sunbathing. But Wavell said musingly: 'The boundary of the Roman Empire?' Stonewall Jackson's march to Mannassas Junction was often in his mind, and he too would have liked to start out secretly at dead of night, riding at the head of a mounted column for a destination that no one knew but himself. But while he liked to picture himself as a cavalier, it was his fate to be remembered as the dour and indomitable slave of duty, condemned to defend one indefensible position after another and always relieved of his command when victory was in sight. His brilliant victories in the Western Desert and in Ethiopia – the first victories of the war – were forgotten in the shade of ABDACOM (the Allied British Dutch and American Command in the Pacific), of Malaya and Burma. But for us, the sturdy courage with which he accepted these strokes of fortune was part of what we admired. At the heart of it was a moral certainty, a distaste for humbug and the shop window, a devotion to truth. But that deep core was adorned and graced for those who knew him by endearing quirks, a tendency to produce impromptu limericks, pleasure in parodies and absurdity.

Soon after he became Viceroy, Wavell pointed out that he was now quite in the dark about the progress of military plans; it was not really enough to depend on what he was told. In view of his past, he suggested that he was hardly a security risk. But his *staff* were civilians, said Lord Louis. In the end, I was instructed to make up for him a weekly package of selected planning papers and signals that would keep him informed. (I too was a civilian – but I was Lord Louis's.) These were to be enclosed in an outer envelope marked personally to the Private Secretary to the

Viceroy and an inner envelope marked with a code-word which meant
that the Private Secretary was to send the package in to the Viceroy un-
opened. With these papers I used sometimes to include for the Viceroy's
entertainment some of the best of the ditties, often rather scurrilous,
with which the planners amused themselves in their less hectic moments.
They seemed to amuse the Viceroy too, since he sometimes added a verse.

One of these, *Lines written in defence of planning as understood by the
ancients*, was written in reproof of myself; I had written some satirical
doggerel about Hannibal planning to march on Rome. My critic reproved
me for thinking that:

>   .... planning by Carthage's eminent SAC
> Was just like today only centuries back.

He continued:

> Now this is not so, as Philip should know . . .

and went on:

> To be sure a commander would ask the advice
> Of his experts, but these were romantic and nice . . .

And after some examples:

> A leader of Romans would go by the omens
> Discovered inside of his victims' abdomens
> And if he were Norse, as a matter of course
> He would watch flights of ravens or talk to his horse.

And a little later:

> The lack of Dakotas and parachutes would
> Not worry a leader so long as he could
> By raising his arms and intoning Hosanna
> Supply his formations with adequate manna.

And the conclusion he reached was that:

> An ancient commander would never find place on
> His staff for an antediluvian Mason.

Sundari Devi on swing. This was taken in May 1942 at Wildflower Hall, Lord Kitchener's weekend home near Simla, when the planners were discussing the Worst Possible Case. If the Japanese had landed in India then, we had nothing to stop them. I could say nothing to Mary about this but did not know if I should ever see her or the children again.

P.M. with the Royal Indian Navy, 1946 and (*below*) with the Indian Army and Air Force. After the War, Auchinleck sent a Services Exhibition on tour in India; its purpose was to help the people of India to think of the Defence Services as their own.

Wavell and Stilwell. This is not the meeting referred to on p. 168 but was taken on Stilwell's arrival in Delhi a few months later when the tide was beginning to turn. P.M. with back to camera.

below left Wavell and George. This is extracted from the group at the wedding of Lady Felicity Wavell to Captain Peter Longmore, at which George was a page. Lord Wavell had already been recalled as Viceroy but was allowed to postpone the announcement until after the wedding.

below right Mary and Philip attain a brief distinction as parents of the page, in their best clothes for once.

Hyderabad. *above left* Watching
the conjuror, at the birthday
party of Barakat, the Nizam's
elder grandson and his
successor.

above right Barakat blowing up
a balloon at a gas cylinder.

right Goodbye to Hyderabad:
Philip, Mary and three children
garlanded at the last party.

At Greenlands Farm, three children at the derelict cottage with fifteen acres where we tried to support ourselves in food.

The view from Greenlands, with the finished house in the bottom right-hand corner.

'. . . the children in the apple tree'.

There was no other senior officer to whom I would have sent this kind of thing.

On the whole these efforts were best when they stuck close to parody, One, addressed to a Director of Plans, began:

> Oh, what can ail thee, D. of P.
>   Alone and palely loitering;
> Thy colleagues twain are long gone home,
>   And no phones ring.

That achieved a certain poetic force, and was followed by:

> I saw the shades of D's of P.
>   Pale warriors, death-pale were they all,
> Who cried: 'The Academic Plan
>   Hath thee in thrall!'

From the same hand came an apposite amendment of Clough:

> Say not that planning naught availeth
>   The labour and the toil are vain
> Discussion faltereth and faileth
>   And as things have been they remain.

It ended:

> For not by mental process only
>   With facts and figures comes the light;
> Imagination swift and lonely
>   May strike the spark to banish night.

And to that Wavell added – without reaching, I am sure, to the bookshelf:

> And not by Eastern planners only
>   Is borne the burden and the brunt
> Consider when you're feeling lonely
>   The chaps who plan the Second Front.

Another ditty, in mockery of the proliferation of code-names for operations, contained the line:

BULLDOG with LIPSTICK got confused.

Wavell drew a picture in the margin of a bulldog confused, and clearly abashed, by lipstick on his face. But not till after retirement did he say anything to me about this unorthodox correspondence.

Of course I cannot explain why I felt such an affection for Wavell. Who can explain such things in rational terms? I can only say that I did, and try to give some indication of what he was like. He came nearest to self-expression in *Other Men's Flowers*, the collection of poems which he knew by heart. The mere scope and variety of these poems tells a good deal about him but his comments tell more. Consider for instance what he says of *Lucy Ashton's Song*, which runs:

> Look not thou on beauty's charming;
> Sit thou still when kings are arming;
> Taste not when the wine-cup glistens;
> Speak not when the people listens;
> Stop thine ear against the singer;
> From the red gold keep thy finger;
> Vacant heart and hand and eye,
> Easy live and quiet die.

On that he notes:

> I have known the jingle many years and could not disagree more heartily with every precept, except perhaps the fourth line. I have found few things in life more satisfactory to look on than beauty's charming. My profession, and inclination, have forbidden that I should sit still when kings, or dictators, are arming. I enjoy the wine that maketh glad the heart of man . . . As for a vacant heart, easy life or quiet death, I desire none of them . . .

Set that beside the last poem in his book, the only one of his own, which he wrote in April 1943, during the few days we were in England before sailing in the *Queen Mary*. In that poem, he speaks of how he has remembered the Madonna of the Cherries through 'long years of battle, bitterness and waste' and of how she has stood for:

> Fruits of the kindly earth and truth and grace,
> Colour and light, and all warm lovely things

– stood, in short, for all he is fighting for. He ends his book with a blessing on that Lady and on 'all beautiful things that help us to forget the dreariness of war'.

But, as I have said, he was quite firm with me and I had to come back to Delhi.

2 Mercy for Traitors

I am trying to display a succession of changing scenes, as though the reader were riding on a grassy lane through a heavily timbered forest, with avenues opening on either hand which give him glimpses of open glades, lawns, streams and distant hills. There is no turning back; it is one journey. And if a prospect opens which resembles one seen before, we shall canter briskly on and slow to a walk at the next. I shall hurry on then to a new scene rather than dwell on the Delhi to which I came back; the Defence Department had grown larger but performed much the same functions as before. The main difference was that Charles Ogilvie had left, and the Secretary was Chandulal Trivedi, who later became Governor of four Provinces in succession, one before independence and three after.

I found Trivedi a good colleague to work with. He was quick and energetic and to me always considerate. I admired his balance; he never forgot that he was an Indian and that India would one day be independent – and in this he had the whole-hearted backing of Auchinleck – but he worked amicably in the Defence Department with British officers who had no such vision in mind. The day came when he was appointed Governor of Orissa; Field-Marshal Auchinleck told me that he would like me in his place. I said he ought to have an Indian; he agreed – but it must be a capable Indian who knew his way round; a failure would do more harm than good. He told me later that it was the ICS who would not have me; they thought I was not sufficiently grown-up – and I can see what they meant; they may have been right. The man appointed was Ambrose Dundas, a good ten years older than myself. I liked him at once. But Ambrose had spent most of his time on the North-West Frontier and knew nothing of the central administration. He had to face, within a few weeks of arrival, a session in the Central Legislative Assembly, the embryo Federal Parliament. He felt he would be at such a disadvantage there that it would be better if I took his place in the Assembly and this was agreed.

The Central Assembly before independence was a curious institution. The Government of India Act of 1935 had stuck at an interim stage, just short of the Federal, because the Indian Princes had not agreed to come into a Federation. The Central Assembly had therefore stuck too, at a stage in the regular constitutional development of a British Colonial Legislature from which it ought by now to have moved on; it was as though a tadpole had failed to grow into a frog. There was a block of nominated officials on the Speaker's right, and then a little group of people representing special interests, followed by a central block of the Muslim League and, finally, on the Speaker's left, the largest single party in the House, the Congress. If the Congress and the Muslims united, they could defeat the Government and the special interests. But sometimes the Muslims would vote with us. If we were defeated, the Government did not have to resign – and therefore it might be argued that the whole operation was like playing with toy trains; it did not matter if the engine fell off the line. There is a good deal in this; politics is about power and the important thing is the possibility of changing the Government peacefully. Can it really be supposed that learning to address one's remarks to the Speaker and to avoid hypothetical questions – all the paraphernalia of Parliamentary procedure – really teaches anyone that balance between anarchy and despotism that we call democracy and the rule of law?

Clearly, the answer must be no; Parliamentary procedure is not enough by itself. But something was learnt, both by the Government and the Opposition. The Government did try to avoid defeat; they did try to avoid justifiable criticism. During the years I was in Delhi, I used frequently to hear the phrase: 'It could not be defended in the Assembly.' That was effective and might put a stop to a proposal. The Assembly was a focus for the attention of the Press and it made the Government more sensitive to public opinion than it would have been otherwise. Criticism from the Opposition was often irresponsible but not always; there were some members who really did seek information; there were some excellent journalists. Auchinleck supplemented the formal machinery by inviting some politicians to gatherings at which they would meet some of his Principal Staff Officers for dinner, discuss matters that interested them and ask questions.

I had two sessions in the Assembly and enjoyed them, something few ICS officers would admit. I enjoyed them mainly because I knew so much more about the subject than anyone else in the House; altogether I had been nearly ten years in the Defence Department and for much of the time I had been drafting answers to questions for other people. It was much more interesting to answer in my own way and see the reactions that arose. Answers in the past had often been designed to give as little information as possible. I tried to give as much as I could. I had so much detailed knowledge, and my opponents were usually so ill-informed, that I rose to answer questions with a sense of exhilaration and enjoyment which the Opposition did not expect from the official benches.

After I left the Assembly, I sat one day at lunch next to Minoo Masani, who in those two sessions had been an opponent on the Congress back benches. He was younger than most of the Opposition and I had been younger than most of the Government side; we had each had more than our share of speaking in the House and had liked and respected each other. I told him that for five and a half years I had felt that the one thing I wanted was that we should win the war – and I thought most Englishmen had felt the same. Nothing else mattered in comparison with that. Now there was a tremendous feeling of release – and I was eager to get on to something new. He said that Indians had just that feeling about independence; until that was achieved, everything else was secondary and once they had it they too would feel that a new life could begin. Both of us were to be disillusioned; neither of us found a new heaven and a new earth. But I recall the conversation at this point because that sense of the war being over and new vistas opening contributed to the mood in which I faced the Assembly, a mood of relaxed self-assurance not sufficiently attuned, I now think, to the fact that for the Indians their war was not yet over.

I was allowed a very free hand and I decided early that I would try as far as I could to be positive, not merely defensive, to take the initiative when I could, and if possible to appeal to emotion and human feeling. There was to be a Victory Parade; the Congress professed to regard this as unnecessary and put a lot of questions about the cost. Finally one of them asked why it was thought necessary to have a Victory Parade at all. The question came to me with some non-committal official draft reply such as that it was thought not inappropriate in the circumstances. I replied, in tones as resonant as I could make them: 'Because, sir, with the help of God and our allies, we have defeated the greatest military power in history.' There were no supplementary questions to that and even the ranks of Tuscany gave it a mutter of slightly mocking approval. They preferred that kind of style to the soberly official.

During those two sessions I had not only to answer questions but to speak in formal debates, usually on matters in which there was a great deal of public interest. I shall refer here to one such matter only; it was of the first importance to the new India that was coming into being.

In Malaya, we had lost an army; about eighty-five thousand men were prisoners, of whom about sixty thousand were Indian. The Japanese themselves hardly ever surrendered; they fought to the last man; they therefore despised prisoners of war and treated them badly. But they thought they could make some use of the Indians; they separated them from their British officers, kept information from them and offered them every inducement to co-operate. The men were told that the war was over and the British were defeated; they were harangued by educated fellow countrymen about the new Asia that was growing up under Japanese leadership; they were offered the choice of joining a new Indian army with Japanese backing or of harsh and degrading treatment, to which there seemed no prospect of any end. Some of the Indian officers were tortured, starved and beaten; Captain P. K. Dhargalkar of the 3rd Cavalry, for example, was confined for eighty-eight days in a cage less than five foot six inches long and the same in width, in which there were sometimes as many as four people. The astonishing thing to me is that more than half of that sixty thousand remained faithful to their military oath.

The fact remained that less than half, about twenty-five thousand, did join what was called the Indian National Army, led by Subhas Chandra Bose, a man of courage, intellectual force and a passionate devotion to the cause of immediate independence. All these men were legally guilty of mutiny, desertion and waging war against the King-Emperor, military crimes for which the penalty was death. But it was quite clear that the great majority – perhaps four-fifths, perhaps more – had been sadly misled as to the facts and that, when they knew their old comrades were still in arms and were driving the Japanese out of Burma, they were sorry for what they had done and wanted to come back. When it was announced that they would not be shot out of hand they surrendered in droves.

But what was to be done with them? Auchinleck convened several meetings with the Home Department – meetings of six or seven people all told – at most of which I was present. Everyone dismissed as out of the question the idea of shooting twenty-five thousand men. Everyone agreed at once that those who had joined the Japanese in order to escape and had done so should be restored to their former rank and continue in service. Everyone also agreed that the principle of fidelity to military allegiance in spite of changing circumstances must be asserted, as much in the interest of the new independent India as of the old. The new India would need a reliable army. And the sufferings of those who had stood fast must not be slighted.

The first of these discussions took place just before the end of the war with Japan, when the public knew nothing of the INA, who were already surrendering – demoralized, starving and in rags. We must be ready to make an announcement as soon as the war ended; it must go as far as possible in the direction of clemency – and whatever happened we must not then give way to agitation and go down the slippery slope of conceding one point after another. We were all agreed on that.

The war ended; we made our announcement. I drafted it myself;

it stated the general principles and went on to the application. Those whom military intelligence classified as 'grey' – those who were misled about the facts and had been half-hearted in their help to the Japanese – would be simply dismissed. Those who had tortured or killed their former comrades, those who had held positions of special responsibility and been fully aware of what they were doing – these were a different matter and would be brought to trial. No figures of course were mentioned but we thought at that time that there would be about a hundred trials which in law might lead to a death sentence. Of course, such sentences, if any were passed, might be commuted or remitted.

The announcement was received not unfavourably. The tone of the Press at the time was usually critical and sometimes abusive, but on this matter comment was at first grudgingly favourable and Pandit Nehru said that it was not bad for the Government of India. Within two months, all that had changed and the public – the newspaper-reading public – had worked itself up into a frenzy of excitement on behalf of the INA who had come to be regarded as national heroes. I have a strong impression that the Congress High Command were as much disturbed by this as we were. They did not realize quite how close independence was, but they did hope to take over a reliable machine. The more thoughtful of them did not regard the policy we proposed as unduly severe but *their* war – the war for independence – was still to be won. A party which for twenty years has been trying to rouse people from their pathetic contentment must necessarily find it difficult to reverse the current. No one was prepared to speak out – indeed, there was no leader of consequence who felt he could afford to be left out of the chorus; but there were clear signs that they regarded the issue as a very hot potato which they would have been glad to drop.

The subject was put down for a debate in the Assembly, and on the Government side I would have to be the principal speaker. It was tabled for discussion quite early in the session, which ran from October to December 1945. I shut myself up alone the previous night and went through what I meant to say till I had it almost by heart – but the debate was postponed, on some procedural pretext. I think the Opposition hoped that interest would die down; personally, I felt disappointed. I was keyed up to a high pitch of tension and I believed that my case was a good one. I wanted to get the debate done with and relax. My recollection is that it was postponed three times, but, instead of dropping, tension mounted. At last the day came; I suppose the Opposition too began to feel they had better be done with it. By this time I knew my speech very well indeed; I had been through that tense nervous preparation over and over. There was no barracking; they listened with absolute concentration. I have spoken a good deal since then, but never to an audience so hushed and so attentive.

I appealed to the Opposition to think of the future, of the new India that would soon come into being and that would depend on the fidelity of its army. I asked them to consider the past. Why were the British in India at all? Not because Indian soldiers lacked courage or skill; not simply because of technical superiority. For a hundred years after Plassey there had not been much difference in the weapons on either side. Nor was it solely a matter of parade-ground drill; that was something the Maratha and Sikh armies had learned too. No, it was certainty of allegiance that had been the deciding factor in battle after battle. However brave he or his soldiers might be, an Indian prince could never be sure that one of his allies or one of his generals might not make peace separately or join the enemy. The men Indians should be proud of were the splendid soldiers who had driven the Germans out of Italy and the Japanese out of Burma. Those were the kind of men they would need in the army of the future – not men who changed sides when things were difficult.

And ought they not to be proud of men who had faced torture and starvation rather than waver in their fidelity? What would they do if confronted with the situation that faced us? Surely there were two essential objects to bear in mind. We must safeguard the reliability of the Indian Army of the future and therefore we must not brush aside as nothing the military crimes of desertion, mutiny and waging war against the Head of the State. Did they not agree with that? But on the other hand we must use imagination and understand the position of those simple men who had seen defeat in Burma and had then been cut off from all information about what was happening. For such men, simple dismissal, without punishment as criminals, was surely right. But for a few leaders – and particularly those guilty of torture and brutality against their comrades – the law would take its course. Was this wrong? Was this not in the interests of the future India as well as the old?

That so far as I remember was the gist of what I said. I do not suppose that it had much influence on the course of events, but it did I think modify the tone of the speeches on the other side and the comment in the Press. I was reported very fully and very fairly. All this was before the trials of the leaders, about which I do not want to add anything to what I have said before; this book is not the place for assessment of policy. Since those events I have heard and read criticism – and sometimes rather contemptuous criticism – of all that took place, though nowhere any constructive suggestion of any better course. This has made me wonder how many of those who criticize have themselves taken a part – however small – in really difficult decisions. It is easy to make lofty pronouncements when all is over but anyone who writes about the past ought, I think, to use all the imagination he possesses to see the situation as it presented itself at the time. Then he must try to understand something that I think of as the drag of circumstance.

Try to picture a simple diagram. The intention of a leader, such as Marlborough or Cortes or Auchinleck, is a force that makes a line in one direction and the drag of circumstance makes a line in another direction; in the angle between them there will be a resultant line representing the actual course of events. So at least it has seemed to me ever since that series of happenings after the war with Japan. We did in the end do what we had said we would in no circumstances do; we conceded more than we had meant to. But the drag of circumstance was strong and I believe it was a good thing we did what we did. There were no martyrs. The Congress forgot the INA as quickly as they conveniently could. Dhargalkar, who had been confined in the cage and who gave evidence against the INA, rose after independence to the rank of Lieutenant-General and represented India in Korea.

3 A Very Odd Character

In the years between the outbreak of war in 1939 and the spring of 1946, when we left Delhi for yet another new existence – as different from Delhi as Delhi from Garhwal – events jostled each other in so crowded a sequence that it has not been easy to recall the order in which they occurred. I have recorded only those that stand out most jaggedly, like rocks from a dangerous sea, and it has been hard to reject so many faces and friends that give me pleasure in memory.

There has not been room – and perhaps it would not be of much general interest – to recount the meagre news we had from home by unbelievably slow mails, nor the painful decision Mary and I had taken that she should go home with the children so that their grandparents might see them. All through these crowded years, the certainties that were the background of my life had been there – and yet – and yet – awareness of them was a little deadened by the numbing effect of war. One day Mary told me of a misfortune that had happened to a woman we knew, though not intimately, and I must have brushed it aside, my mind being full of other things. She looked at me sadly and said: 'Once you used to be interested in people.'

The end of the war restored that interest. To the general relaxation, to the renewal of interest in life, was added the prospect of an entirely new career; *Call the Next Witness* was picked by the Book Society of those days as their choice for the month; after the two sessions in the

Assembly I had had four months' leave to England and had used it to write *The Wild Sweet Witch*, a novel about Garhwal, on which I had been brooding for some time, sketching scenes in my head and trying to fit them together. That had good notices and a Book Society recommendation. I felt no doubt that the ICS would wind up – at least for its English members – and I looked forward to a new life as a writer. But before I come to the last chapter of my life in India, there is one portrait I cannot omit, because of its outstanding oddity.

It was before Ceylon that I first met him. Someone came into my room and asked to see a certain document that was secret. I looked up and was astonished. There before me was a figure that a Japanese cartoonist might have drawn if he wished to portray a British officer. His uniform was formally correct – but it was not what people wore. Others in GHQ at that time of year kept as cool as possible; they wore shorts and soft bush-shirts of cotton twill with badges of rank in worsted. This man was in starched khaki drill, with a tunic, long stiffly creased trousers, a collar and tie; he looked as if he were going to a ceremonial parade. His badges of rank were of burnished brass and heraldic antelopes pranced in brazen splendour on the lapels of his tunic. He looked very uncomfortable. His hair was brushed straight up *en brosse* and, as I recall his face, it appears that there was a moustache rather like that of Kaiser Wilhelm II or Mephistopheles – but this may be an imaginary embellishment. Rather coldly I asked to see his pass and read: Major J. E. Powell. It seemed in order but I was still suspicious. Really, everything about him was so very unusual. I rang the Directorate of Military Intelligence. Yes, they said, he was quite genuine.

Much later, we remembered this incident together and laughed at it. 'You thought I was a spy,' said Enoch, but it was not quite as definite as that. I thought he looked *wrong*. When I came to know him, I disagreed with almost everything he said but I came to like him. Indeed, a friend remarked that I seemed almost obsessed by him and it was true that I was fascinated; I was trying to *understand*; he was an enigma. Part of the solution, I think, was that he had made up his mind that he would not – like most wartime officers – try to behave as though he too had been to Cheltenham and Sandhurst. No, he would not be like other soldiers, he would be what he was, an exceptionally gifted boy from the West Midlands who had become a Professor of Greek at Sydney and who could do a military job better than a soldier. There was much in this to be admired but the desire to be original sometimes led him into strange postures. I happened to say that the mid-afternoon in Delhi in the hot weather, when temperatures in the shade might approach 120°F, was not the best time for hard mental work.

'On the contrary' said Enoch at once 'I find it a very good time for work – provided that I have had a sufficiently heavy lunch.'

'And what do you mean by heavy?' I asked, full of curiosity.

'Steak and kidney pudding followed by jam roly-poly,' he replied. This I thought was going too far – and he probably did himself, because it was accompanied by a smile that held a good deal of self-mockery.

By that time he was a Brigadier and a member of the Army in India Reorganization Committee. Auchinleck had appointed this Committee to report on the size of army India would need after the war and he wanted on it someone with a good brain who was not a professional soldier. Its headquarters were in Dehra Dun, about a hundred and twenty miles from Delhi, and I went more than once to stay a night in their mess and spend the following day discussing things with this Committee. Once I arrived to find Enoch the only one in the mess. He said, in a rather stilted voice:

'Will you have a whisky and soda? I have observed that that is what an English gentleman considers suitable after a journey.'

Remarks of that kind were meant to assert his independence of convention and to proclaim his rejection of a tradition which is the backbone of English history – the tradition of aping the gentry which ran through our society for centuries and by which Tudor shopkeepers and Victorian brewers became Earls and Marquesses. It was a rejection in which he did not persist. Even then he would show by a laugh that he was aware of some absurdity in his pose as the incorruptible plebeian.

But what weight should one give to other opinions expressed at the same time? Power, he told me, was the only thing that counted; the mistake we had made in the last war was fighting it. We should have agreed with the Germans to divide the world between us. But might there not have been some divergence of view as to how the world should be run? I enquired mildly. Was there no difference between the Nazi philosophy and our own? He laughed at my naiveté; power was all that mattered. Today, the Rt Hon. Enoch Powell would repudiate such Nietzschean views. Any man may change his opinion; for my part, I wonder how deeply he held his views at the time. He was an Anglican atheist, he told me; he no longer believed in God, still less in Christianity, but there ought to be a church and the King should be head of it. That too he would repudiate today – but should such sayings be classed with the jam roly-poly? Was he pulling my leg or was it all an elaborate bid for an identity that would command his own respect and the attention of others? And where does one fit in those wistful little poems in the manner of *The Shropshire Lad*? I still find him a fascinating psychological puzzle.

He dominated that Committee about the future of the army, not by monopolizing the discussion – on the contrary, he behaved beautifully at meetings – but by getting up very early in the morning and drafting the next chapter. One such chapter was almost entirely his own work and I remember it because it illustrated a habit of mind that is surely dangerous. It was about the number of officers that the army would require. The Committee had weighed the threats India might be expected to face and had estimated the forces that would be required to meet them; this meant the army would need, let us say, five thousand officers. An officer must have a certain educational qualification. During the war, there had been in India so many men of military age with that qualification. Now of these only – let us say – three per cent had held commissions in the army. That gave a fixed proportion of three per cent on which to work. The total number of men with the right qualification could not increase by more than two per cent per annum – a committee had just reported and that was what it said. Therefore the number of young men suitable to be officers could not increase by more than two per cent either. This would not provide the required number of five thousand officers; it would be twenty-five years before there were enough. Therefore India would need to draw on Britain for officers for the next twenty-five years.

This was an argument which proceeded logically, step by step, from certain assumptions taken as axioms, like a proposition about the three angles of a triangle. But it reached a conclusion that was absurd if one took into account human factors. India was not going to wait twenty-five years for independence, and no independent country would agree to accept half her officers from abroad. The conclusion being outrageous, a more flexible mind would have questioned the earlier links in the chain and perceived two flaws. Many Indians, particularly the educated, had regarded World War II as Britain's quarrel, not theirs; far more might be ready to join the forces of an independent India. And predictions by committees about rates of growth are not infallible. Auchinleck dismissed this chapter as altogether off the mark and it discredited other recommendations too. I lost touch with Enoch later but I continue to watch with surprise that quick, logical and powerful mind arguing remorselessly to conclusions which demand rethinking in the light of human sympathy.

But we are about to leave Delhi and before that let me recall one trivial incident. There was a young man at the University of Lucknow who had had the astonishing good fortune to win a scholarship to the United States. What was almost more difficult just then, he was allotted a berth in a ship. His fortune was made! All he had to do was to go through some formalities in Delhi. He hurried there – and was told it would take three weeks to get a visa and he must have a bond for a thousand rupees signed by some responsible person guaranteeing his return. The ship would leave Bombay in two days' time and his scholarship would lapse and he did not know anyone in Delhi. He was in despair. What could he do? You will have guessed; he was a Garhwali. It was seven years since I had left the district and he had then been about thirteen. It was the eve of independence. But the Deputy Commissioner was his father and mother and would rescue him. It was only a matter of a few telephone calls and signing a bond – and he caught his ship. He went into India's Foreign Service and for years wrote to tell me about his progress.

XI

BELEAGUERED ROYALTY

1 'We are so cosmopolitan . . .'

It was someone's birthday and the children were playing 'Oranges and Lemons'. Uncle Yusuf and Aunt Fatima held up their hands to make an arch; they were enjoying themselves as much as the children and Uncle Yusuf seemed to have forgotten that he was a member of the Cabinet and that he was formally addressed by a tremendous title that meant he was a leader in battle and victorious in war. 'Here comes a chopper to CHOP off his head!' Their hands came down and they had caught a merry struggling little urchin who was trying to escape. 'Oranges or Lemons?' they whispered in his ear and with peals of laughter he joined the tug-of-war team behind Aunt Fatima.

'Who is that little boy?' I asked my nearest neighbour and she told me a name I have forgotten, but a name unmistakably Hindu, some Ram Swarup or Jag Deo.

'But he's wearing the wrong sort of hat!' I exclaimed in astonishment. He was wearing a Turkish fez, like an inverted red plant pot with a black silk tassel, which in Northern India was always the sign of a Muslim.

'Oh, here in Hyderabad we do not care for things like that!' said my neighbour gaily. 'It is one of the nice things here that we are so delightfully cosmopolitan.'

She was right for the moment and up to a point. None of us knew that it would be only five months till the end of nearly two centuries of stability. It was like the spring of 1789 at Versailles. At the buffet suppers that the grandees of Hyderabad enjoyed so much, the men were elegant in black *sherwanis* or gorgeous in gold brocade, the ladies wore saris of sapphire or flame-colour or starlit blue; they moved here and there between flowering bushes, enjoying the scented dusk, just cool enough after the heat of the day, clustering like bees round their queen in the flood-lighted centre of the gathering, or stepping for a moment away from the bright centre to rest the eyes or to look up at the brilliance of the stars. Everyone seemed to be happy and witty and amused; the tables were covered with Persian pilaos, Mughal kebabs, Indian curries,

French salads – dishes to suit every taste. There were Arabs, Persians and Turks as well as a scattering of French and English. And of the Hydera-badis themselves, the people of the state, there would be among the guests some Hindus, the daughter of a high court judge perhaps, with her young banker husband, or there might be the descendant of some Maratha freebooter who two hundred years ago had led his cavalry to fight for the Viceroy of the Deccan and had been rewarded with an estate. But nine out of ten would be Muslims, descendants of men who had come into India from Persia or Afghanistan or Central Asia, many of them still pale as ivory, each treasuring a crescent sword from Damascus that was the symbol of his family honour, a reminder that he was really a noble and a warrior even though by day he worked in the Secretariat as a civil servant. It was a state of the same size and population as Spain, Muslim in culture and language. Its ruler maintained that his was the largest Muslim state in the world – but there was one little fact that he did not always remember, that he had fifteen Hindu subjects for every Muslim.

Long ago, in the time of Clive, the Nizam-ul-Mulk, the Viceroy of the Deccan, had become the faithful ally of the British. Indeed, it had become part of his style and titles – Faithful Ally. Before that he had shaken off all but the most shadowy allegiance to the Mughal Emperor in Delhi. For every practical purpose he had been an independent ruler. Now he was the Premier Prince of India, His Exalted Highness, Faithful Ally, Invincible in War, Ever Victorious; he was the Head of his State, the Head of his Army, supreme within his boundaries – so long as he behaved with some discretion – but not exactly independent, because he could no longer make war nor conduct foreign affairs. He had given up his independence as effectively as the King of Oudh. But it was a hundred years since Oudh had been annexed and its King had gone into exile. Hyderabad continued; Hyderabad had sent help to the British at the time of the Mutiny, in the Kaiser's war, in Hitler's war. In return, the people of Hyderabad had had security. For a hundred and seventy years there had been peace. The Hindus knew better than to raise their heads. They were tolerated; they became judges and vice-chancellors; they made money; they practised their religion; some of them were even invited to parties. They lived quietly. The Muslims did not fear them; they too lived quietly. They had given up their independence and they had tranquillity instead. Now it was 1947 and in five more months the British would be saying that all that was over.

It was through Sir Walter Monckton that I was there. He had sat in the Viceroy's box once when I was speaking in the Assembly in Delhi; we had met afterwards and talked and he had wondered if I meant to go into politics. Everyone understood that before long we should all be looking for new careers. But I was clear that I did not want that; I wanted to live somewhere in the English countryside and write novels. I thought this would need an openness to impressions, a receptive ear; if you join a political party, there are arguments, aspects of life, to which you must close your heart. He understood that. But soon afterwards Mary and I were asked to dinner at Hyderabad House, a great palace in Delhi; Walter was there and the Prime Minister of Hyderabad, Sir Mirza Ismail, and at some stage of the evening the proposal was broached.

There was a problem and Sir Mirza had a solution. He was a great man for solutions – reasonable, civilized, elegant, unhurried. He had been born in the state of Mysore towards the end of the last century and when he was about seven or eight the ruler of the state had died, leaving an heir of just Mirza's age. The Government of India had appointed a wise old gentleman of the Indian Civil Service to be Tutor and Governor to the young Prince. He was to bring him up with some six or eight boys of his own age, of whom Mirza Ismail was one; they would learn English and geometry and Urdu from Indian masters but the Tutor and Governor would supervise all their work and see that they learnt to ride and play games and behave like young gentlemen; he would be a father to them and would see that they were educated like Renaissance princes – with a touch of Eton and a rather lesser touch of Rugby. This had been an outstanding success; the Maharaja of Mysore had been a most enlightened prince and for a long time Mirza Ismail, the companion of his boyhood, had been his Prime Minister; the state had had the reputation of being one of the best administrations in India – peaceful, progressive, liberal, remarkable for many reforms and in particular for fountains and public gardens in its cities.

Since then Sir Mirza had been Prime Minister of one of the great states of Rajputana and now he had come to Hyderabad, the premier state of India. Here one problem overrode all others. His Exalted Highness ruled over about sixteen million people, of whom one million were Muslim; the army, police and civil service were predominantly Muslim; much of the countryside was ruled by feudal nobles, most of them Muslim. Some of these nobles maintained their own law courts, their own police, their own system of Land Revenue, and even their own soldiers. All this had hardly changed since the eighteenth century; the British had made no reforms here. And suddenly – no one knew when but very soon – this feudal aristocracy would have to come to terms with India – a country with hundreds of millions of subjects and a powerful army, a country which surrounded them on all sides and which would undoubtedly be ruled by the Congress party. The Congress professed to be democratic and egalitarian – and Hyderabad was neither. The Congress professed to be secular – and Hyderabad was an Islamic state in which God was sovereign and the monarch His deputy. And – secular or no – the Congress was composed of people most of whom were born Hindus. That was the great problem.

But of course there were plenty of others and it was one of these that concerned me. His Exalted Highness had long cherished the ambition to be regarded one day as the Khalif of Islam, the Shadow of God upon Earth, an office which had fallen into abeyance when the last Emperor of Turkey was forced from the throne. With this in mind, he had married his elder son to the daughter of the last Emperor. Her Highness the Princess of Berar had left Turkey as a child when her father was exiled; she had been brought up in Paris. She was more French than English, but thoroughly at home with any Englishman who could respond with pleasure to that slightly mocking air with which an educated French woman is liable to regard him. She had travelled in America too; she was, in short, cosmopolitan. But her husband, the Prince of Berar, knew little of any world but Hyderabad; he had been brought up hap-hazardly, as was too often the way with Indian princes; he had learnt more from servants and toadies than from tutors. Husband and wife had little in common. She had made a noble resolve that her two sons should be preserved from the corruption that so often grows from continual flattery and from wealth without responsibility. 'I have given up my life; I will not give up my children,' she said to me once. The elder was thirteen, the younger was eight. Her Highness would have liked them to go to school abroad but neither His Exalted Highness nor their father saw any need for the boys to have a better education than themselves. It was forbidden. At present, they did just what they chose; there was no one in the whole state to say no to them except their mother, whom they did not always attend to, and their grandfather, whom they did not often see.

This was the situation when Sir Mirza became Prime Minister. He regarded the education of a future ruler as of the first importance. So far, he saw eye to eye with the Princess, but it would have been sur-prising if his mind had not turned to the solution that had proved so successful in Mysore fifty years ago. He suggested that I should come as Tutor and Governor. He painted a glowing picture of the attractions of Hyderabad; I should be able to write most of the day, merely keeping an eye on the boys' development. To have me there as a confidant would be a consolation and support to himself; he had a heavy burden of responsibility and no one to whom he could talk frankly; everyone in Hyderabad belonged to someone's party. Walter Monckton came only occasionally for a few days at a time; he was no longer a member of the Government in Britain and came as a barrister, as a constitutional adviser. Sir Mirza told me that he and Sir Walter saw the main problem of Hyderabad in much the same terms. The state would have to reach some agreement with the Congress Party in India sooner or later. Their best chance was to make a bargain quickly. The terms for a settlement that the Congress would consider in March would be too high by April and would drop month by month. But so far His Exalted Highness would not consider anything the Congress would be likely to look at for a moment. To talk of such things to me would mean a great deal to him, Sir Mirza told me.

I was aware, of course, that there was an element of flattery in this but that was true of most conversations in India, and he clearly wanted me to come. I also perceived that the arrangements for the education of the young Maharaja of Mysore had been made when everyone took it for granted that things would stay much as they were for ever – but no one could think that in 1947. However, I agreed to visit Hyderabad and see the Princess.

I met a most impressive person, a few years younger than myself, a commanding figure, handsome of feature, with a clear fair complexion and auburn hair; she wore superb saris, which suited her imposing height. No one could ignore her or slight her. She was always, essentially and indefinably, royal, and it seems to me that if fate had so willed she might have been one of the great queens of the world. She would have been as imperious as Elizabeth I of England and she would have demanded as much from the young men of her court, sent them as readily to their death on the Spanish Main, teased them as merrily and as cruelly. She would not have seen so clearly the virtues of compromise. I came to know later that she had skill – which she neglected – as an artist and a wide appreciation of painting and that she could observe with humorous detachment any situation that did not too closely concern the future of her children. Formally, of course, she was a Muslim but she was a good deal influenced by philosophical Hinduism, of the school which has much in common with Buddhism and Sufism. But this was our first meeting and the important thing was that we should clearly understand each other about Sir Mirza's plan.

Neither she nor I was enthusiastic. Everything was so different from Sir Mirza's boyhood. His Tutor and Governor had had the British Government behind him; I should not have that advantage. With companions and schoolmasters from Hyderabad, how could the Princes ever face real competition and get real self-confidence? How limited an education it would be, compared with the best that was available in Switzerland, which was what she really wanted! For my part, I was very frank; I explained that I felt it was time I ceased to be an official; that I wanted to live through a year of English seasons, to feel the spring come and see the leaves turn in autumn and spend Christmas at home. I hoped I could earn a living by my pen – but after twenty years it would be silly to throw away the pension I had earned and so I wanted to wait till the ICS was formally wound up. I could stay in Delhi, where I had a job that would generally be thought more important than this. But I had never been in a state, nor in the south of India. 'If I came, it would be for the wrong reasons,' I said, 'it would be from curiosity, to see a new life, perhaps to write a book.' I did not think I should want to stay more than two years at most. If she would have me on those terms, I would do the best I could to make Sir Mirza's plan a success. It might have advantages for the boys as a preparation for sending them to school. It appeared to be acceptable to His Exalted Highness and in any case I would write a report after a few months and make suggestions for their future.

'That suits me very well,' said the Princess. 'I would rather have you than some old Colonel who would make a job of this and want to stay for ever.' The Princess and I were usually very frank with each other. I told Sir Mirza my doubts about his plan, though more diplomatically. But he was sure I should like Hyderabad so much that I should not want to leave.

I had no scruples about leaving the Defence Department. The sooner an Indian was in my place the better; he would need all the experience he could get before independence. To leave Delhi was to leave a centre of power, but that was not to me the wrench it is to many people. If money were everything, the proposal was undoubtedly attractive. In Delhi I always ran into debt and Hyderabad would be a chance to get straight. Mary and I and our three children would live free in the household of the two young Princes, which I would control, with all its stewards and cooks, horses and motor-cars. There was an established precedent that an ICS officer on deputation to Hyderabad drew the pay of his previous appointment – and it would be all pocket-money. It would be a charming interlude. Anything might happen!

It was a time when good-byes were being said every day and when everyone knew that bigger changes still were in the air. One of the last public occasions in Delhi at which we were present was the wedding of Lord Wavell's daughter Felicity, at which our son George was a page, being almost of an age with the Viceroy's grandson Francis Humphrys. It was immediately after the wedding that the announcement was made that the Viceroy had been recalled, an event that seemed to intensify the thunderous doom-laden atmosphere, and made it easier for us to go.

We were to start our new life in Ootacamund, a hill station in the Nilgiri Hills; that would be in a few weeks' time and meanwhile I had to feel my way into Hyderabad society, see the masters who would teach the boys, arrange the household, see the eight boys and all their parents. It was all new, not very demanding, but often frustrating. Sir Mirza had promised me everything I wanted and when I went with some request to an official he would always be charming. He would promise – but nothing would happen. For the least thing, I would have to prod and prod. It was like fighting a featherbed. At last I went to Sir Mirza in a flurry of irritation. I apologized for bothering him with matters so trivial – it was absurd, all about inkpots or desks or blackboards or teachers' pay – but I was making no progress.

'My dear fellow, what is it you want?' he said, in his bland, reasonable tones. 'Dictate to me. I am your stenographer. Dictate the order you need.' So I did, and he wrote it out and signed it and we went on to talk about the political scene. It moved very quickly, and almost all my knowledge came from him. I cannot doubt that he was right in thinking that all the time things were moving against any prospect of Hyderabad's future as an independent Muslim state. Sir Mirza believed that, early in 1947, the Congress would have agreed to allow Hyderabad, not indeed independence, but some degree of self-government not very different from what then existed. To have announced such an agreement with the premier state in India would at that stage have been a successful stroke; other states would have followed. But His Exalted Highness wished to be entirely independent; he would have liked to be referred to as His Majesty and perhaps to have been Khalif of Islam; he thought he might strike a bargain by which he could obtain access to the sea; he talked of buying Goa from the Portuguese; he hoped to recover the province of Berar, which had long been administered by the British. He could not see that he had very little to offer and that day by day it was getting less; soon he would have nothing that the Congress could not take from him without giving anything in return.

It was in March that Lord Mountbatten came as Viceroy with instructions to achieve independence by 1948. That date in itself reduced His Exalted Highness's power to bargain. Soon afterwards came the announcement that independence would be a year earlier, in August 1947, and that there would be two dominions, India and Pakistan. The lesser princes began hastily to accede to one dominion or the other; Hyderabad had lost the chance of showing the way. There was talk of a link with Pakistan; to envisage a Muslim block in South India was not much more bizarre than a Muslim block in East Bengal – or, at least, would not have been except for those inconvenient millions of Hindus. But Mr Jinnah's views on an Islamic state were very different from those of His Exalted Highness. Further, Mr Jinnah had made a very bad impression when accorded an audience; he had crossed his legs and lolled in his chair and even lighted a cigarette, all crimes against proper behaviour. So Hyderabad continued in an isolation that grew daily more dangerous.

I had supposed that His Exalted Highness might wish to say something to me about the education of his grandsons. How little I knew! Walter Monckton told me later that he had made several visits to Hyderabad – flown out from England, been lavishly entertained for several days, paid fees as high as any barrister could dream of – but denied an audience. It had been more than a year before he had been allowed to meet the Nizam. We were somewhat luckier. Suddenly one morning we received an invitation to tea that afternoon, at a palace some twelve miles outside Hyderabad, where the Viceroy sometimes stayed but which was usually more like a museum. A Rolls-Royce came to fetch us – a very old one, but a Rolls is a Rolls. We sped along wide, empty streets, cleared of all traffic, police whistles blowing, loyal subjects lining the pavement. His Exalted Highness was somewhere ahead of us, followed at about a mile's distance by the British Resident, and after another mile by ourselves.

The palace was on top of a steep conical hill; we drove up a spiral approach and stopped at the foot of a lofty flight of steps. On either side of the steps were rank on rank of courtiers; they wore silk *sherwanis* in cream, dove-grey, palest blue, belts of gold and silver brocade, tall hats shaped like tulips and of all the colours of all the tulips in Holland – crimson and gold, russet, pink and lilac. They made two pillars of tulips, stretching away, up and up in a narrowing perspective to the great doors at the head of the steps. It was an impressive scene, but in India there is often some discordant note in a carefully arranged occasion; sure enough, there was such a note here – an ill-dressed little man in an old nondescript *sherwani*, rather dirty, not buttoned up to the neck, with a dingy cap, hanging about at the foot of the steps. He seemed uncertain of his role and indeed to have no place in the proceedings; we thought it tactful to ignore him and addressed ourselves to the stairs. But elegant, agonized ADCs appeared at our elbows, hissing, like geese or samovars: 'His Exalted Highness!' So we turned and presented our humble duty.

His Exalted Highness showed us round the palace himself, accompanied by the Nawab who was Minister of Works. There was an extraordinary mixture of treasures, lovely pieces of Chinese jade, costly jewels, Victorian musical-boxes, curiosities that had caught someone's fancy a hundred years ago. And in every room, His Exalted Highness would direct our attention to the floor or the chandelier or the moulded decoration on the walls – once to the bell-pull – and turn to the Minister of Works and say:

'Nawab Sahib! Nawab Sahib! What would it cost to replace that?'

'It's really impossible to say, Your Exalted Highness,' the Minister would reply. 'The workmen to do such work could never be found nowadays.'

'You see? You see? Couldn't be replaced. Priceless.'

After that we had tea with delicate cucumber sandwiches. We were careful not to cross our legs or loll in our chairs like Mr Jinnah. But the education of the Princes was not mentioned.

2 Education of a Prince

The education of the elder Prince was the more urgent. He was thirteen; he spoke English, French, Turkish and Urdu fluently but did not write any of them correctly; he could ride any horse with confidence, could dive from any height, had shot a tiger, could drive a Jeep and take an engine to pieces but could not catch a ball, and if you asked him the simplest question in arithmetic he had recourse to counting on his fingers. He had hardly ever done anything he did not want to do at that moment, and would have been something of a problem for any school for normal boys of his age. Of course I was not an expert in education but it was assumed in India that anyone in the Indian Civil Service could become an expert in anything at once, like Cabinet Ministers in England. At that time I would have said confidently that a boy must learn a mental framework on which he could later build. Once he had mastered the framework, he could pursue his own interests, as I had done under Neville Gorton; but for the framework, it would be an unusual boy who would not need external pressure and some plain hard drudgery. That framework the elder Prince would need before he went to school.

I worked out a time-table which would fill the boys' time from the moment they got up till bedtime. There was a ride before breakfast, on the lovely rolling downs of Ootacamund, among the blue gums and the scented wattle; we soon had eight quite accomplished young horsemen. 'Sir, look at me!' I remember young Haidar crying. He was about twelve and small for his years; he was cantering downhill with his stirrups crossed on the saddle, his arms crossed and a loose rein. Twice a week we followed the hounds and on those days, if there was a run, work in school might begin a little late. We all breakfasted together, the eight boys and our own children, Mary and I and Captain Hamid Beg, a cavalryman, a kind of equerry. School usually began at nine, and we started with one of a series of prayers, which I wrote with some care, trying to make them acceptable to Hindu, Muslim or Christian. There were five masters for the eight boys, so they had a good deal of attention. We had a drill sergeant and boxing instructor who gave them some physical training in the middle of the morning – but I had to be present; the six companions did as the instructor told them but the two Princes would not exert themselves for him and he dared not rebuke them, so he begged me always to be there.

After lunch, the boys went off to carpentry or cricket or something of the kind, arranged by the kindness of the head of a large regular school. There were more lessons in the evening. Sometimes I read them stories or told them tales. At weekends, we usually went for picnics on the downs; they would make a bonfire and we played stalking and tracking games. One game in particular, which we called Looking and Not Looking, was very popular. You need a hillside with scattered boulders or gorse bushes or patches of bracken; everyone hides except one boy, who stands in a prominent place, takes a good look round and then shouts: 'Not looking!' when the rest have thirty seconds to get a little closer to him without being seen. Everyone enjoyed these expeditions but no one more than Barakat, the elder Prince. It was a good thing he did. One day the mathematics master, a big jovial man with a reddish-brown face like an Afghan, told me Barakat still did not know the multiplication tables and that all his work was held up because of this. I gave him two days – but he still did not know them by Saturday. So he stayed behind in tears with the maths man, while the rest of us went on a picnic. I never had to do it again.

They were good boys at heart – Barakat, the elder, far more withdrawn than Karamat, a plump little boy of eight who was distinctly a wit. A specialist in Harley Street remarked to Karamat about a year later that he was rather stout for his age. 'In my position,' Karamat genially informed him, 'I can afford to be.' Barakat was outwardly a more conventional boy, deeply interested in engines, really loving his rides on the downs and his weekend picnics. He understood that he might never be ruler and quickly accepted the idea that he would have to pass examinations. Indeed he reproached me on one occasion because I used once a week to try to stir up their wits by setting them some puzzle to which they could find no answer in their books. 'It won't help in our exams, sir,' he said.

I heard him once exulting to the others about the energetic life they lived; friends in Hyderabad, he said, could not even imagine so tough a life as this – and clearly he was proud of it. There was a deep inner reserve to Barakat. We were very lucky; we had no broken bones and they all put on weight. By the end of the season Barakat and Karamat were entirely amenable to external discipline and I think much closer to self-discipline.

There were three large bungalows, fairly close together. In one, the masters lived and the boys did their lessons; in the second, we lived as one large family with the boys; in the third, the Princess lived with her mother, the last Empress of Turkey. Her Majesty spoke Turkish and a few words of French, no English. Mary curtseyed, I bowed; we said: 'Your Majesty', and then she sat smiling, a placid, loving grandmother, and the conversation flowed round her. She was particularly fond of our son George, not yet four; so indeed was the Princess and there was a famous occasion when George, who was a tiger at the time, crawled out from behind a sofa, roaring, and then said to me in a pained voice: 'Tell that Princess to be frightened when I come out roaring.' She was delighted. George could sometimes be observed talking earnestly to the gardener in what must have been Telugu, a language no one else in the establishment could speak.

So our life was a mixture of nursery and school. I did not have so much leisure as Sir Mirza had foreseen, because I spent more time with the boys. But I still had far more than I had had in Delhi and I read more widely and broke new ground in my reading. I had time to reflect and to absorb impressions. I used some of my leisure to write *The Sword of Northumbria*, an adventure story based on the old game of the Heptarchy we had played at Oxford and on stories I had told the children. It was full of gallops and fighting. When it was published I sent a copy to Lord Wavell, who replied with a staff-college commentary on some of the battles.

Ripples reached us sometimes from Hyderabad. Once an intrigue was started against one of the assistant masters. It was he who was in charge of the Islamic instruction they received on Fridays and someone tried to persuade His Exalted Highness that he was not sufficiently orthodox. He came to me in great fear. I had to pretend I knew nothing about this intrigue and also to avoid entanglement in Muslim theology but I felt I must support this man, who had the approval of the Princess and whom the boys liked. I wrote a letter to the Minister of Education thanking him for deputing such excellent teachers and asking that HEH might be informed of the progress his grandsons were making under their excellent tuition. I had a polite formal reply from the Minister; it seemed to work.

One trivial incident comes to mind that illustrates the extreme oddity that was apt to crop up wherever our placid lives touched the machinery of the Nizam's Government. There was a splendid palace in Ootacamund built in the high Victorian period by the Nizam's grandfather. It belonged not to the state but to the Privy Purse. His Exalted Highness was reputed to be the richest man in the world and in gems, treasure, gold and silver, it may have been true. He never came to Ootacamund himself and the custom had grown up of lending this palace for two months in the most trying season of the year to the British Resident in Hyderabad. This courtesy to the Resident was felt, no doubt, to be of value to the state and when the Resident occupied the palace the state – that is the tax-payer – paid rent for it to the Privy Purse.

Now it so happened that I wanted a piano so that the boys could learn simple tunes and sing choruses; a later generation will say that I should have arranged for a teacher of Indian music, and perhaps that argument adds to the incongruity of the whole episode, but it did not occur to me at the time. I had found a music mistress but there was no piano to be hired in Ootacamund. Then I heard that there was one in the palace the Resident occupied. I asked him if he ever used it; he did not and had no objection to my borrowing it. There was an official of the Hyderabad Public Works Department called the Superintendent of Palaces. I asked him to have this piano moved to the school bungalow – one of the 'palaces' in his charge. He was clearly embarrassed – indeed frightened. All the furniture in the big palace was the personal property of His Exalted Highness; he dared not move it. I talked to him quietly and soothingly. When he was over the first shock, I asked him what it was that he feared. Did he think that, if His Exalted Highness knew that the instrument was being used for the instruction of his grandchildren, he would insist on a payment of five rupees a month to the Privy Purse from my budget – which was met by the state? It was a cruel question because he was torn between truth and loyalty to his Sovereign. In the end he put his hand on his heart in a moving gesture and said: 'Sir, I am ashamed to say, Yes, that is what he would do.' But he took the risk and it was smuggled up the hill on the understanding that no one should be told where it came from.

Sometimes on Sundays we went with the boys to lunch with Her Majesty and the Princess, and these were pleasant family occasions. Sometimes we gave a small dinner party, and very sumptuous such parties were in a quiet way, since we had a steward and two chefs, one for European food and one for Turkish and Mughal. In this atmosphere of domestic royalty – on a small scale, rather as I picture Balmoral in the time of the old Queen – it was hard to remember that every day the crisis was coming nearer. Sir Mirza had resigned. 'Sir Mirza was a traitor!' said the Princess, her eyes flashing. She would have cut off his head if she had been Elizabeth I of England. I still think he appreciated the situation far more realistically than any other adviser except Walter Monckton. His place was taken by the Nawab of Chhatari, a landowner from the Western UP whom I had known long ago. He had acted as

Governor of the UP and was a perfect picture of a Muslim nobleman, tall and handsome, charming, courtly, politeness itself – but not the man for such rough waters as these.

It was not surprising that there was bitterness. The India Office devised a pedantic but convenient dogma: 'Paramountcy cannot be transferred.' This meant that Hyderabad must make its own arrangements with India, which was like telling a rabbit to make its own arrangements with a tiger. The alliance that had lasted a hundred and seventy years was called off, and of that discourteous decision, the Faithful Ally and his advisers learnt (so Walter Monckton told me) only from the newspapers. During that summer, the right-wing Muslim organization called the Ittihād-i-Muslimān, the Union of the Faithful, grew more and more strident in its demands. It was said – I have no certain knowledge – that whenever His Exalted Highness was given unpalatable advice – and at this stage, that meant whenever he was given realistic advice – he would say that he would consider the matter and that he would then pass the word by the back stairs to the Ittihād-i-Muslimān, who would at once stage a demonstration. Next day he would announce that he could not go against the wishes of his people.

His Exalted Highness and the Ittihād alike moved in a realm of fantasy. The rabbit had lived so long in so secure a hutch that it did not know it was a rabbit. One day soon after independence Walter Monckton went to an audience to outline a legal point he hoped to make to Delhi. His Exalted Highness greeted him with the news that he had made up his mind; Berar was his and he had only lent it to the British. He would resume possession. He would order his troops to march in and that would end the legal arguments. Sir Walter pointed out that this would be an act of war and asked that the Commander-in-Chief should be summoned. He was an Arab, a soldierly man. Walter explained the proposal and said: 'Please tell His Exalted Highness how long the Hyderabad Army could hold out against the Indian Army.' The Commander-in-Chief looked at his toes. Walter insisted: 'No, you must say and you must say what you really think.'

'Three days,' he said, reluctantly, and some fifteen months later that proved to be exactly right.

In Ootacamund, no one would have known that anything had happened when India became independent on 15 August 1947. We read sadly of terrible slaughter in the Punjab, but it was almost as remote as it must have seemed to those in England. I did not think there would be changes in Hyderabad for a year or two; in any case, as regards the boys, the only course was to make the best recommendations I could for their education on the assumption that all would go on as before. No other hypothesis would have been considered. I wrote a full report, broken up into short incisive paragraphs – like a planning paper or a military appreciation. I described the arrangements made and the life we had lived; I said I was confident that all the boys had benefited, and particularly the Princes – but I did not think the experiment should continue; it had served its purpose. There was not enough competition; it was much too narrow a circle; there were only four boys of each age group. And the assistant masters, excellent though they had been, belonged to the Hyderabad educational system and it was impossible for them not to show some deference to the Princes. If the boys were really to be educated for the modern world, I felt they should go to a school abroad. But I did not think it would be right for the elder Prince to be pitch-forked at once into the rough-and-tumble of a conventional English school. Perhaps a school that had been recently started with some less conventional features, such as Bryanston, might be better. Even there, I thought it was desirable to have some introductory period; he might perhaps board for a year as part of the family of a married housemaster. He was an affectionate, home-loving boy. If something on these lines was chosen, I would be happy to act as a guardian in England, going to see him at half-term, discussing his progress and so on. That was my recommendation; if it was not approved, then I suggested, as a second-best, a school in Hyderabad of about fifty boys instead of eight. But this would be a school, and it would need a schoolmaster at its head. If the second course was preferred, I would try to start such a school but should like to be released as soon as possible.

This report, I learnt to my surprise, would be considered by the Cabinet. The Nawab Sahib of Chhatari, now the Prime Minister, with his invariable courtesy, asked me to be present, to meet the Cabinet Ministers beforehand, and to be available if any questions arose. I drove down from Ootacamund to Hyderabad. One by one the Cabinet Ministers took me aside. Each one said the same; he congratulated me on the clarity of my paper and my understanding of the situation. He preferred my first proposal – but he would vote for the second. Why? His Exalted Highness would not like the first. So I was not surprised when the verdict reached me.

We moved down to Hyderabad and for two or three months lived in a splendid palace that had been redecorated for us. There was room for the boys and ourselves to live there and for classrooms. I set about recruiting the new masters we should need and the new boys to bring the numbers up to forty or fifty. But I wanted to get home. I really believed that for Barakat and Karamat my first solution would have been the best; in a general way, it must surely be best for an Indian boy to be

brought up in contact with his own culture, but for these two, as Hyderabad was at the time, something else was needed and both had the intelligence and stamina to stand meeting others on an equal footing.
This special school for Princes, though better than nothing at all, was a
poor second-best. My heart was not in it.

Head and heart were mixed in those last days in Hyderabad. As to
India in general, I believed it was time for the British to go, time for
India to settle her own affairs. So much that needed doing could only be
done by Indians. I read an article in some British weekly regretting that
the Indian Civil Service should leave, but to me it seemed essential that
we should; if we did not, no one would believe that British rule was
ended. It must be absolutely clear where responsibility lay. And I could
not deceive myself into thinking that in the new India there could be
room for the Hyderabad whose life I had briefly shared. An absolute
monarch, feudal nobility, the domination of a Muslim minority – they
would be anathema to the professed ideals of the Congress and at the
same time a target for their greed. All this I saw clearly but with it went
many regrets.

It was like looking at seventeenth-century England. Reason says that
Charles I was impossible and yet he steals our sympathy by his dignity in
adversity, by his good manners, his taste in art, his style. It was much the
same with the nobles of Hyderabad. Their courtesy and good humour
were unfailing; their clothes were enchanting. There was a special
pleasure in talking to the ladies, the mothers of the Princes' companions,
for instance; you could never tell when there might not be a sudden
change of note. You would be talking to a Victorian high school girl
who would quote Tennyson and remember passing the Higher Cambridge – and then she would vanish and there would come some salty
comment on the ways of men and women that would be more French
than English. It was distasteful in the extreme that the British should
behave to these people with such contempt for past obligations and such
callous disregard for the decencies of diplomacy. 'In Hyderabad, it is
permissible to stab a man in the back but you must never be rude to him'
– a Muslim in Delhi had said to me. We did both.

We were sad to say good-bye to many friends but I was confident that
I had fulfilled my obligations to the Princess. Perhaps she had already
some outline in her mind of the plan she eventually carried out, though
she cannot have foreseen all the circumstances which made it possible
for her to steal the boys and put them surreptitiously to school in England.
If some such idea was already in her mind, it was a convenience to her
that I should go. Certainly she did not encourage me to stay. 'It is not
as though this was really your métier,' she said. On my part I was entirely

frank with her about my desire to get to England but I do not think I enlarged on one aspect – I really was suffering from a surfeit of grandeur. I wanted to get away to a simpler life, to dig and plant things and watch them grow.

There was something else too, something of which I certainly said nothing to the Princess and which I did not formulate clearly even to Mary or to myself. India hits you full in the face with misery. There is misery everywhere; starved, mangy dogs, gaunt lame ponies; beggars that sicken the beholder. In the back streets of the towns, people are huddled together in hideous squalor; there are flies everywhere, wasted limbs, festering sores. Unless you take the way of St Francis of Assisi, you cannot live as a sane man with open eyes among such sights. You must close your eyes, harden your heart and do what you can. If you are in any sense a ruler, you must make your heart harder still, because any just system of rule must make laws and treat all men according to categories. A just judge cannot play father to the prodigal son. Hard cases make bad law, they say, and, if that is so, good law makes hard hearts. Just as Indians felt that all their problems would be solved by independence, so I felt obscurely that to leave India, and to stop being an official, would release me from a burden of which I had taught myself not to think. But it is not a burden of which one can ever be quite rid; it is part of being human.

The children needed England too. It was traditional for the British in India to send their children home at about the age of seven and we were coming to the time when that separation would have faced us even if there had been no political changes. It would not have been good for them to stay on. There were too many servants, they got their own way too easily. And they were growing up in ignorance of their own country. 'Does the milk have to be boiled in England?' asked Penelope, always a practical child. 'Don't be so silly, Penny,' said Sundari Devi. 'In England, the milk comes ready boiled from the cow.' But she was uneasy about living in England, land of wonders though it was, because the countryside seemed to be infested with fierce monsters, stoats and foxes, which preyed on the innocent bunnies and hedgehogs of her picture-books.

To say good-bye always means hardening the heart and one of those to whom we said good-bye with most regret was Captain Hamid Beg, who had been attached as a kind of equerry to Her Highness and the two boys, and was devoted to their interests. He had lived with us as part of the family. He was a devout Muslim, constant in his prayers, and by a deep inner simplicity and integrity kept himself aloof from the intrigue which surrounded him. He asked me before I left to give him copies of the prayers with which we had begun the day. He seldom volunteered an opinion, but if he gave one it would be always worth hearing. He said nothing about the state of feeling in Hyderabad in the autumn of 1947 until one day, when my bearer was packing, it occurred to me that it was silly to take to England two rifles and a pistol (which had always been locked up in a safe, quite useless). I asked Hamid Beg if there was an arms dealer who would buy them. 'Let me take them,' he said. 'I will sell them better privately.' And in a few hours he was back, with about three times the price I had expected. No one had showed any sign but the city was already seething with fear.

At the last minute, there was a difficulty. Our plane was to come down at Istanbul and we needed a Turkish visa. But the day before we left, the Hyderabad authorities returned our five passports without visas; no one knew the international status of Hyderabad and we should have to get our visas in Bombay, where we had only a few hours between planes. However, I climbed into the airport bus, leaving Mary with the children, determined to make myself a nuisance in the Bombay Secretariat and do my best to get the visas, but I was not very hopeful. I shared a seat with a Bombay businessman, an Indian; I did not know him but he recognized me. He remembered the time when my name had been in the headlines almost every day; he had been in Delhi and had come to the Assembly to hear me speak on the INA. I told him about my errand to the Bombay Secretariat and he said at once: 'I have a car with a driver waiting where the bus stops. I shall take you to the Secretariat; I have a friend there and he is in the passport department. I shall stay with you till you get the visas you need.'

He did and I was back at the airport in time to catch the plane. That act of kindness, to a stranger, some three months after independence, marked my last day in India as a member of the Indian Civil Service.

XII

AN END
AND A BEGINNING

'You look as though you'd been working,' said a comfortable person with a basket as I sat down in the bus. She had been shopping in Bridport and was coming back to Charmouth; she spoke with approval, though with a touch of amusement, no doubt feeling that a professional would not have got in quite such a mess. I had been spreading fertilizer by hand on one of my fields. The sun had been warm for a spring day and I was not used to moving bags weighing a hundredweight; I had sweated a good deal and the fine grey dust had blown on my face and hair. I had cut the skin on one hand and the dust had turned the blood black. I did not look at all as I had looked at the wedding of the Viceroy's daughter in Delhi. But I was very proud of my fields and determined to treat them generously.

This was more than a year after we had left Hyderabad; we were living for the moment in a cottage in Charmouth that was normally let as seaside lodgings. On most days of the week, I sat at my desk and wrote till midday and then I would go by bus or bicycle to the holding of fifteen acres or so which clung to the shoulder of Stonebarrow above More-combelake. The builders were at work there on two tiny cottages which we hoped to make into a habitable house. The thatch had got so bad that someone had put corrugated-iron sheets over it; there was no inside tap and no inside sanitation, so a good deal had to be done. The estimates grew steadily more frightening. Meanwhile, I did what I could with the holding, growing vegetables, keeping hens, trying to improve the long-neglected hedges, preparing for the day when we should live there and keep cows.

At first, we had been on leave, not too sharply concerned with getting a living nor even in too great a hurry to find a home. For both of us it was a delight to explore the West Dorset countryside near Mary's home at Charmouth; for me, it was important, after nearly twenty years, to see something of my father and mother. My father had borne a heavy burden during the war. He was sixty-two in 1939 and now had two partners, of whom one was my brother. Both these younger men went into the army when war broke out. The elder left behind a wife who was a qualified doctor, but she had children and could not leave them at night. So my father had to take all the night calls for a three-man practice and by day add half my brother's work to his own. There were first-aid classes and air-raid precautions too, over and above the practice. All this would have counted less if life had been easier at home, but it was almost impossible to get help in the house and my mother's health had got steadily worse. For some time before the war, she had been suffering from a sclerosis, of a kind quite different from my sister's. It first affected her right hand; she had beautiful hands, with which she had been skilful. Long after it began, she went on with her work for Women's Institutes and the Rural Community Council, tiring herself to the point of utter exhaustion. She would come home hardly able to speak, and sit, nursing that painful hand, now thin, white and wasted, till she was a little revived by rest and tea.

Part of this I had seen on a short leave before the war. But the trouble spread to her legs and by the latter part of the war she was unable to leave her chair or even to turn over in bed without help. My father would come home, after a heavy day and often after a disturbed night, to find he must nurse my mother and perhaps get his own supper and wash up; all this he did with unfailing gentleness and devotion. He was sixty-seven when the war ended and had grown very thin. But he was brisk and cheerful; the sparse diet of wartime suited him, he told me. He could never have done it if he had been a man who worried. He had always had the gift of making up his mind quickly, doing all he could for his patient and then going on to the next without harrowing indecision or afterthoughts.

I have spoken before of his forbearance. Now it struck me more forcibly than ever and I remembered – with an ashamed amusement – an example of it on my first leave from India. Mr Binns of Duffield House next door had grown no less acid with the years. The garden that had belonged to the two houses when they were one was surrounded by a high wall of warm old bricks; it was divided down the middle by a much more recent fence. Mr Binns conceived a tiresome little animosity, believing he had been wronged by some alteration to this fence. My father told me of this sudden unreason. I had spent a lot of time lately on disputes about boundaries and was full of all that Boy Malcolm had meant by the phrase: 'Why did God give me two ears?' I said:

'Well, Father, I've heard how you see it. But in my experience there are always two sides to every dispute and I can't give an opinion till I've heard Mr Binns.'

Someone ought to have kicked me, but my father looked at me, smiled his kind smile and said nothing. One of Mr Binns's sons ended – or at least silenced – his father's grievance by working out that the value of the land involved was twelve and sixpence.

That had been fifteen years ago. Now my father's forbearance was often needed because my mother's acute, active and restless mind seemed in her illness to focus increasingly on small things that were close. She wanted the house to be run as it had always been and it caused her irritation amounting to distress if the Georgian silver teaspoons did not appear on the tea-tray with the right Crown Derby teacups. She had once been able to show people how to do things properly and had trained them to exact obedience; she could not get used to being unable to move herself and having no permanent trained servant. It was difficult, as one saw this concern and frustration, to remember how once she had rejoiced in mountain tops and heather and running streams.

My father's patience was endless. He had more leisure, now that the other two were back in the practice. He had no intention of retiring. People still wanted his sympathy. He told me at about this time of a woman who had been his patient but now lived many miles away on the coast. She had just made the long journey back to see him because she was frightened; her new doctor did not seem interested and merely sent her to hospitals for X-rays and reports. But he was planning to move out of the old house in the village and let my brother move in; he had bought a plot of land where he was making a garden and hoped to build a small bungalow. Now he would give time to growing beans and peas, some asparagus, a few strawberries and many roses. I found in his company the same kind of pleasure that I had found long ago when he came back from the Kaiser's war in 1919. We talked about his garden and the steps he was taking to lighten the heavy clay. We talked, too, about his early days at Barrowden and about Greenlands, my holding at Morecombelake, and about my hopes for making us, as near as we could, self-sufficient in food. Into these usually earthy subjects, he sometimes injected a note of absurdity of a kind all his own. I mentioned a large pig farmer who found overtime so expensive that he fed his pigs only six days a week. They had plenty of water and on Sundays had nothing else. He found it made little difference to the time they took to reach the right weight. 'And it might help to make the bacon streaky,' said my father.

To buy Greenlands had been a sudden decision. The need to find a convenient dry nesting-place had become urgent overnight. There was a small film company, THIS MODERN AGE, a subsidiary of the Rank organization, which made short documentary films, the kind of thing now done by television but then shown in cinemas. They asked me to write 'treatments' for two documentaries on India and Pakistan and proposed that I should go with the camera teams for six months. This fell through in the end, but at the time it seemed important to make up our minds before I went. We wanted a house with four or five bedrooms, an old vicarage perhaps, with a big garden and a field or two where I could keep pigs and hens and a cow. When we explained this to house agents they laughed. In 1948 they had hundreds of buyers on their books looking for that kind of house and when one came onto the market it would be sold that afternoon. So at first we waited and hoped and then, when there was to be this long absence, we went round to look at the places they had on offer, the ones they couldn't sell – it was usually easy to see why. Then suddenly we heard of Greenlands.

It was high on the shoulder of Stonebarrow, a long narrow triangle of steep land, with two cottages and a cowstall. One of the cottages had one room up and one down, the other had two up and two down. They were all small rooms and in poor repair. Until lately, a man had lived there all alone, without chick or child; he had kept a cow or two and a horse and cart. He made clotted cream and sold that, but not much else; he went down with his cart to the beach and loaded seaweed to strew on his grass. Once an artist had lived there and painted postcards which he sold at the post office. Ted Love at the garage told me his grandmother had lived there; she had told him how once they caught a pheasant and cooked it and burned the feathers every one; she had been sent up the hill to keep watch while they burned the feathers, because the wind played tricks on that hillside and a person coming along the track might have smelt burning feathers and told the gamekeeper or the policeman.

There was everything against it but I fell in love with the place. The Vale of Marshwood stretched away at your feet ten miles and more to Pilsdon Pen, the highest hill in that part of Dorset. The Vale was a zigzag patchwork of crooked little fields and woods with a great circle of hills all round, Coneygar and Coney's Castle and Lambert's Castle to the west, Chardown, Hardown and Lewesdon to the east. When clouds came sailing in from the sea on a sunny day – 'cloud-puffball, torn tufts, tossed pillows' – their shadows made new patterns, overlying the quilted texture of hedge and bank and coppice, shifting and changing as they drifted away to the north-east. Close at hand by the cottages, there was a little stand of oak and ash where there were always treecreepers and nuthatches; up the hill, where once the Roman road had run, the fine downland turf filled my mind with such joyous memories that I did not stop to think whether it would carry much keep for cows. 'Isn't it rather steep?' people said doubtfully and I was surprised. I had grown so used to Himalayan hillsides that it did not seem steep to me. But I found there was hardly anywhere on the fifteen acres where you could put down a bucket without its rolling down the hill.

A builder had bought it as a speculation. He meant to restore the cottages on the quiet, asking no one's leave, running up a load of bricks at night from some authorized job and putting in a few days' work when he had men to spare; wartime controls were still strict. He told me it would cost £350 to make the place habitable; in the end we spent ten times that. The whole concept became much more ambitious when we brought in an architect. Because of the slope, the three small rooms on the ground floor made one straight line. He proposed to extend the middle room to twice its size, building it out on the lower side and turning the ground plan into a T. The best bedroom was built above that projection; it stood out like the stern cabin in one of the old sailing ships, full of light and air, with a wide window looking straight across the Vale to Pilsdon Pen. We replaced the thatch with cedar shingles, which are reddish at first but quickly weather to a silvery grey that is almost lavender in some lights.

The architect's estimates were turned down out of hand by the authorities; he wrote them indignant letters and made no progress. At last I told him that designing houses was his profession but writing letters was mine, and I thought I might do better than he at getting round officials. He reluctantly allowed me to intervene; I went to see the key man in Bridport, threw myself on his mercy and asked his advice. He told me to apply again with a lower estimate of the total. 'But must I cut off a bedroom and crowd all my children into one room? Surely that isn't what you want?' I pleaded with a sob in the voice. Not at all, not at all; we needn't alter the plans, only the estimates of what it would cost. It was a nudge, a wink, an invitation to dishonesty – not to bribery, but to disobeying the regulations. These, I suppose, were intended to concentrate building resources on repairing war damage – but there was no war damage available for our local builder. We put in our application again with 'reduced specifications'; that was the phrase. Bridport approved. But there was a regional authority at Reading. I set off for Reading; here we went through much the same ritual. They were most considerate; they saw that it was my own money I wanted to spend; I was not asking for a grant. But even with reduced estimates the cost was not much less than the cost of a new council house. And – in a burst of confidential candour – 'council houses are not for people like you'. Who, I wondered, were people like me? But I did not ask the regional authority. I played my old card about crowding the children all into one bedroom and met the same response as at Bridport. Reduce the specifications. They were most obliging; they told me the figure they would pass. So we applied again with estimates that were flagrantly false and Reading approved. I had to get bundles of notes from the bank and pay the builder in cash; I felt degraded. If I had needed a demonstration of the futility of over-government, this was it.

Still, the day came when we moved in. There were paraffin lamps for the first year and there was trouble with the water. There was a well up the hill which siphoned to a tank at the top of the house; if we used too much in too short a time the siphon would suck dry and had to be started again, at first with a hand pump. But those were difficulties to be overcome and it was worth it. It was quiet up there, almost as quiet as on a high mountain. We could not hear a sound from the traffic on the road from Bridport to Charmouth down the hill. We had only to walk through the top field to be on Stonebarrow, with the sea crawling towards the cliffs five hundred feet below us to the south and open downland all round. There came a spring morning when I stepped out to so fresh a scent of dew and grass and fern that I said to Mary:

'It's just like a morning in Upper Garhwal!'

'You mean,' she said, 'one of those mornings in Upper Garhwal that we used to say were just like a spring morning in England?'

I had not supposed I could make a living out of fifteen acres, but it seemed worth trying to grow our own food. Almost everything was still rationed; butter, eggs, cheese, meat, sugar; such things as raisins, tinned fruit, tinned meat, were on 'points', which meant they were interchangeable but there was a limit on the total. Clothes were rationed, too, as was food for animals. The world was still short of ships and two ounces of dried egg powder took up less room in the hold of a ship than the eight ounces of corn that a hen would need to lay an egg – so I was told by the agricultural adviser. A beginner could not get rations for hens or pigs or cows unless he bought a holding which already carried rationed animals. All I could do at first was to get the minute allowance for the cottager who kept his own pig and a dozen hens. It was meant to supplement domestic scraps and what you could grow in the garden.

That at least was a start. So I began in a very small way as a domestic producer. I grew cabbages and potatoes to help. I was full of ideas about organic farming and I wanted my hens to lead as natural a life as possible, so they had a wooden house in which they were supposed to sleep and lay eggs while by day they roamed the fields and hedges as they chose. But hens, like gipsies, have a gift for squalor. They make a chain of dust-baths and contrive in a few weeks to make a pretty hedgerow look like a backyard. If they run free, they must be let out in the morning and shut up at night; they refuse to go to bed until the light has faded to the exact moment they think proper and if you don't shut the door a fox will slip in. Once they start to lay, they will steal their eggs, as the country saying goes, and you will waste your time searching the hedges until one day you find a nest of twenty in a clump of bracken – and some will not be fresh. I began very soon to perceive that what seems to a beginner a charmingly natural way of doing things takes up much more of his time than the professional method he will learn in the end. When I had fifty hens – dotted about my fields in batches of a dozen – it took two hours a day to feed them. When I had a thousand it took two hours a week.

The cow came and I learnt to milk her; Mary made butter and cheese and clotted cream. There were some young pigs to drink the buttermilk. Rationing became a little easier and I was allowed rations for twenty hens provided I kept fifty. I mixed fish-meal with potatoes to supplement the ration; the fish-meal was made from heads and backbones and sold as a fertilizer while the potatoes were dyed blue because unfit for human consumption. I begged bags of rye from a farmer who was breaking some new rough ground and was glad to sell the rye for cash; it is just as nourishing as wheat but neither hens nor men will eat it if they can get wheat. We began to sell eggs. There were ducks – dark chocolate-brown ducks, beautifully marked, who laid splendidly.

We bought a hundred day-old cockerel chicks; I fussed over them like a hen with only one and lost nearly half (we learnt later to rear about ninety-eight per cent), but when the survivors were growing nicely a mysterious predator began to attack them, tearing out the throats of one or two every day. I thought the murderer was a stoat and set traps for him in drainpipes. But one afternoon, when I was three fields away, planting blackcurrants, Mary saw him at work – a monstrous crow, swooping down from the sky; the first time, his terrified prey fled squawking and managed to dodge him. He soared and swung round to strike again but by now Mary was waiting for him, crouching fiercely in a patch of bracken with my gun. She brought him down and the children were intensely proud of her. Very grim and black he looked and we hung him up by his heels as a warning to his wife.

Once we took some runner beans to the grocer in Charmouth and he gave us such a wonderful price that next year we grew rows and rows of them – but that year runner beans were cheap. Daffodils too we planted by the thousand; daffodils are a joy to grow but send them to the market and you find that though you may get a good price with the earliest of the early, it will drop in a week or ten days to a third or less. And the monotony of packing daffodils in bunches! Each dozen must be arranged by three and by three and by three. We even sent holly to Covent Garden, rolled up in great prickly bundles of sacking in time for Christmas.

Apples were to be the main crop; our north slope would roll the dangerous frosts of early May down the hill before the sun reached the blossom. I chose early, middle and late varieties and learnt a great deal about which variety must be pollinated by another if the fruit is to set. And of course there were four hives for the honey bee. We planted a hundred and fifty apple trees and set them about with wire – of which the lowest six inches must be buried – and in the wire we laced binder twine, dipped in a liquid that was supposed to smell of fox and keep the rabbits away. I became an artist with wire-netting and my hands were like sandpaper. I sprayed those trees three times a year to keep off saw-fly and capsid, aphis and codlin-moth, wilt, lichen, scab and bitter-pit. I pruned them with anxious care to build up shapely trees when at last they came to fruit. When at last they did, I had come to realize that it was time to go.

I was trying to have it both ways. I spent three or four hours at my desk in the morning before I turned into a peasant and worked with gnarled hands at planting potatoes and broad beans. Every ten days or so I would put on my dark pinstripe suit and a bowler hat – protective colouring for a country bumpkin in the dangerous city – and go to London. It was eight miles to Axminster station and then four hours in the train to London. There I would see a publisher or someone in the BBC or do some work in a library.

There was one period when my journey to London would be to see the Princess. She had stolen the boys at just the right moment. She brought them to London to have their eyes tested; it was a dogma that Indian Princes went to Harley Street to have their eyes tested and for that she had permission. The net was closing on Hyderabad and soon after she reached London communication was interrupted. The Princess and Her Majesty, with the two boys and Captain Hamid Beg, were staying at the Savoy. Clearly she could not take them back to Hyderabad when no one knew what would happen next; nor could she allow their education to be indefinitely interrupted. So she acted on her own initiative and did what she had always wanted to do. With remarkable perspicacity, she chose Harrow – Pandit Nehru's old school. She saw the headmaster and arranged that Barakat, the elder, should start at Harrow at once as a day boy, while Karamat went to a prep school near by. They continued to live at the Savoy and Hamid Beg took them to school every morning by Underground and met them in the evening. I was several times asked to lunch at the Savoy, to give advice, which was seldom taken. Once Barakat's housemaster was there; he wanted him to become a boarder. I entirely agreed but that was a subject on which the Princess was adamant. She would not give up her children.

Those lunches at the Savoy made a strange contrast with Greenlands – elegance and luxury in a private suite instead of sandwiches under a hedge. The occasion I remember most vividly was when the crisis was over; Hyderabad had been swallowed; the Indian Army had overrun the state – in three days, exactly as foretold; His Exalted Highness had kept his titles but lost almost all his power. One of his first acts was to instruct the Princess to bring back his grandsons. She was furious. She strode to and fro, flashing with emeralds. She looked magnificent.

'Look at the telegram His Exalted Highness has sent me!' she cried. 'Imagine the vulgarity of my in-laws! He says he will pay my bill at the Savoy if I bring the children back!' She did not take them back but flew to Delhi herself and saw Nehru before she saw His Exalted Highness. She had her way. She was a gallant woman and I wish she had been an Empress before democracy became the fashion. The boys, in their different ways, did well at Harrow.

Once in Piccadilly – or was it in front of the Dorchester? – a sudden scent of freshly cut turf assailed me. Someone was laying out a scrap of ornamental lawn and the country smell hit me sharply with a pang for home. But there is a limit to the number of lives one can live at the same time. We were as happy at Greenlands as we had been in Garhwal. There was a moment of triumph when we entertained some old friends to lunch on melons, chicken, salad, potatoes, raspberries, butter, cheese, clotted cream – all home grown. It was satisfying – at that age – to end the day, tired it is true, but not with the sick fatigue of hurry, frustration and compromise; tired, rather, physically and mentally, with effort from which one could see some results, conscious that so many pages had been written, so many eggs picked up, so many potatoes planted. But we had not made up our minds what to discard. I had not plunged, finally and for ever, into the life of a peasant. I kept the morning sacred for writing books and paid a man to help me. He did the early milking and feeding except at the weekends. In the later part of the day, there were often fencing jobs for the two of us to do together or the young pigs to be moved or some new quarters to be built for hens. He went at five; I was often doing things till dark.

But every mouthful we grew was costing us five times what it would have cost in the supermarket.

A smallholding of fifteen acres on marginal land cannot carry a hired man. Not only that, it is too demanding for a writer. There is thought as well as physical labour to eat into one's time and energy. I was constantly exploring the possibilities and drawbacks of keeping geese and goats, the value and price of new kinds of feedstuffs and of manure; above all, ways of dealing with the bureaucratic regulations that beset us. It called for constant initiative and emergencies were always arising. Once at midsummer, Mary and I had both been out of doors, long after the

children were in bed, constantly finding just one last thing to do before
coming in to supper; as dusk began to fall – the lovely midsummer dusk
that comes so late and slowly – we sat wearily down and drew up our
chairs to the table. A knock came at the door.

'Your heifers are out!' said a neighbour's voice. And we had to drive
them back through the gap they had made and then mend the gap.

So there was not much leisure to cultivate that sensitivity to personal
relations that I had felt would suffer if I went into politics. We were
happy; we were all happy and we were sure it was good for the children
to run wild for a year or two in so beautiful a place, for George to gaze,
as he sometimes would, for an hour or two, sitting quite still, at a new-
born calf or a baby duckling. We were all of us aware of:

> The voice of the hidden waterfall
> And the children in the apple-tree.

But I could not bring myself to want my four children to be peasants for
ever, and if they were to have the education we had planned it was no
good selling bundles of holly to Covent Garden and writing books that
the critics praised but no one bought. I must earn more. For six months,
I spent four nights a week in London, sitting by day in a publisher's
office, writing *The Men Who Ruled India* before breakfast and after dinner,
and straightening things up at Greenlands on Saturday and Sunday.
But that was no way to live. It slowly became borne in on us that we must
either plunge in deep, with the water over our heads, and give up any
idea of the children going away to school, give up hiring a man, give up
writing for a time and simply toil at the holding – or we must give up
Greenlands and the holding as a way of life. We must move nearer
London and start again. It would still be country; there would be a field
or two perhaps but the fields would be only a hobby.

There had been an evening, when we had first bought Greenlands
and before we lived there, when I walked back to Charmouth over
Stonebarrow. I had been using a pickaxe to dig a ditch that I hoped would
clear the water from the roots of two old apple trees; it was stony ground
and my hands were sore and my back ached a little. But my spirit lifted
as I reached the top of the hill. There had been some snow a few days
back and rags of snow still lay here and there on the north side of a bank
or of a gorse bush. There was a clear sky and it would soon be freezing;
the blue Atlantic twilight was drawing in over the sea and in the last
rays of the winter sun the snow was indigo and the bracken red as a fox.
I thought of the ways I had not taken, the doors I had not opened, in
those last days in India. They had presented themselves, doors I might

open, secure ways of living, with a regular income, comfortable surroundings, servants who would bring a drink in the evening. But I was glad
I had not opened those doors. I had no regrets.

Now, three years later, when we had made up our minds to go, to
start once more a new life altogether, I did have regrets, deep regrets,
not for those doors not opened, but because to leave Greenlands was a
defeat. I had wanted to stay there for ever. Sundari Devi had called it
'our forever house' – but perhaps that desire had been rather infantile
on my part. I had tried to do too many things that were incompatible
with each other; 'a condition of complete simplicity' costs 'not less than
everything'. It is a sign of growing up to make a choice and cut out what
will not fit in. So it was, I concluded for the second time, a defeat. And
it was bitter to say goodbye to the cloud-shadows sailing over the Vale
of Marshwood. There was, nonetheless, a good deal to take away and
we were going to a new life.

> What we call the beginning is often the end
> And to make an end is to make a beginning.

One memory, in especial, I should keep. That too had been of a winter
evening with the sun near setting; its light had taken on the warmth of
colouring that comes with its last moments. I was stooping over my
digging when I heard the steady beat of wings. I looked up and saw
something I have never seen before or since – three swans low overhead
lighted from below by rays which warmed their wings and underparts
to ivory, almost to gold. They flew away eastwards, against the pale
sky, making perhaps for the great swannery on the coast at Abbotsbury,
where there have been swans for a thousand years.

NOTES

p. 22. G. O. Trevelyan: *The Competition-Wallah*.

p. 49. Anthony Powell: *Infants of the Spring*.

p. 51. 'couched Brazilian jaguar'. T. S. Eliot: 'Whispers of Immortality'.

p. 51. Henry Brooke: later Lord Brooke of Cumnor, Home Secretary 1962–4. Walter Oakeshott: High Master of St Paul's, Headmaster of Winchester, Rector of Lincoln College.

p. 54. James Fergusson: Sir James Fergusson of Kilkerran, Bt, later Keeper of the Records of the Crown of Scotland.

p. 55. Robert Birley: Headmaster of Charterhouse, Headmaster of Eton, and later Professor of Education at the University of the Witwatersrand.

p. 90. '. . . an undeclared, intermittent and surreptitious civil war . . .' I am afraid this is a quotation from myself, in *The Guardians*.

p. 91. I have told this story, from a slightly different point of view, in *Call the Next Witness*.

p. 97. On this relationship of patron and henchman, I have written in the foreword to O. Mannoni: *Prospero and Caliban*, Methuen 1956, a translation of *La Psychologie de la Colonisation*, a book to which I owe a great deal; and also in *Patterns of Dominance*, OUP, 1970. There is a Hindi word *jajman* which properly means the person who employs a Brahman to perform sacrifices and covers the relationship of some patrons to their henchmen but not all.

p. 100 et seq. 'their motives were usually only too clear . . .' In these pages I had in mind E. M. Forster's idea that Indians are mysterious and incomprehensible. Yes, but no more than all one's fellow-creatures.

p. 104. 'For most of us . . .': T. S. Eliot: *Four Quartets*: 'The Dry Salvages: V'.

p. 117. 'Four things greater . . .': Kipling: *Barrack-Room Ballads*: 'The Ballad of the King's Jest'.

p. 135. 'Too tender a morsel for the fire . . .': Sir Thomas Browne: *Urne Buriall*.

p. 142–3. The story of the road, the District Board and the Congress I have told before in *The Guardians*, though from a slightly different angle. But I had to repeat it.

p. 144. *The Man-eating Panther of Rudraprayag*: Jim Corbett: OUP.

p. 145. *The* tiger. As one woman for Sherlock Holmes was always *the* woman.

p. 145. Nisár: the accent is on the second syllable, as in Hurrah!

p. 151. 'I think there is probably . . .': Lord Linlithgow, quoted in *The Viceroy at Bay*: John Glendevon: Collins: 1971.

p. 158. 'Where either': *Othello*: IV.ii.59.

p. 164. '... the moon and the tides.' As I was finishing this book, I renewed acquaintance with one of the planners who had spent much time on a plan for invading Sumatra when in Japanese occupation. He told me that after the Japanese surrender he had talked about this plan to the Japanese commander in Sumatra. Using British Admiralty charts, tide tables and astronomical information, both the Japanese and ourselves had arrived at the same date as the best for such an operation.

p. 170. 'I said it very loud and clear...': *Alice Through the Looking-Glass*. One of Humpty-Dumpty's poems.

p. 182. Admiral Sir James Somerville and the Bofors guns. There is a slightly different version of this story in *Fighting Admiral*, the biography of Sir James by Donald McIntyre, Evans 1961. But my version has good authority and is more vigorous; the other may have been bowdlerized.

p. 183. Bernard Fergusson: later Lord Ballantrae. Governor-General of New Zealand.

p. 200. *Sherwanis*. I usually avoid Indian words. But there is no exact equivalent for *sherwani*, the elegant formal garment buttoning up the front and fitting the body closely. *Sherwani* is a Persian word and used generally by Muslims but there is a similar garment traditionally worn by Hindus called *achkan*. It used to be regarded as vulgar and disrespectful to come before a superior with the *sherwani* unbuttoned.

p. 214. '... a Muslim in Delhi had said to me'. It was General Iskandar Mirza, later President of Pakistan; I left his name out of the text as it would have held up the flow of my narrative.

p. 217. The wedding of the Viceroy's daughter... See illustration.

p. 219. '... a convenient dry nesting-place...' This was a phrase my father often used. *Jemima Puddleduck* had been my favourite Beatrix Potter when I was a small boy. It seems to me now that I showed good taste. It is a story symbolic of man's pilgrimage. Jemima is always in search of a convenient dry nesting-place but she becomes ensnared by a foxy-whiskered gentleman who means to devour her. It is written with pervasive irony; *we* know, even at four years old, what a silly she is, but nearly all the story is written from her point of view. And the tension mounts to a sinister denouement which takes place off stage, in the classical Greek tradition. There is room for a thesis on irony in the works of Beatrix Potter.

p. 220. '... cloud-puffball, torn tufts, tossed pillows...': G. M. Hopkins: *That Nature is a Heraclitean Fire*.

p. 223. '... a monstrous crow...' It was a carrion crow, which says Pork, pork, pork, because he does like a bit of pork, not a rook. It really did seem as black, and almost as big, as a tar-barrel. *Alice Through the Looking-Glass*.

p. 226. 'The voice of the hidden waterfall...': Eliot, *Four Quartets*, 'Little Gidding. V.'

p. 227. 'a condition of complete simplicity...': Eliot, *Four Quartets*, 'Little Gidding. V'.

p. 227. 'What we call the beginning...': Eliot, *Four Quartets*, 'Little Gidding. V'.

INDEX